Comics and Conflict

Comics and Conflict

PATRIOTISM AND PROPAGANDA FROM WWII THROUGH OPERATION IRAQI FREEDOM

Naval Institute Press
Annapolis, Maryland

CORD A. SCOTT

Naval Institute Press
291 Wood Road
Annapolis, MD 21402

Library of Congress Cataloging-in-Publication Data
Scott, Cord A.
  Comics and conflict : patriotism and propaganda from WWII through Operation Iraqi Freedom / Cord A. Scott.
    pages cm
  Summary: "The comic book, which emerged in its modern form in the 1930s, was initially a form of simple, visual entertainment that gave readers, especially children, a form of escape from daily life. However, as World War II began, comic books evolved into a form of propaganda, providing information and education for both children and adults. Comics and Conflict examines how comic books were used to display patriotism, valor and adventure through war stories, and eventually to tell of the horrors of combat from World War II through the current conflicts in Iraq and Afghanistan"— Provided by publisher.
  Includes bibliographical references and index.
  ISBN 978-1-61251-477-2 (hardback) — ISBN 978-1-61251-478-9 (ebook) 1. World War, 1939–1945—Social aspects—United States. 2. Comic books, strips, etc.—United States—History—20th century. 3. Comic books, strips, etc.—United States—History—21st century. 4. Superheroes—United States—History—20th century. 5. Superheroes—United States—History—21st century. 6. Propaganda—United States—History—20th century. 7. Propaganda—United States—History—21st century. 8. War and society—United States—History—20th century. 9. War and society—United States—History—21st century. I. Title.
  D744.7.U6S46 2014
  940.53'1—dc23

                                                                                        2014015534

(∞)Print editions meet the requirements of ANSI/NISO z39.48–1992 (Permanence of Paper).
Printed in the United States of America.
22 21 20 19 18 17 16 15 14   9 8 7 6 5 4 3 2 1

First printing

This book is dedicated to my loved ones who did not live to see it completed and to those who did.

Contents

Preface

Popular culture is a curious subject for history as customarily defined. Until the widespread availability of inexpensive reproductions and printed texts, beginning in the sixteenth century in the West, relatively few artifacts of popular culture survived for later historical analysis. Traditional history was largely based on what past elites believed was worth saving, and for earlier periods it still is. Even supplemented by random survivals and often hard-to-interpret archaeological remains, such histories necessarily reflect the ideologies of those at the apex of power. Scholars working centuries later, and with quite different ideologies, remain restricted by the extant sources. By contrast, popular cultural history draws on a broader base of materials and a more complete record, especially for the past two centuries (a period roughly coterminous with the existence of the United States of America). Thus, as historical subjects get closer to the present and the depth and breadth of evidence expands, it is increasingly possible to write history that reconstructs the mental universe in which ordinary people lived.

A major part of this record consists of popular narrative forms, which reflect—in a less self-conscious way than elite writing and art—the beliefs, hopes, aspirations, and fears that shaped humanity's past. In short, the materials of cultural history are exactly those that had previously been unavailable or underappreciated by conventional methods of historiography. What might seem to be simple, ephemeral stories originally intended for rapid disposal after their particular historical moment had passed may instead offer today's historians unique insight into the mind-set of their readers. This wider culture, here represented by the comic book, cannot be captured entirely by the reigning ideologies. It is too big and various to police effectively, and much of the time it occurs "under the radar." Even after mainstream historians analyze it, some part of popular culture always escapes control, representing a relatively unfiltered record of the past. Among popular narratives, comic books are particularly revealing, as they directly reflect their audience's fantasies, nightmares, and delusions.

Comic books often conceal secret gems of historical import. At their beginning and for a long time afterward, war comics depicted combat in heroic terms: noble causes, courageous soldiers, and the "good death." Deliberately suppressed were the harsher realities of combat: cowardice, low morale, illness, and madness. Writers of comics did not reconcile these inconsistencies until much later, when the fictional exploits of such characters as Sgt. Rock and the Haunted Tank included nuances of combat that had not been openly discussed.[1] Besides the stimulation offered by those colorful and violent panels, comic books sparked my lifelong interest in history, particularly military history, war, and its impact on the culture at home. This book looks specifically at how war-themed comics developed from early newspaper strips and military cartoons and caricatures into the comic book format initially geared toward children. I also explore what the comics' depictions of conflict tell us about American society and values.

Children's entertainment has been an important, yet too easily dismissed, aspect of American life over the last sixty years—because it is not just for children and not just entertainment. The comic book has served as a way to introduce young readers to adult topics and yet allow them to retain some sort of separation from reality. The comics have never been as direct, or effective, as advertising, but the ideology of support for American doctrine and the American military is still there. However, the audience of the comic book has changed over the years. According to the New York Comic Book Museum, the average comic reader is twenty-four years old and has more disposable income than the average American.[2] This has an impact on which reader the comic is geared toward, and it is most likely not the perceived audience: children. As long as they are considered a "children's medium," at least partially directed toward that demographic, however, the comic book will serve as an active way of teaching them. It remains to be seen whether this is for the betterment of mankind. Even adult comic book readers still wish to indulge their childhood feelings but read about adult themes at the same time. Adults today also look at comics as a type of investment, given the auction prices of such comic books as the first issue of *Action Comics*, which recently fetched $1.5 million at auction.

Over the course of their history, comics have gone far beyond simple stories aimed at children; they comprise satire and criticism, as well as patriotism and hypernationalism. Sometimes, the comics' producers toed the line of gung-ho patriotism, but at other times they took issue with government abuses and the misuses of state power. (Paradoxically the comics themselves were sometimes instruments of that power. The government has long recognized the potential of the comic book to distract, inform, or indoctrinate readers.) As mirrors of diverse attitudes toward warfare, the comics are like movies or books. Some of the creators (writers, illustrators, and publishers) of comics tried to depict combat in its horrors, while others glorified war. Comics dealing with the horrors of war became a subfield unto themselves in the 1950s and 1960s, specifically in the titles *Frontline Combat*, *Two-Fisted Tales*, and *Blazing Combat*.[3]

For the purpose of this book, I narrowed the field of comic books under analysis. The war-themed genre is as varied in comics as it is in novels, films, and other forms of fiction. The war comic books discussed here concern conflicts that were occurring during the years these comics existed. The conflicts of the last seventy years have a special place in comic book history. World War II, Korea, Vietnam, the Cold War, and Operations Desert Storm and Iraqi Freedom have all found a place in comic book literature. The comic books reflect the ways Americans at large have viewed the military's role in society and how individual creators interpreted the nation's many wars. Comics from 1938 (the beginning of what is commonly referred to as the Golden Age of Comics) through current publications will be discussed as well. Of course, not all war comics can be considered, but as large a sample as possible has been used to examine and better understand how the genre developed.

To look at the history of the medium, one must first look at what reading comics accomplishes. Comic books—and even the strips in newspapers from which some of them evolved—serve several functions for readers. Steeped in patriotism and propaganda, they often depict fighting for moral or political purposes. Indeed, as World War II began, comic books became an integral part of wartime propaganda, providing information and education for children and adults alike through colorful pages filled with characters whose wartime adventures excited audiences, promoted patriotism, and exposed the horrors of combat. From World War II through the conflicts in Iraq and Afghanistan during the first decade of the twenty-first century, comic books have played a crucial yet overlooked role in shaping the broader cultural perceptions of these conflicts. For the creators of such comics, inspiration was easy to come by, their imaginations piqued by reality that played out before them on newsreels, the nation's newspapers, nightly television, and more.

For those who read comics during times of war or conflict, these books promote different ideologies or specific economic or political positions. Although such points of view often varied from conflict to conflict, comic books could educate the masses about the errors of Nazism or Communism or radical Islam. The one common denominator in the struggle against each opponent was patriotism. The flag-waving patriotism of America during national holidays or other events can be seen as a first step toward fanaticism. Crisis also encourages people to rally around an image or icon. Such patriotism often verges on—or becomes—idolatry. For example, the American flag—either as tangible object or iconic talisman—becomes a vehicle for nationalist sentiment, sometimes even xenophobia. Its colors alone become symbolically charged. The concept of a flag-themed superhero is primarily an American invention.[4] American comic book characters who sport the red, white, and blue (and/or the stars and stripes) include the Shield, Captain America, and, to a lesser extent, Uncle Sam, Wonder Woman, and SuperPatriot.[5]

Such characters also exist in comic books from other countries. Canada has the Canadian Alpha Flight team, the Vindicator, and—most notably—Captain

Canuck (whose costumes are red and white, featuring a maple leaf). In the United Kingdom, there is Captain Britain (whose costume incorporates elements of that nation's emblem), as well as Union Jack and Jack Staff, whose very names refer to their nation's flag.[6] These characters allow the reader to identify with a country and its ideals as embodied by the hero. How much do these works of art merely tell us about their particular creators, and how much do they reveal about their larger audience? Are they products of individual creative minds (artist and/or writer) with limited or local appeal? Alternatively, do they express some collective ethos or ideal? Are the characters merely vehicles for the artists' credo or critiques? Surely these artifacts may illuminate personal psychology, but they also tell us of the times and values in which (and for which) they were created and in which they were consumed. Furthermore, they were both document and dogma; they not only represent reality but also promulgate particular moral or political, personal, or pluralistic ideals. The conduct and character of the heroes serve as guides for proper action in a democracy.

If comic books excite positive feelings through identification, can they also prompt revulsion and revilement? Do the characters in comic books inspire fear or hatred in their readership? Do they effectively sell the reader on the dangers of the "enemy"? By reinforcing stereotypes of degenerate villains, as well as American purity, comic books inculcate the reader in America's goals and golems. Indeed, propaganda has long been a staple genre. For example, 1940s comic book depictions envisioned the evil nature of the Axis powers. These comics show the depth of bigotry and hatred toward these vilified "Others." Furthermore, the propagandistic endeavor of the comic book could go beyond the frame of the narrative. Advertisements in the comic book during World War II, for example, called for people to buy war bonds, engage in scrap drives, and participate in other war-related events. The idea of a drive or call is an important aspect of propaganda. Besides the patently commercial ads or military-themed toys, some promoted patriotic clubs, such as the Sentinels of Liberty with Captain America and Bucky, his sidekick.

Why is this study important? Reflect for a moment upon George Santayana's dictum "Those who do not learn from history are doomed to repeat it." Only recall the crises-of-empire of prior powers (Athens, Rome, England, China, and Prussia). How do historical and fictional accounts of war relate to the decline of empires or the rise of new ones? What was the impact of Thucydides' documentation of the dereliction of Athenian ideals? Consider the efficiency of comic books as a delivery system that can disseminate a message to the relatively uninformed and unformed—the barely literate or illiterate. Had children and youngsters been inculcated sooner and subconsciously, that empire might have continued longer. We must not ignore the impact of illustration and word on the attitude and behaviors of the citizenry.

The political history of the United States is obviously mirrored by comic books; their advent did not merely coincide with the rise of the United States as a global power. Rather, the comics arose in part to explain an increasingly confusing and dangerous world, at first to children and teenagers and later to young adults as well. The time frame that is the focus of this book, 1938 to the present, shows not only the repeated involvement of the United States in armed conflict but also a repetition—with variations—of interactions and responses on the part of the citizenry. I divide these seventy-six years of cultural history into smaller periods, along themes that coincide with particular instances of American military intervention. This diverse panorama of time and place illustrates how certain themes and interactions, certain aspects of patriotism and propaganda, cycle throughout our history.

The comics reflect the changing power of the United States, yet the comic book creators underwent a transformation too. At first, they were quasi-propagandists. Early comic books were written to create a broader, stronger spectrum of patriotism among readers. Images and dialogue, plot and character, as well as extratextual elements such as advertisements, all worked to inform or influence the susceptible reader. In recent years, however, they have often been critical of U.S. policy abroad, and some questioned the patriotic cause and conventional wisdom as early as the Korean War. During the 1950s, smaller comic book publishers were the most willing to challenge the official line, but they were not commercially successful and eventually went out of business. Starting in the 1960s, however, some of the larger producers started to publish more daring story lines that ran counter to American policy, a trend that became predominant by the 1990s.

Both the verbal and visual elements of the comic book are analyzed in this study. I have identified particular themes or motifs that add nuance to the chronological study of these texts, which give a sense of the character of their creators and consumers, as well as the changing nature of the genre and our nation. Thus the depiction of the Iraq War will vary from the description of World War II. These changes, addressed within each chapter, reflect the integration of current culture and the time of the creators' presentation in each era's comics.

Any work of this nature must include an analysis of the comic book's history, whose origins can be traced to original cartoon strips, the pointed and often satirical illustrations found in newspapers, and various representations of soldiers during wartime. During World War II, comic books became an essential part of military experience, either as an informational or training tool for soldiers of varied education levels and intellectual abilities or as inexpensive entertainment. By the early 1950s, the comic book's propaganda value was acknowledged by the defense establishment. These aspects of comic books continue to this day, and I will return to them throughout this book, as they are markers of the evolution of the genre.

The cultural influence of comic books continued throughout the 1950s, either as a perceived threat to youth (dubbed the "ten-cent plague") or as an outlet for teenagers and young adults to adapt to conditions around them. Writers and artists sought to use the comic book as a platform for their political agendas or to express their concerns about war, political indoctrination, or the nefarious depiction of enemies of the United States. By the late 1960s, comic books contained messages both overt and covert. They called for a reevaluation of American military might and the end of the patriotic narrow-mindedness rooted, in the eyes of their creators, in the triumph over the Axis. As the Reagan era came into full swing during the 1980s, some comics reveled in revanchism, demanding revenge for the ill treatment of Vietnam-era soldiers by the Vietcong or imagining the recovery of national pride after the disaster of that war. Other comics managed to view the government with complete cynicism and distrust. If necessary, comic books would create an enemy if one did not exist. As the Cold War ended, comic book writers often used the threat of a "New World Order" to represent a serious danger to mankind, or they revived older villains. In the past decade, story lines often capitalized on fears of terrorists wreaking havoc with stolen atomic weapons.

Finally, the events on September 11, 2001, drew comparisons to the attack on Pearl Harbor at the beginning of U.S. involvement in World War II. It was predictable that comic books would revert to the patriotic mode as a way of showing (and fostering) solidarity with an outraged America. As the call to punish terrorists eventually engulfed Iraq, which could not be shown to have been responsible for the initial attack, the comics again took another tack: distrust of the administration in power. Given the problem of fighting a new "moral" conflict, publishers revived such characters as Captain America, Sgt. Rock, and Iron Man.[7] This reflects not only on the comic book industry but on the American psyche as well.

To illustrate my argument, I considered all available sources, including early military vignettes and short comics sequences, as well as the later and artistically more complex comics series. I will investigate how the artists interpolated both personal prejudice and the values of society at large. In doing so, they both documented and determined transformations in American culture. The comics are descriptive of their times, and shifts in American values are as evident as the changes in the automobiles, airplanes, and artillery depicted. These changes occur over periods of more or less blatant satire, variations in the portrayal of American machismo, and diverse depictions of violence and death—particularly of American soldiers. Enemy casualties, of course, were always expected and usually celebrated.

From all of the potential sources, I selected those I felt were necessary to address the topic of this book—the ones most focused on contemporary military action by the United States. These comprise comics that appear intended to inculcate patriotism or to disseminate propaganda or legitimate protests against the actions of the government. The examples are chosen to reflect the war at the time of publication or within recent memory (for example, stories about the Revolutionary War published during the Vietnam War are excluded). From the specific eras and series, I have singled out authors who have captured the essence of war comics and represent excellence or extraordinary contribution to the field. For World War II, these creators include Will Eisner, Joe Simon and Jack Kirby; all were Jewish and had a stake in defeating the Nazis. By the 1950s, the era of Jewish involvement had diminished, and Joe Kubert, Wally Wood, and John Severin took the field further. This shift focused on the experiences of combat, rather than a specific goal of the American military. In the Vietnam era, a significant illustrator of war comic books was the prolific Sam Glanzman, who drew on his own combat experience. By the Reagan era, many comics creators—such as Don Lomax, Wayne Vansant, and Larry Hama—used their experiences in Vietnam to reflect on and reform the genre. Finally, by the end of the century, artists such as Garth Ennis helped reinvigorate and reinvent the field in the post-9/11 world.

Examinations of other popular art forms have been used to expand our understanding of history, from Lary May's analysis of film's role in shaping conceptions of democracy to Lewis Erenberg's discussion of the cultural and economic impact of jazz and swing music.[8] Similarly, William Savage, Roger Sabin, Bradford Wright, and Jim Steranko have sought to tie comic book readership to a wider cultural history.[9] John Dower used comic illustrations by both the Japanese and the United States during World War II to examine the role of race in that conflict.[10] I look to expand on these pioneering works (particularly Savage's) to show how the comic books both mirrored and manufactured popular attitudes to war. Most histories of the comics deal with how the industry developed; they do not address depictions of war or the propagandistic endeavor of the comic book.

Cultural history delves into mores and mind-sets, values, levels of patriotism, and cultural standards. My cultural history of comics will examine the methods of moral education, the concept and substance of propaganda in actions and costumes, and how the depiction of current or recent events competed with news and entertainment media (newspapers, movies, and television) to inform and form cultural values. I will show how cultural views were colored and crafted by those entertaining stories of soldiers and superheroes. These slanted depictions of America hooked and hoodwinked their readers by promoting patriotism and promulgating propaganda of a more dubious character.

Not the product of a single person, this book reflects the contributions of many who helped in its creation and refinement. While the final results (and mistakes) are mine alone, I was assisted by *many* people whose help and input must be acknowledged.

First and foremost, I would like to thank my wife Rachel for all the assistance and encouragement that she has offered over the years. She has kept this project and me going through the rough times.

I would like to thank Darlene Ulmer, Ron Wade, and Mark Holroyd from IADT–Chicago for their encouragement to write and teach the two classes (History of Propaganda and History of Comic Books) that led to this book. They were great bosses at a crucial time in my academic career.

I also wish to thank Dr. Lewis Erenberg, Dr. Ted Karamanski, Dr. Peter Karsten, and Dr. Michael Neiburg, who offered encouragement and advice on the subjects of cartoons and the military. From the Naval Institute Press, Adam Kane and Adam Nettina were outstanding for their enthusiasm and quick responses to my queries no matter how seemingly inane.

Sections of this book were previously published in the *Journal of Popular Culture* (spring 2007), the *International Journal of Comic Art* (fall 2008), *Captain America and the Struggles of the Superhero: Critical Essays*, edited by Robert Weiner (spring 2009), and the *Greenwood Encyclopedia of Comics and Graphic Novels* (spring 2010).

My colleagues have served a critical role in developing my thoughts and concepts. In particular, Kevin Kaufman, Pat Mallory, Stella Ress, and Jay Ward have all kept me going and offered insight. Lee and Cindy Windsor gave me an entirely new perspective on how to look at comic books while on a battlefield tour of Italy. To them and many others I again say thanks.

My family served as a source of strength, especially during the many times when I felt that the book would never see publication. My dad, Jerry, and his wife, Renée Scott, offered encouragement and suggestions. My brother Micah has never ceased to amaze me with his keen observations of my work (his intelligence and talent continuing to confound me). My relatives (especially the Volk and Veilleux families) were always there for encouragement. Paul Mache offered great comments and the great break for other topics when needed.

My greatest thanks must go to the corps of "Wonder Women" who got me through this. Lauren Mache gave me positive thoughts and observations as she went through the dissertation process twice (!). My daughters Zia and Jayna pointed out all sorts of "odd things," yet let Dad work when needed. Finally, my Aunt Peggy Smetana and my mom, Linda Scott, assisted in ways big and small. I cannot express my gratitude to these pillars of strength. I only hope that I have done them all proud.

1 Entertaining and Informing the Masses

America is addicted to wars of distraction.

—BARBARA EHRENREICH

The interrelationship of comic illustrations and political commentary runs deep. While the practice of drawing may be as old as human culture itself, its earliest extant use for political or military propaganda dates to at least the time of Xerxes in ancient Persia in the sixth century BCE. The Greeks and Romans often depicted their commanders as superior, even superhuman, in their physical forms and heroic action. By the early modern period, humorous drawings were regularly produced to report executions and other public events, as seen in London broadsheets from the seventeenth century. These drawings had mass appeal, especially among those with limited literacy (including children). The English colonies were heir to this tradition, and the eighteenth century saw the first true modern political cartoons in colonial America. One pioneer of the art form was Benjamin Franklin, who—in an effort to promote colonial unity—published his seditious "Join or Die" cartoon in 1754.[1]

The History of the Medium

During the nineteenth century, artists increasingly incorporated humor into their political cartoons. Perhaps the most influential of these artists was Thomas Nast, who published his best-known work in *Harper's Weekly* in the 1870s. While the cartoons did not have a sequential narrative, they had a consistent purpose: exposing corruption in New York's Tammany Hall. In fact, the most frequent target of Nast's attacks, Tammany boss William Tweed, noted that although his constituents could not read, they could easily understand "them damn pictures."[2] Political cartoons also used grotesque ethnic stereotypes to appeal to their readers' racism and xenophobia. For instance, the Irish were depicted as ape-like to highlight their foreignness and supposed cultural degeneracy. While such images are considered grossly insensitive today,[3] even accomplished artists such as Nast promoted what in the mid-nineteenth century was a widespread view of the Irish.[4]

These political cartoons eventually developed into the general-entertainment medium known as the comic strip. While Nast used the political cartoon for the specific purpose of lampooning government and business corruption, the comic strip became valued as much for entertainment as for information. Comic books eventually played a large role in shaping modern American society, at first among younger readers but gradually for the larger public. Themes drawn from history and current events were used as "hooks" to attract a wider readership with the promise of an enlightening experience. In addition to Nast, artists such as Richard Outcault (creator of *The Yellow Kid*) and Windsor McCay (creator of *Little Nemo in Slumberland*) generated substantial circulation gains for their papers and raised the medium to unprecedented heights in the age of the newspaper wars of the late nineteenth century.[5] So important a cultural fixture were these early comic strips that the term "yellow journalism"—now used to describe the sensational newspaper reporting of that time—emerged from the fight between two newspapers for the rights to publish *The Yellow Kid*. In that era, adults made up most newspaper buyers (even though the newspaper had a much wider readership).

Although cartoons preceded the comic book, comics historian Roger Sabin notes that cartoons represent a curious paradox: the seemingly childish images in panels, comic strips, and books concealed adult themes such as inside jokes and political humor satirizing contemporary events.[6] Such was the case with *The Yellow Kid* and other popular comic strips, including *Katzenjammer Kids* and *Little Nemo in Slumberland,* which were created soon after on Outcault's model. Because these cartoons often featured children as their principal characters, they became identified as a children's medium; because they were written in such a way that immigrants and less-educated people could understand them, illustrated stories also became associated with the lower classes. And because of this perceived readership, strips such as *The Yellow Kid* were able to comment on political issues in a way that seemed harmless at first glance. Yet they became more sophisticated than was supposed, belying the common misconception that comics were solely a children's medium, too simplistic and lowbrow for serious adult readers.

Although depicted in a fantastic manner, the fighting and other violence in comic books generally had some basis in current or historical events. Nevertheless, the fictional medium of the comic strip was never intended to be strictly accurate in a documentary sense, and it allowed artists license to exaggerate aspects of war for effect. Events were often distorted, just as the characters usually had enhanced bodies and unlikely or impossible abilities. Popular images of war, as Daniel Perlmutter has noted, were metonymies, in which the images of the event signified the larger condition of the conflict. Individual figures represented more than themselves—they were means to show the viewer the greater cause. Both heroes and villains were drawn according to legible pictorial codes, so that the reader immediately recognized who represented good and who represented evil.[7] As with any visual medium, reality could also be altered to highlight the worst aspects of the enemy. The enemy might be portrayed with an unnatural skin tone or strange physical features, or associated with the monstrous inversion of cultural norms, as in the case of stereotypical racist depictions in political cartoons, comic strips, and comic books.

The legendary comic book artist Will Eisner took this metonymic art form one step further. He noted that a comic illustrator could depict the nature of the character, good or evil, by the very weapon that he carries. For example, if a character carries a serrated blade that looks "foreign" or exotic, then he is unusually bloodthirsty. On the other hand, if the character carries a simple-looking knife, he is a pragmatic hero. His weapon is a utilitarian tool wielded only to complete a task, even if that task is killing an enemy. The weapon, in short, symbolizes its user's motives.[8] Such popular illustrations open a window into the society in which they were produced, because comics served as both propaganda and a barometer of social attitudes toward American military intervention. The comics instilled young readers with the concept of an America worth protecting: a place where regardless of their upbringing (presuming it was white and European), they could attain a better home, job, and life than their ancestors had had. At the same time, comic books helped their readers to identify threats to the United States.

Before World War II, the main perceived threat to American society was domestic crime. The comics depicted this internal "enemy" through his acts of violence and dangerous nonconformity and, ultimately, as an evil entity that must be destroyed. By using the comic book as a form of propaganda, one could depict an enemy through derogatory illustrations more powerfully than with words. The enemy could signify anything from corporate greed to barbaric violence on the battlefield. The historically based comic books produced by Dell Publishing typified the strategy of using real events as material for comic book stories. By World War II, racial and military conflicts had become intertwined in the comics as they were in the country: the enemy could be perceived at once as internal and external. At the height of wartime hostility against the Japan, supposedly treasonous American citizens of Japanese descent were often drawn with fangs and other bestial features. The comics added to the tense political climate by tacitly defining, however obliquely, what did and did not count as "American." Such popular illustrations helped determine the attitudes of Americans toward issues in the real world, including the use of military force abroad.

In addition to this summary of the history of comics, a few definitions are in order. The most common art form discussed here is the *comic book,* which is most commonly a thirty-two-page magazine consisting of one or more stories. Most comic books are published monthly, with print runs of ten thousand to half a million copies, depending on the popularity of the title or character. Most people are familiar with individual *comic strips* featured in newspapers. Comic books are composed of a collection of these basic narrative units, each with a series of illustrated boxes that, read sequentially, tell a story. It was the republishing of these strips, originally from separate issues, by printing them onto a single news sheet folded three times—eventually with a cover printed on glossy paper—that established the standard comic book dimensions most are familiar with today. A comic book exceeding sixty-four pages in length and consisting of a single, self-contained story is called a *graphic novel.* Going forward, the format under discussion will always be a comic book unless specifically designated as a comic strip, graphic novel, or otherwise.[9]

This book analyzes a select group of characters and stories in militarily and politically themed American comic books published from the mid-twentieth century through the first decade of the twenty-first century. Because of the profusion of titles and characters created during this span, the ones discussed here are drawn from the most famous, most representative of a given period or are the most significant for the development of the genre. Finally, although the comics discussed here were largely produced in the last century, many of them depicted much earlier events. For instance, the war comic *Two-Fisted Tales,* published by EC Comics in the 1950s, included historical war stories such as the Battle of New Orleans in 1815.

World War I and Cartoon Illustrations

During the early twentieth century, American artists frequently summed up an entire national character in the form of a single iconic figure. Just as the "doughboy"—slang for an American soldier—could symbolize American heroism, his call to patriotic duty could be embodied in the venerable figure of Uncle Sam. This image was immortalized in the popular World War I recruitment poster painted by James Montgomery Flagg in 1917 and inspired by the British poster of Lord Kitchener.[10] The large pointing finger was meant to directly involve the viewer. If Uncle Sam represented America's virile masculinity, Columbia gave citizens a feminine form for the abstract concept of the nation. Many saw her as a representing all that was best in America. Throughout World War I, posters depicted Columbia as an armed woman rising to her duty. In one early propaganda poster, a Boy Scout hands her a sword.[11] In another, she is a helpless maiden ravaged by a bestial figure wearing elements of the German enemy's uniform, such as the spiked helmet.[12] Animals also served as symbols of national types, for instance the resolute British bulldog or the German "beast," in the savage form of the ape. These personifications of national types, among others originally drawn for posters, later became comic book characters during World War II. An example was Uncle Sam, who became a comic book character by 1941.

Before World War I, comic strips were usually devoted to condemning moral vices such as gambling and drinking (or supporting the American cause during foreign conflicts). Bud Fisher's comic strip *Mutt and Jeff,* which debuted in 1907, is an excellent example of this focus. From its inception, originally under the title *A. Mutt,* the comic strip dealt with gambling, in the form of playing cards, betting on horses, or playing other games of chance. These strips targeted an older audience: a child may have been familiar with betting, but he or she was hardly likely to understand the subtleties of the subject.[13] Fisher made his living as the creator of these comic strips, collecting royalties even when he was not actively drawing. When the United States entered World War I, he wanted to enlist, as he considered the war a "big show" that would bring both excitement and comic fodder for further Mutt and Jeff strips. The American military denied him the chance to simultaneously serve and draw the strip. Instead, he joined the British Army—as an officer no less—and continued the comic strip. Fisher's wartime comics continued to depict adult vices such as gambling and drinking, which soldiers engaged in when not on the battlefield.

His characters served in the various Allied armies in Western Europe in World War I. In one story arc, Jeff, the shorter and scruffier character, joins the U.S. Army Air Corps and tries his hand at bombing practice. As the concept of aerial bombing was still new, pilots often tested their skills by using various kinds of dummy bombs. In this strip, Jeff drops a sandbag and succeeds in knocking Mutt out. While the story relied on a pratfall, the image's more serious message of the character doing his part for the war effort was probably not lost on the reader.[14]

The Interwar Period

For those back home, the widely accessible format of the comics opened windows into the soldier's life on foreign shores, allowing readers of all levels of education to participate virtually in a fight they had supported remotely. One such example of early war visual arts is *Halt Friends!* (1924), a pamphlet produced as a charitable moneymaking venture for unemployed ex-servicemen. (Americans purchased copies of *Halt Friends!* to support World War I veterans, just as many today buy copies of the paper *Streetwise* from the homeless.) *Halt Friends!* describes the experiences of ordinary doughboys and contained a series of poems, ditties, and recollections of the combatants.[15] While not a true comic book in the sense of juxtaposed pictures telling a story, it did feature caricatures of officers, servicemen, and the conditions that the men encountered in France. While the publication's readership was largely civilian, it also contained jokes that only those with an intimate familiarity with military culture would find understandable.

Another example of soldier life told through humorous pictures was *Happy Days,* by Capt. Alban Butler of the American First Infantry Division. Originally published in 1928, Butler's book contained various vignettes of soldierly life. It offered a humorous portrayal of the troops of World War I, as well as a voice to those frustrations that all soldiers face: inhospitable living conditions, lack of access to official military information, and the seemingly cruel or arbitrary actions of superiors. Butler's creation of this comic was significant for two reasons. First, as an officer he could convey information that the average foot soldier did not possess—such as the tactical purpose of plans and intentions and of the morale of a wider body of troops. Second, he included pioneering comical drawings, almost akin to slapstick. This kind of "big foot" approach in humorous illustration was common in newspapers from the early 1900s and a basis for many early comic books when they entered the mass market in the mid-1930s.[16]

Butler's book contained art far more meaningful than the simple sight gags might suggest. The moral and political complexities of war were underlying ideas in many of the cartoons, which many readers, especially younger ones, would not have comprehended. One such cartoon was a single panel showing German children ranging in age from roughly two through ten years old. Underneath the caption was the phrase "future machine gunners." This particular panel was not without significance. It documented the frustrations of American soldiers concerning the Versailles Treaty of 1919, which some feared too heavily favored the Great Powers. Many who served considered the treaty grounds for the next war, since the agreement inflicted monetary punishment on the Germans and placed many restrictions on their political sovereignty. In retrospect, therefore, Butler's book was remarkably prescient. German children of the late 1910s and early 1920s eventually became the backbone of the German army, the SA (or Brown Shirts), and the notorious SS, which best represented the Nazi ideal of the "Aryan" soldier. Many American soldiers saw the Germans generally as nameless "Huns," but the most brutal among them was the machine gunner, who could inflict massive death and injury. The cartoon's reference was very significant to the military readers, who would see the potential connection between this development and the emergence of German killers later on in life.[17]

The Need for Entertainment in the Depression

While many veterans of the Great War were adapting to life back in the United States, rising forms of entertainment competed for status in the city and country alike. The newspaper funnies served as a form of escape from the gloominess of daily news events, especially after Black Thursday and the start of the Great Depression. The comics, usually two to four panels organized as a horizontal column—whence came the term "strip"—provided the reader with all sorts of information and humor. Pratfalls like those of the Keystone Kops, the raucous pranks of the Katzenjammer Kids,[18] and the exploits of Flash Gordon and Terry and the Pirates entranced readers young and old with daily adventures in near and faraway lands.[19] Comic strips gave readers an entry to a happier alternate reality. This audience included adults, who looked to escape bad news from the front page of the newspaper, and children, who might not understand the adult concepts but understood the story through pictures.

In 1933 salesman Max Gaines noted that a standard newsprint sheet, folded three times and stapled in the middle, produced a cheap format in which weekly comic strips could be resold in booklet form. He secured the rights to some popular strips, hired Eastman Color Printing, and released the first true comic book, *Famous Funnies: A Carnival of Comics,* in 1933. While merely reprints packaged in a new format, the comic book was an immediate success at the newsstands.[20] It presented no new stories, but children who might not regularly see newspapers or have access to some popular strips could now buy a series of short illustrated stories for a very low price. In a way, comic books were analogous to the adult pulp novels of the day, minus their lurid and sensational themes. *Famous Funnies* was so successful that many publishers copied the new format. As comic books proliferated, they began to explore different genres aimed at different readers—just as newspaper cartoons, comic strips, and serials had before them.

Of these new genres, the most popular was, and largely still is, the superhero comic. Its characters were defined by their superpowers and devotion to fighting for social justice. During this early evolution of the comic book, National Comics (now DC, but as it was known at the time) quickly established itself as the leading publishing house in the field with the largest readership. DC's *Action Comics* #1, released in June of 1938, featured the first appearance of Superman, the creation of writer Jerry Siegel and artist Joel Schuster; *Detective Comics* #27 introduced Batman. While these characters had broad appeal, comic book creators also devised a variety of superheroes to fit the tastes of niche readers, maximizing potential sales. Other successful superheroes from this early period included Captain Marvel, Hawkman, the Flash, and Plastic Man. The popularity of the superhero comics led companies to plagiarism, usually with doppelgängers of existing popular characters, occasionally leading to lawsuits threats over copyright infringement.[21]

Typical story lines centered on crime fighting. Some superheroes—such as Prince Namor, the Sub-Mariner, and Jim Hammond, the Human Torch—even fought each other when not fighting crime. These two superheroes fought crime with the help of futuristic technologies, which addressed an important topic at the time: the implications of scientific progress. Namor, the child of a sea captain and a mermaid princess, could breathe on land and under water and had the ability to fly. The Human Torch was an android who could catch fire if exposed to enough oxygen and then would possess all the powers associated with flame: he could fly, weld or melt metal, and shoot flame balls or jets of flame.[22] Despite their struggles, often billed as the fight between fire and water, the two had a moral center that ultimately allowed them to combat evil through their genetically or scientifically enhanced bodies.

A considerable problem that comic book scholars have encountered is making meaningful distinctions between the comic book and the comic strip. This difficulty is especially evident in such comic books as *Famous Funnies,* which were themselves compilations of newspaper comic strips. As the popularity of the comic books grew, the genres of the comic book and comic strip increasingly crossed over. Two examples are the Superman comics, which started out in comic books but were adapted into a daily comic strip format as well, and Will Eisner's *The Spirit,* which started out as a comic strip but was quickly adapted into a comic book. The crossover was important for increasing the exposure of the characters to a wider and more varied audience. Moreover, by transitioning from the newspaper-based strips to the longer comic book, the plots could develop into more detail, and the characters could show greater emotional depth and the reasons behind their actions. Eisner was instrumental in developing the longer, self-contained comic book, later called the graphic novel.[23]

Regardless of the format, by the 1930s the comic also became a significant engine of social change. For example, the cartoon strip *Little Orphan Annie* appeared in the *Chicago Tribune* syndication network and inspired readers to voice their opinions on social issues that affected the protagonist. How to resolve Annie's poverty precipitated a story-line fight between *Chicago Tribune* editor Joseph Patterson and the creator Harold Gray. The poor orphan is virtually adopted by Daddy Warbucks, a wealthy tycoon. When he is away on business, she is watched by the Silos, a family that lives on a modest farm. Patterson initially cancelled the strip over his objection to Annie staying permanently with Warbucks, according to Gray's original plot. Despite Warbucks' wealth, their relationship was cold and formal, as opposed to the warmth and affection Annie experienced with the Silos. The strip was reinstated when many readers protested its cancellation. Patterson later asked the audience to weigh in on Annie's fate. Opinions were split evenly—with one side adamantly supporting the financial stability offered by Warbucks and the other arguing for the paramount value of the love offered by the Silos. In the end, Annie goes to live with Daddy Warbucks.[24] For the readers of *Annie,* the character had become a bellwether of the conditions and hard choices of the Depression.

From their inception, comics' story lines have interjected references to current events or concerns. An example would be political events from overseas, such as the rise of Adolf Hitler. Even as a form of escape, the comic book allowed readers to fantasize about punishing real-life wrongdoers. Since the Depression was the overriding concern of Americans during the 1930s, readers enjoyed seeing superheroes fight against those who exploited the bad times for their own financial benefit. For example, early characters such as the Green Lantern, Superman, and Batman often took on corrupt businessmen who mistreated poor and desperate workers in the late 1930s. One story involved Superman's revenge on a mine owner who allowed unsafe working conditions to prevail in his mines. Only after Superman saves the miners trapped in a cave-in are the conditions of the overall business exposed and the guilty brought to justice.[25] Although the Depression had already slowly abated by then, its memory was still fresh in readers' minds in 1938 and 1939 when these stories appeared. These superheroes took on the industrialists and made them behave in a socially conscious manner.[26]

The key to success for many comic books and strips was the fact that they represented strong characters, which symbolized stability during a time of chaos. As William Young has argued in his article "The Serious Funnies," strong figures such as Tarzan and Steve Canyon represented a force of order, especially in the untamed wilds of Africa or Asia. Imposing order onto the chaos created by the "savages" of the uncivilized world, or the brutal Axis armies overrunning Europe and Asia, was a recurring theme in many comic story lines throughout the 1940s. The most important message of Depression-era comics was that such chaos could be contained and defeated. Men who might harbor private doubts about their courage would rise to the occasion, and those who promoted chaos would ultimately fail.[27]

Toward the end of the Great Depression, comics served as a way to warn of the Japanese assault on China and the encroaching German menace in Europe. Comics such as Milton Caniff's *Terry and the Pirates* (first published in October 1934) dealt with the adventures of American men in different locations around the globe.[28] Yet, for the most part, the Axis armies were merely sideshows to these exotic backdrops—not active parts of the stories. Before the United States joined World War II, most Americans felt insulated from the danger and violence, such as the Japanese occupation of China in the late 1930s. Many of these early comics were closer to action-adventure stories than true war comics were. There were gunplay and fights, yet the stories did not necessarily read as war narratives. Instead, the comics were merely about men acting for the "right reasons" and helping the underdog.

One aspect of real life that transferred into the comics was the enlistment of American pilots in the Royal Air Force to fight the Germans before the U.S. entry into the war. These protagonists were extensions of the action hero type, who did not conform to the regulations of the American military. The stories portray Americans looking for adventure and seeking to fight for what was "right" in world society—as in the case of the Americans who volunteered to serve in the Canadian and British armed forces and with the Flying Tigers, who fought for the Chinese air forces between 1940 and 1941.

Comics often depicted an idealized image of war: fighting the good fight for the betterment of society. Enemies, in this case the Axis powers of World War II, were depicted as stereotypes of all that was wrong in society. These caricatures prevailed in all forms of entertainment, and comics were no exception. The combat in early comic books was not bloody, and if the hero died, it was an honorable, not needless, death. One common subject was about fractious squad members quarrelling within their own ranks. Once a member of the squad was killed, however, the unit would set aside its differences and rally to avenge its dead comrade's sacrifice. The greater good of society, of which this scenario is a microcosm, was a major theme of wartime entertainment and propaganda.

As comics developed during the Great Depression, their stories initially centered on domestic threats: evil corporations, nefarious individuals, and criminal groups. The portrayals of the Germans, who were almost always depicted as Nazis, and the Japanese, however, externalized American anger and extended these themes into World War II and foreign politics. Neither the Germans nor the Japanese were significant elements in comic story lines until the late 1930s, when the various Axis land grabs made headlines and alerted Americans to the possibility of an imminent war. Prior to this period, the main antagonists that crossed the pages of American comic books were criminals, especially those from the FBI's list of "public enemies." They were sensational and violent, and criminals John Dillinger, "Baby Face" Nelson, Bonnie and Clyde, and others became the initial models for many of the earlier flashy comic book villains.

With the advent of the war, artists draped these established tropes onto new enemies. The Nazis actively menaced surrounding countries, bullied weaker people, and opposed American ideals. Depictions of the Japanese, building both on their physiognomy and as racist stereotypes, portrayed as vicious and subhuman the people who had invaded the city of Nanking and attacked the USS *Panay*. While news reports tried to downplay events abroad, these racial stereotypes presented the German and Japanese as everyone's enemies, vicious even to women and children. As John Dower noted in *War without Mercy*, perceptions of the enemy's viciousness made it possible to hate them for what they did *not* represent. American values, such as fighting honorably against enemies, prevented Americans from stooping to the level of the Japanese and retaliating against "mistakes" like the *Panay* incident.[29]

As the fear of war became more pronounced, Depression-era businessmen were courted by greedy military industrialists willing to fund anyone who could further their profits. An excellent example of the fictional portrayal of this situation is the Red Skull's initial appearance in the Captain America series. The Red Skull is a Nazi sympathizer named George Maxon who is willing to sell anything to the Germans. While the Red Skull is killed in the story, this connection to the Nazis in a time of deep anti-German sentiment made the Red Skull a great villain—leading the writers to revive the character.[30]

Before World War II, the interests of comic book readers reflected the isolationist attitudes that prevailed across the country. War-themed comics were not particularly popular. Indeed, readers were far more interested in adventure stories at a time when the most active combat arm of the United States was the Marine Corps. Marines' exploits would be occasionally referred to in comics, and the Marine Corps would play an increasingly pivotal role once the United States entered the war. The popular comics closest to the war genre were action comics such as *Flash Gordon* and *Terry and the Pirates,* which featured adventurers, gunplay, and the high technology associated with modern combat.

The story lines of *Terry and the Pirates* by Milton Caniff, *Tailspin* by Hal Forrest, and *Barney Baxter* by Frank Miller (not to be confused with the contemporary comic book artist of the same name) all sought to transport readers into exciting, exotic locales. Not only did these comics illustrate the theme of bringing order to chaos, they also foreshadowed future military conflicts. The setting for all three comics is Asia. The main characters serve as pilots or adventurers in some capacity, reflecting the widespread desire for physical, social, and economic mobility in Depression-era society.[31] *Tailspin* and *Terry and the Pirates,* in particular, were drawn with lavish attention to detail. In these comics the accurate, even technical, depiction of planes and uniforms became a point of pride. When the war finally reached America, the comics quickly and effectively embraced military themes. The fictional Barney Baxter participated in a bombing raid on Japan approximately six weeks before the real Lt. Col. James Doolittle raided Tokyo in April 1942.[32] As the war began, the traditional superheroes got involved, albeit most frequently on the home front. Over time, however, war comics emerged as a standalone genre, whose popularity waxed and waned over the following seventy years, largely depending on the nation's involvement in wars.

The Comics Expand

As comics had to meet tight deadlines and because the genre was expanding at an exponential rate, the books often took on a cheap, slipshod appearance. The

fast production schedule also meant that colors were sometimes printed outside their intended borders. Readers who looked at art with a critical eye saw
the comic book as the epitome of lowbrow. The art was sloppy and ill defined,
the characters trite and formulaic, and the stories often ridiculous. The artists
themselves did little to counter this perception, as they had no contractual
commitments to any particular publishers. It was still a freelance business, and
comic book artists and writers often worked for several companies to make
ends meet. As the medium was not yet considered fully legitimate, many writers and artists worked under pen names. Some feared that if they were known
to work in the comic book industry, they would have trouble getting work
in graphic design or fine art. Another theory for the aliases was that as comic book artists often had to freelance, using the same names might get them
in trouble, especially if they worked on similar comic characters for different
publishers. The need to produce comic books in an expedient manner sometimes required teams of artists in order to finish projects on time.

Finally, the majority of artists and comic book creators came from Jewish backgrounds, and anti-Semitism could still be a problem. They often Anglicized their
names rather than risk alienating anti-Semitic readers. As a result, many of the
most famous names from the golden age of comics were actually pseudonyms:
Stanley Leiber became Stan Lee (writer, hereafter indicated by "w"), Jakob Kurtz-
burg became Jack Kirby (artist: "a"), and Batman creator Bob Kahn became Bob
Kane (a). Some Jewish comic book creators, however, such as Will Eisner (a), Joe
Schuster (a), and Jerry Siegel (w), worked under their real names.[33]

Comic Books and the Fascist Threat
Though American comics were a form of escapism for many people, for the Nazis
they were an unachievable or even ridiculous fantasy. During a Reichstag speech,
German propaganda minister Josef Goebbels claimed that as Superman was a creation of Jews, he epitomized all that was wrong with American society in general. Nazi
leaders considered it an affront that Americans dared represent themselves by such
an amazing character, when "real" Americans were lazy and crass creatures. Hitler
believed that the popular culture of the United States was grossly inferior to that of
even the least cultured European countries. He noted that even the English, with their
regrettably lowbrow tastes, were more refined than the jazz-listening, mongrelized
Americans. The comic book was another example of how Americans cheapened art,
lowered standards, and were therefore unable to uphold proper Aryan ideals. Furthermore, the Nazis considered this a betrayal: most Americans qualified as members
of the Aryan race, yet they allowed themselves to be controlled by Jews and blacks.[34]

Most comic book creators were quite young—many in their late teens or
early twenties—thus hardly older than much of their readership. For instance,

Jerry Schuster and Joel Siegel were only in their late teens when they sold the rights of Superman to DC Comics. As a result, creators and readers tended to see things in the same way. Stories advocated social justice and how to make a difference. Superman made corrupt officials or business leaders change their evil ways and, once the war began, fought against the tyranny of dictators.[35] These youthful ideals often helped to gain a younger audience.

Comic book writers discussed, albeit in simplified terms, the need for the U.S. government to become involved in political issues at home and abroad. At the same time, they expressed the revenge fantasies provoked by the death of a loyal sidekick or group member. One only needed to listen to the radio or look at a newspaper to understand that the clouds of war were gathering in Europe. Japan's invasion of China, and not just the exotic locale, was an important reason *Terry and the Pirates* was set in Asia. The *Destroyer,* by Atlas Comics (later Marvel), described the fight against Nazism within Germany and depicted fantasies of freeing people the Nazis had imprisoned in concentration camps.[36]

Jack Kirby (a) and Joe Simon (w), creators of the iconic *Captain America,* were also very young. Kirby was barely twenty-one when the comic book took off in early 1941, and even when he returned to drawing comics after his Army service in Europe, he was considered an "old man" at twenty-five. Simon was slightly older than Kirby but still was in his early twenties when World War II began. Stan Lee, nephew of Atlas Comics publisher Martin Goodman, was only seventeen when he started as a gofer for Simon and Kirby. By *Captain America* #4, he was scripting some pages of the comics; by 1943, he was writing some complete comics such as *Captain America* and the *Destroyer.* Lee's story lines showed remarkable political and historical knowledge. Like several other Jewish comic book creators, he used the comics to advocate U.S. intervention, but on the basis of doing the right thing, and deemphasized rescuing their Jewish relatives suffering in Europe. Lee wrote comics until he enlisted. He then served in the Army stateside and remained involved in the comic medium.[37]

Other early comic creators wrote about European battles in their stories. One of the earliest such comics, and perhaps most viable in terms of sales, was *Wings Comics* from Dell Publishing. Dell was one of the first comic book companies, as well as one of the more successful. *Wings Comics* contained several mini-stories, which told of the adventure of war. Vignettes included stories of the Skull Squad, an Allied bombing group in Europe. There was also "Jane Martin, nurse," whose identity was later changed from a nurse to a spy. Clipper Kirk was an adventurer whose stories, like those of *Terry and the Pirates,* centered on the Orient. Grease Monkey Griffin had the technical expertise that enabled him to fix and fly any plane.

The story arcs of all these comics emphasized the Axis efforts to rule the world, with an emphasis of the German threat to the world. Of the first eighteen issues of *Wings,* the Japanese were cast as the enemy in only two characters' story lines: those of Clipper Kirk and Grease Monkey Griffin. Even in those two stories, the Japanese were depicted as mere dupes of the Germans. This assumption was common throughout early war comics. More often than not, while the Japanese were seen as cruel overlords in Asia, they were little threat to Americans or the American mainland. The Japanese did not even figure in *Wings Comics* #18, which came out immediately after their attack on Pearl Harbor on December 7, 1941.

One of the most prolific artists who would eventually convey the experiences of the average soldier was Bill Mauldin, who started sketching as an Arizona high school student in the late 1930s. Mauldin worked in comic panels rather than in strips or books, and his work was generally published in small publications, including his high school newspaper or *Arizona Highways* magazine. Mauldin often took aim at political issues in the Arizona area, but his grasp of the wider political world was insightful, especially for a high school student. After graduating, he joined the Arizona National Guard, which later became a part of the Forty-Fifth Infantry Division. By the time he attained fame as the creator of *Willie and Joe* and *Up Front,* he was still a mere twenty-one years old.[38]

Equity and Comic Book Work

As the comic book industry took off in the late 1930s, many artists drifted from company to company in search of better conditions, more money, and greater artistic collaboration. One publisher that developed a reputation for fairness and decent wages was Phoenix Studios. Run by Will Eisner and Jerry Iger, Phoenix produced comic books that were popular and at the same time offered artists the chance to expand their creative horizons. Eisner himself wrote for several famous comics, the most popular of the day being *The Spirit,* about a quirky private eye.[39] His other scripts yielded adventurous characters and stories that tied into the real news of war. The most famous was *Blackhawk,* written by Eisner and drawn by Chuck Cuidera. The first issue, published in 1941, tells the story of a Polish pilot shot down by the evil German Baron von Tepp, who goes on to strafe the farmhouse of the pilot's family. After witnessing this and hearing about other German atrocities, Blackhawk vows to punish all Germans. As the story line progresses, he recruits a crew of fighters from around the free world, constituting a virtual United Nations to fight the Axis menace. They somehow build a secret island base, from which Blackhawk and his band fly advanced fighters against the Nazis.

The story included all the key elements of contemporary American propaganda: German atrocities, Allied war goals defined by the UN concept, vengeance against the evil enemy, and most important a sense of adventure and excitement. Though the story stuck to the standard script, this did not mean that all was well or that the war was without consequences. In the comics people are captured, lose family members, are wounded, and sometimes die. But these sacrifices are never in vain, as they help advance a cause, and characters who fail at first get the chance to redeem themselves in combat.[40]

The role of the sidekick emerged early in the development of comics, as they served as an important link for younger readers. By identifying with a sidekick of similar age or slightly older than themselves, young readers were able to envision themselves fighting on the side of right and vanquishing America's foes. During the run-up to the American entry into the war, young characters were often shown in various combat roles. While this is disconcerting today in an age when the abuse of child soldiers is well known, at the time it was seen as a useful type of propaganda, as it encouraged younger people to work their way into support or even fighting roles as the war progressed. Such sidekicks included Bucky (Captain America), Zippy (the Black Terror), Robin (Batman), Toro (Human Torch), and even groups of young fighters such as the Boy Commandos and Young Allies. While there was always an adult supervisor, at times these sidekicks and auxiliaries fought real battles on their own.

A particularly popular plot device was brainwashing, an example of which appeared in the story "Grease Monkey Griffin" in *Wings* #15. This issue exhibits one of the most confusing adaptations of racial ideology imaginable. On the cover, a Zulu-like African warrior stands in the cockpit of a flying plane and throws a spear at an Allied plane—while carrying a copy of *Mein Kampf* in his other hand. In the story line, it is revealed that the tribesmen have been brainwashed by Nazi agents in the heart of the African jungle. This sort of indoctrination was frequent in comic books and showed how effectively it was believed that Hitler could sway people to his cause. It also implicitly assumed that Africans were simple-minded and easily duped, and therefore they needed American or European protection (part of "the white man's burden").

Comic book publishers noticed the appeal of stories about bravery and started publishing stories about the exploits of explorers, heroes of old, and even Canadian soldiers fighting for freedom in Europe. Dell and the Parents Magazine Institute (publisher of *Parents Magazine* among others) were the two biggest producers of this kind of comic. Both companies tried to promote these comics as visual learning devices and not merely vacuous entertainment as so many adults believed. The Parents Magazine Institute attempted to use comic book stories to emulate history texts in both the *Real Heroes* and *True Stories* series.

Many of the early stories were based on events from American history, such as George Washington's battles, the actions of Rogers' Rangers, and other factual sources.[41] The stories were often centered on uplifting events and on the eventual triumph of the American spirit over evil and adversity. As the series progressed, the story lines shifted to the heroism of American and Canadian military forces in combat. *True Comics* eventually subsumed *Real Heroes* and published eighty-three issues before ending its run. Comic writers also introduced their readers to different lands. After Pearl Harbor, they ran the country profiles that detailed life for South American U.S. allies, among others.[42] The *True Comics* style was emulated by other companies and even took hold in Canada, where the series *Canadian Heroes* was produced. These comics were a way to enlighten younger or less educated readers about current and historical events.

The Shift to War

Not long after December 7, 1941, a comic book titled *Remember Pearl Harbor* was published that illustrated the horrific events of that day. Readers were shown not only the events as perceived at the time—often not very accurately—but also stories of real and fictional individuals with whom the reader might empathize.[43] Several comic books capitalized on the Pearl Harbor attack or fears of another such attack, this time on the mainland, as a way to boost their readership. Comics soon came out that promoted for various war material drives, for example *Boys and Girls Can Help Uncle Sam Win the War!* This comic book told children about basic steps that they could take to contribute to the war effort. Many of the comics switched over to a "war footing," paralleling the larger society. Yet the Japanese were mentioned relatively little before Pearl Harbor and less than the Germans even afterward. Once the United States entered the war, the majority of American resources were deployed to the European theater.[44]

The comics produced during the war defined "the American way"—a place where science and equality prevailed over ignorance. It reinforced the idea that America was a place where people who worked hard to better themselves could become successful, while looking out for the oppressed at the same time. Yet many comic book stories were also what Lary May called subversive narratives, pointing out how domestic corporations and criminals—not just foreign villains—sought to undermine American ideals.[45] Right after the war began, some comics attempted to build support among skeptical Americans. Stories were often about a central character, ambivalent or hostile about the war, who learns the error of his ways and comes over to the side of justice and equality. As the war continued, story lines and advertisements continued to emphasize the superiority of the Allied cause. As the comics of World War II reached the newsstands for sale, they were eagerly purchased by a public in need of hope and entertainment.

2 Fighting for Freedom (1939–45)

John Liberty—Professor of American History—is stirred by the evening headlines! "Innocent workers killed by fiends who seek to destroy American Democracy!" What we need to battle America's enemies are the spirits of old!—to keep
the ideals of American freedom alive!—with a *man* to lead them!

—SYD SHORES, PHIL STURM, AND JOE KLEIN,
Marvel Masterworks: USA Comics

Immediately before the war, the most notable development was the dramatic increase in the number and variety of patriotically themed superheroes. These included the major character Captain America and such minor
characters as the Shield, Uncle Sam, the Defender, Spirit of '76, and Major Liberty (the latter quoted above). These characters aimed to instill patriotism and
build support on the home front during a time of national crisis. They did so in
part by battling exaggerated internal threats to the United States from Bundists
and Axis spies. Unlike the real armed forces, which sometimes missed warn-
ings of pending attacks, the costumed characters always avert disaster at the
critical moment.

In the story "Human Torch and Sub-Mariner Fighting Side by Side," written
by Carl Burgos and illustrated by Bill Everett, the Japanese and Germans use
Allied prisoners of war as slave laborers to dig a massive tunnel through Alaska
and Canada to invade the American West Coast. Just as the Japanese are about
to launch their attack through the tunnel, the Human Torch and Sub-Mariner
go on the offensive and roundly defeat the enemy army.[1] Of course, only the
superheroes can stop such a devious and improbable project and always at
the last second before absolute calamity strikes. Superheroes reassured Americans that they could feel safe. This particular story also illustrates how two
traditional enemies—the Torch and Sub-Mariner, representing fire and water,
respectively—could unite for a common cause. The message was clear: the
Axis was the greatest threat of all.

Calls for U.S. Entry into the War

At first the war in Europe affected Americans only indirectly. However, as events in Europe and Asia became more violent and unpredictable, the country slowly shifted its stance to a war footing. More people actively called for war, but others vehemently opposed it. In this environment, most comic book creators tried to include more information about the conflict, while others used the war as a staging ground for fantasy and entertainment. Unlike most Americans, the majority of artists and writers of comic books favored American intervention in Europe and Asia.

The comic book heroes of the 1930s functioned as enforcers of a high moral and social order, as superheroes including Superman, Batman, and the Green Lantern battled unscrupulous corporate profiteers. It was a natural progression from fighting corporate greed to fighting enemies of all things "American."[2] Friends and family members who had escaped from Europe told the artists about Nazi abuses and cruelty, which were not usually reported in the press. Joe Kubert, who started illustrating *Hawkman* in the early 1940s, recalled hearing of Nazi atrocities around the dinner table in his house in New York.[3] Of utmost importance, as noted in chapter 1, many comic book creators came from Jewish backgrounds and were especially appalled and disgusted by what Hitler was doing to Jews in Europe. Comic books became an outlet to vent a desire for vengeance, as well as a medium to mobilize the American people against Nazism.

One artist, Peter Kuper, has postulated that Jews writing comic books were trying to push American entry into World War II when most Jewish movie moguls at the time were hesitant to do so.[4] Given the apparent threat that the comics represented to the Nazis, as demonstrated by Goebbels' comments to the Reichstag concerning Superman, the impact of comic books was significant. They did more than merely boost the morale of the American reader.[5] These pro-war comics argued that superheroes needed to "do the right thing" for America. Like members of other immigrant groups, comic book creators wanted to be successful in American society. The comics were a means to that end, both financially and socially. They made the case that their assimilation reflected ethnic and religious pluralism and a broader and more profound tolerance and was therefore a reason to fight for the ideals of America.

Even Theodore Geisel, better known as Dr. Seuss, the famous illustrator of children's books, took a strong pro-intervention stance before the war. While Geisel's real fame came in the 1950s with his first children's book, *Horton Lays an Egg,* he argued in his earlier work for the leftist New York newspaper *PM* for the need to stop Hitler.[6] The whimsical characters that accompanied Hitler in his *PM* illustrations appealed to both youngsters and adults, regardless of their education. Geisel later used these *PM* characters (most famously Private Snafu) in a new format—short, animated training films for the U.S. Army made in conjunction with the Walt Disney and Warner Brothers studios.[7]

Comic Books after U.S. Entry into War

The American people's anger after the devious Japanese attack on Pearl Harbor led to a powerful desire for revenge. The comic books, which had already shown Americans fighting the Axis in limited ways for several years, now shifted into high gear. Comics, like other popular media, now attempted to rally the populace to support the troops, conduct recycling and war bond drives, and to hate the enemy generally. The comics had several propaganda goals: to unite people behind the war effort; to encourage vigilance against enemy spies; to rebut Axis propaganda; to portray the enemy as immoral, brutal, and—especially the Japanese—subhuman; and, finally, to assure the population that the Allies were fighting for a just cause.

Readers were looking for realistic depictions of the conflict in which their family members, coworkers, and neighbors were engaged, yet they also wished to escape from the horrors that war entailed. At times this was a difficult balancing act for the artists. The lines between entertainment, reportage, and propaganda often blurred. Accuracy also mattered. Prewar comics could get by with invented details, but now even younger readers were often familiar with the armaments, uniforms, and lingo of the new war. Action, however, trumped realism, and the subject was so immediate and compelling that the stories still held the readers' interest. The various German uniforms might not always be the proper color, but given the sales of *Captain America, USA Comics,* and the like, it seems that such inconsistencies could be overlooked.

Using a "ripped from the headlines" approach, comics gained immediacy by telling of heroic acts of real men or women in combat through fictionalized versions of their stories or with more accurate but abbreviated versions in such comic books as *True Comics.* In the former case, comic writers noted the barbarous use of child soldiers, while American children had pursued the nobler goal of supporting the war by watching for spies rather than fighting in combat. Comic book artists promoted World War II as "the good war" (as oral historian Studs Terkel later described it), by illustrating the war's aims and how the home front could work for victory. Comic books were used to enlist everyone into the total war effort. One suggested that children could assist by buying war bonds and stamps (the latter were available in denominations as little as a dime). It provided a list of what the bond might pay for: "$150 buys a submachine gun for the marines, $1.00 buys an entrenching shovel, and $65 buys a .45 pistol, with five rounds for ten cents!"[8] The standard comic cost a dime.

Members of the Axis powers were usually portrayed in caricature: the German officers were effete, aristocratic, and cruel; the Italians incompetent and manipulated by the Germans; the Japanese monkey-like and treacherous. The Japanese, in particular, were presented as the worst kind of stereotype. These characterizations portrayed enemy villains in such a way that all social, educational, and age groups could set aside the war's complex political issues, if necessary, and support it. While not the only reason for the use of stereotypes, this was an effective way to shape attitudes toward the enemy.[9] Negative stereotypes were not confined to enemies, however; Africans were drawn with grotesque features, and they were unable to speak except in short, simple phrases. Anyone who was thus seen as inferior to the white American ideal obviously needed protection. This attitude was typical of Western society for a long time before the war, as exemplified by the heroes of H. Rider Haggard's novels and Edgar Rice Burroughs' Tarzan, who easily dominated the "savages" of the African interior.[10] Such tales of noble white men protecting civilization and white womanhood against dangerous aborigines became part of the comics' legends. This theme was carried over to *Terry and the Pirates* and Shock Gibson, among others.[11]

The depiction of Americans in the comics was just as one-sided and simplistic as that of the dastardly enemy or simple-minded, yet threatening, native. Especially influential was Norman Rockwell's "The Four Freedoms" series of paintings, which inspired many forms of mass communication and propaganda. They depicted average Americans exercising and enjoying freedom of speech, freedom of worship, freedom from want, and freedom from fear.[12] The men in comic books, and war propaganda more generally, were illustrated with the best "American" qualities: handsome chiseled features, broad shoulders, and a superior knowledge of science and technology. That this characterization closely resembled the Nazi *Übermensch* was doubly ironic: a major reason the Nazis disliked Superman was that he was created by Jews. Despite his obviously superior attributes, the Germans claimed he looked like a Jew, a serious contradiction to their racial ideology.[13] At least Captain America, another idealized character (and Jewish creation), was as blond and blue-eyed as the Aryan ideal.

One notable feature of these wartime superheroes was their red, white, and blue attire. Ordinary soldiers took to the battlefield in olive-drab uniforms and sought cover whenever possible. By contrast, the superhero awes and challenges the enemy by going into battle conspicuously emblazoned with his colors like warriors of old. Yet writers and artists had to walk a fine line in how they portrayed these characters and how they showed them fighting the enemy. If a superhero was too successful at a time when the war was going against the United States, people became demoralized and sales dropped. If the superhero only fought imaginary or relatively nonthreatening foes (such as domestic criminals), he appeared to be shirking his wartime duty. This balancing act became even more difficult when women entered the defense-related workforce, as well as the comic book genre. The paramount attribute of American superheroes— and, by extension, all American fighting men—was their unwillingness to use their skills, technology, or equipment for any immoral or illegal act. In stark contrast, enemies of the United States had no qualms about using all means at their disposal to conquer the world.

The subtext of these depictions could be read as subversive, albeit not intentionally so. The United States was purportedly fighting against the Nazi racial ideology, yet comic books presented almost identical Aryan archetypes as stereotypical Americans, albeit these qualities were especially exaggerated in superheroes. In addition, Jews devised nearly all of these characters during a time of widespread anti-Semitism in America. The subordination of blacks and the vicious race-hatred directed at the Japanese, including the internment of Japanese Americans, only underlined the hypocrisy of American propaganda—including many comic books.

Comic Books during World War II

By the time the United States became embroiled in full-scale fighting in 1942, the comics that had pushed for its involvement developed story lines around the valor of the Allied countries. The comics presented to Americans superheroes who took on the enemy or their sympathizers. If comic books before the U.S. entry into the war called for intervention, after Pearl Harbor they explained how people could work for a common cause: world freedom. While the comics incorporated real stories of American heroism, the creators also memorialized Allied soldiers. For example, especially after the Battle of Britain in 1940, comic books glorified the efforts of the British, the Free French, and the Free Poles (and other refugee governments based in London). It was in this environment that the Polish American comic book character Blackhawk emerged.[14] Will Eisner and many other artists, including Joe Simon, Jack Kirby, and Reed Crandall, quickly brought superheroes into the war effort when the United States finally entered the war. Many writers joined the War Writers Board (WWB), which was established to promote government policy as well as discourage profiteering.[15] While a private organization, the WWB quickly joined forces with the Office of War Information (OWI). Headed by Elmer Davis, the OWI focused on coordinating all media for the war effort.[16] The comic book creators cooperated with the prevailing attitude of supporting the war.

The OWI wanted to give people generally accurate details of the war (overt government censorship was technically limited to military information). At the same time, it worked to prevent the publication of images that might discourage or demoralize the public. Movies and cartoons for adults remained upbeat and invariably patriotic, and comic books did the same but in an even more obvious way. The comics aimed to do more than merely give children hope about the outcome of the war; they also promoted collecting scrap paper and metal, as well as war stamps, to foster the sense that "we're all in this together." (Stamps denominated in cents could be bought incrementally and eventually converted to war bonds.) Such comics as *Young Allies, Captain America,* and the *Boy Commandos* constantly reminded readers to be vigilant against enemy spy rings or to watch coasts or borders against possible enemy invasion.[17] The earliest war comics—*Captain America,* for one—stressed the need to look out for foreign elements. Companies placed advertisements that urged support for the war effort. Of course, some might have been motivated by a desire for profits, as in the case of Captain America's Sentinels of Liberty. For a dime, one could assist Cap and Bucky in their fight to save American civilization by joining the Sentinels. Later on, the appeal shifted to pleas for the purchase of war bonds, a common type of advertisement in most comics throughout the war. The comic *How Boys and Girls Can Help Win the War* explained why Nazi propaganda was not to be believed, while it stressed, "You can trust the official statements of the United States Government and the United Nations!"[18] *True Aviation Stories* gave instruction on how to distinguish between Allied and Axis aircraft. One comic even gave a chart that showed each plane's bomb load, flight ceiling, and armament.[19]

Other advertisements in the comic books were also war-related. A reader could send for a children's version of a bombsight to attach to a model airplane. Ads offered junior air-raid warden kits, aircraft recognition flash cards, and related items. Drives were also of great importance. Paper, war bond, and scrap metal drives were all supposed to help children feel like they were doing their part for the war effort. However, guilt over not participating could be debilitating. This is illustrated by an anecdote about a third-grade boy who was asked to bring a dime to school for a war bond drive. The next day, when the teacher asked the students for their money, the nine-year-old—who had forgotten to ask his mother—responded that he did not have it. The teacher asked him to come to the front of the classroom, then told the entire class that he was "helping Hitler win the war."[20]

Money was also a source of friction with Marvel Comics, especially for Simon and Kirby. One early advertisement asked kids to send a dime to help fight the Axis by joining Captain America's Sentinels of Liberty. Money poured into Marvel's offices, but it was most likely kept for company finances, not shared with the creators of Captain America.[21] It had not been specifically promised to the war effort. The drive to join the Sentinels of Liberty could be described as war profiteering, even though war profiteers were a frequent target of comic books—including Marvel's many titles. Between *Captain America,* the *Young Allies,* and the *Boy Commandos,* patriotism abounded and sales soared, to the financial benefit of the publishers, not the writers and artists.

Conversion Themes in Comic Book Characters

The Shield, the first truly patriotic character introduced to American audiences, first appeared in January of 1940, preceding Captain America (the character most associated with patriotism during the war). Harry Shorten (w) and Irv Novick (a) created the Shield, the secret identity of Joe Higgins, an agent of the Federal Bureau of Investigation. Like Captain America, by Joe Simon (w) and Jack Kirby (a), the Shield wore a patriotic costume of red, white, and blue. The Shield's origin and character were innovative. In *Shield* #5 (May 1940), readers were introduced to the superhero's origins. Young Joe is forced to face life's cruelties when saboteurs kill his father, who had served in Army intelligence during World War I. The villains make his death look like dereliction of duty, but FBI director J. Edgar Hoover believes in the elder Higgins' innocence, and he reassures and comforts young Joe. Meanwhile, Joe experiments with chemicals and accidentally acquires superhuman capabilities, such as fantastic speed, imperviousness to bullets, and heightened senses. As the Shield, he uses these powers to find his father's killer. Later Joe becomes an instrument of Hoover, the only person who knows his true identity.[22] Stories in *The Shield* contain a mixture of fantastic and realistic elements, which (along with evil Nazis) were a recipe for reader popularity.

The villains that the Shield encounters were often amalgams of genuine threats, specifically German spies. The criminal elements, especially those who threatened war production (which Roosevelt was gearing up in the years before Pearl Harbor) or engaged in profiteering, were perceived as major threats. A more typical enemy was the fictitious Mosconians (obviously representing the Communist threat), who sought to bring war to the United States. Like the Mosconians, most villains were European. This lack of a Japanese threat was common in comic books of the period. When the Japanese were depicted, it was nearly always as a threat within Asia, specifically to China. Despite the severe economic sanctions that Roosevelt placed on Japan, average Americans did not consider the Japanese an immediate threat to the United States. Meanwhile, the view was growing that war with Germany could not be avoided. Therefore, the threats depicted in the prewar comics were either from Nazis, those assisting them, or villains taking advantage of the turmoil to make money as war profiteers or spies.

Prewar Shield stories allowed juveniles to associate real people from the newspapers, such as FBI agents, with the fantasy scenario of defeating a dangerous enemy. For adults, the Shield's origin story reflected two important contemporary concerns: the FBI in its counterintelligence role and current ideas about using science and technology to create the superhuman. The popular culture of the day usually presented science as the way to a utopian future. Science and the scientific method would lead to the betterment of American society and, eventually, that of all mankind. Furthermore, science suggested that an average person could develop into a hero if given the right environment.

When the war in Europe began in 1939, American comics began to incorporate real villains into the story lines of their imaginary heroes. At first, these included both Nazis and Communists, considered equally dangerous at the time, a view reinforced by the Soviet invasion of Finland and the Baltic states. These comic book villains had exotic names, with lots of "vons," suggesting both class elitism and cultural strangeness. In *Shield* #5 (June 1941), the Shield's enemies wear monocles and sport neatly trimmed facial hair. Moreover, the speech balloons parallel the visual clues. Such sentences as "Den ve haff lost notting except de lives of some vorthless Americans" were clearly identifiable as German to children as well as adults.[23] Oddly, however, the monocled Mosconians seem partly modeled on Prussian stereotypes from the age of the Kaiser: arrogant, aristocratic, and malicious toward anyone not of their class.

At the same time, artists were very careful with details of military items, such as uniforms. The Mosconians, for example, wear uniforms that resemble contemporary Russian military costume. Readers familiar with newsreel images would surely notice the accuracy (or otherwise) of these images. The differences in uniforms might suggest who was a bigger threat. Between the world wars, most Americans saw Communists as a bigger long-term threat, so their uniforms may have been a way to implicate them was well as the Nazis. Even Sen. Harry S. Truman reportedly weighed in on the subject when he suggested that if it came to war between the Germans and the Soviets, it would be in the best interest of the United States to back the losing side until the two simply killed each other off, a popularly held sentiment of the day.[24]

The so-called science of eugenics—the attempt to shape the human race through selective and subjective breeding practices—was not solely a Nazi doctrine. It had been developed and, to an extent, practiced in both the United States and Europe before the Nazis took power in Germany. Some American scientists believed that the use of eugenics could weed out inferior genetic predispositions, such as mental retardation, criminal deviancy, and other problems both physical and moral. This culling would ensure that everyone else could be a productive member of society. Selective breeding, forced sterilization of the "defective," and other "improvements" on natural selection were originally American ideas and had found their way into popular culture. During the war, however, the Nazis were demonized for very similar beliefs about the creation of superior beings.[25]

While the term "eugenics" was rarely used, the general concept was nevertheless addressed in comic book stories where America's superior scientists employed genetic engineering to defeat their Axis enemies. In American hands, unlike in the Nazis,' science would be used for good. In comic books at least, creating a super-being was a reasonable American goal. "Well-meaning" scientists experiment on Steve Rogers, changing him from a weakling unfit for combat into Captain America, able to use his superpowers to defend the country. The character mimicked the transition that the United States needed at the outset of World War II, going from a weakly armed country concerned only with itself into a powerful fighting nation able to defend itself and crush the enemy for the world's good.

Although he was introduced to readers in March 1941—a year after the Shield—Captain America became the most famous and enduring of the patriotically clad superheroes (despite several ups and downs). He sought to fight the enemies of the United States directly, both at home and abroad. Writer Joe Simon and artist Jack Kirby adapted themes introduced in earlier comics: Rogers, a physically unfit, underweight, and presumably 4-F (unfit for service) Army candidate, becomes an experimental subject for Professor Reinstein, an exiled German scientist. The character's name is an obvious play on Albert Einstein, who was already the most famous scientist in the world long before he came to the United States in 1933.[26] Reinstein's "Super-Soldier Serum" transforms Rogers from a weakling into a being with incredible strength, agility, and endurance. Before an American army of enhanced soldiers can be created, however, Nazi spies track down and kill Reinstein, and the formula—known only to him—is lost. Reinstein had christened Rogers "Captain America" before he died, however, and the name and the mission stuck.[27] The Super-Soldier Serum recalls the eugenics theme of *The Shield*. More prosaically, it also recalls Charles Atlas' 1940s get-fit-quick advertisements that promised to turn "98-pound weaklings" into virile he-men.

Unlike his predecessors, Captain America does not work alone; he has a constant sidekick, twelve-year-old Bucky Barnes. This gave readers, often around the same age as Bucky, a chance to imagine themselves in the action. Captain America took on the stereotypical villains, as well as some bizarre ones, including giant Asian zombies. Nevertheless, most of the villains appearing in these issues were somehow related to the war. On the covers of many of the first ten issues, Captain America beats up Hitler, fights storm troopers, or does battle with representatives of other Fascist regimes. The level of violence in these issues is striking. Americans and allies are shot between the eyes, stabbed, or even tortured—and only the superheroes can rescue the victims or avenge their deaths. The virtuous superheroes fight by Marquess of Queensbury Rules and invariably win, while the enemy always cheats and loses. The enemy undermines itself through its ill-formed concept of a superior race, with which it justifies the worst atrocities against "subhuman" groups; Americans insist on fair fighting. This assertion of American moral superiority permeates most war-themed media.

The popularity of Captain America, along with similar characters from *U.S.A. Comics*—such as the Whizzer, the Destroyer, the Angel, the Sub-Mariner, and the Torch[28]—led to a spinoff of sorts when Simon and Kirby created the

Young Allies. The writers, later including Stan Lee, again used a formula that worked: youngsters thwarting the enemies of America. The Young Allies were a sort of "Dead-End Kids" group: at times ill-behaved and mischievous but ultimately on the side of good.[29] The Young Allies consisted of Bucky; Toro, the Human Torch's sidekick; "Knuckles" Percy Bartwell, a scrappy kid from the Bronx; Washington Vanderbilt Jefferson, the smart kid who can create any technological item needed; Tubby Tinkle, a former circus freak who uses his girth to escape from danger; and Whitewash Jones, the African American kid—or "Negro," as described in the comic—who "can make a harmonica sing and watermelons disappear."[30] The Jones character was important to stress the concept of racial and ethnic pluralism fighting against the putative racial purity of the Nazi superman. In practice, Jones provided racially stereotypical comic relief, as his nickname makes clear. Occasionally shown wearing a zoot suit, he is a slow, easily frightened bumbler who only manages to assist the team by accident. In interviews, Kirby later explained that the characters were suggested by his own New York City upbringing, when he was involved in street fights with members of rival gangs.[31] The Young Allies had a theme song that expressed their esprit de corps: "We fight together, through stormy weather, we're out to lick both crooks and spies. . . . We won't be stopped, we can't be topped, and we are the Young Allies!"[32]

The story lines in this type of comic portrayed conflicts within the groups as well as against the Nazis. Individuals from specific ethnic, geographic, and socio-religious groups learned to suppress their differences to become a cohesive group fighting together for American ideals. This parallels the conversion process historians identified in wartime movies. Through the process, an American perceived as "ethnic" or "undesirable" in earlier America now became part of the concept of the melting pot, as well as the team player fighting for American ideals. On the screen, one might see the mixed ethnicity unit that ultimately coalesced into an American fighting unit, rather than a group of guys who clung desperately to their own individual or regional ideals.[33]

May's conversion process was certainly evident in more realistic war comics, especially those depicting various Allies working together.[34] The Girl Commandos, the Boy Commandos, and the Young Allies defeat Nazi spies within the United States, and after the war starts, they fight spies around the world.[35] They also break up war-profiteering rings, help increase production of war materials, and boost morale. However, superheroes are not shown working in factories, actively battling troops overseas in combat zones, or promoting the cause of full racial, ethnic, or religious equality. Superheroes did not fight against racism within the United States, reflecting the de facto official policy of fighting for American ideals of equality abroad while accepting inequality at home. This conversion narrative, while nominally promoting equality in contrast with the racist enemy, helped to suppress dissension about the same issues at home. For the moment, at least, minorities fighting to make the world safe for democracy needed to accept their place within American society.

Eisner's character, Blackhawk, also introduced new themes into the war comics. If the destruction of his friends and family at the hands of his *bête noire*, Captain von Tepp, did not provide enough motivation for the superhero to destroy his nemesis, the presence of the obligatory blonde nurse did. This unnamed English maiden introduced another time-honored motive for fighting to the war comic: preserving a woman's honor. In typical fashion, the girls are once again left behind as the men go forth to fight for them and the free world, setting up a final showdown against the evil von Tepp. Blackhawk recruits a gallery of outcasts to join his misfit force of flyers. The team includes representatives of all the Allies at the time, with some Americans participating in the uniforms of other countries. The team members resemble the Allies themselves: they often squabble like siblings, but the Nazi menace keeps them united. As May notes in his article on World War II films, some members of the group are initially shunned as unworthy of the goals and beliefs of America. After the war starts, however, they put aside their differences to contribute to the overall war effort and conform to the American ideal. They have no choice. Only through unity could the Allies defeat an army of seemingly maniacal skills and abilities.[36]

Toward the end of the first issue, Blackhawk lands his plane to engage von Tepp on the field of honor, just as the Germans are about to execute the English nurse and another flyer. The two meet at dawn and prepare to duel with pistols. Wearing a fitted black uniform, Blackhawk shoots the gun from von Tepp's hand as if he were Tom Mix in a Saturday matinee western.[37] The coloring of the uniform is important. It gives a heroic meaning to the all-black uniform previously associated with Hitler's SS and sets Blackhawk apart from other members of the U.S. military. Blackhawk's squadron even has a theme song of sorts: "Over land over sea, we fight to make men free, of danger we don't care, we're Blackhawks."[38] By 1942 or 1943, Blackhawk's origin story was changed; he had become a Polish immigrant to the United States or even American-born of Polish extraction. At the time of its inception, this comic book was written to be as inclusive as possible. It was an excellent early example of the (first- or second-generation) immigrant's conversion to the American ideal, as the Blackhawk group was a United Nations in microcosm: a Frenchman, a Pole, a Swede, an Englishman, and even a Chinese—albeit as a stereotypical houseboy.

Blackhawk represented for comic books what May described as a "conversion character" in World War II films.[39] The character develops in the same way. Blackhawk fights for the right reasons, and his squadron sets aside their divisive domestic or international disputes to fight for the unified ideal. At the same time, Blackhawk is a subversive character; he and his comrades are

ne'er-do-wells who work outside society's conventions, undermining traditional authority with unconventional fighting. Instead of fighting as part of
the military of a particular country, they operate from an island airbase in
the middle of the Atlantic Ocean where the rules of American society do not
automatically apply. The idea is that characters such as Blackhawk will rise to
the occasion when society needs them to uphold its ideals. Although Blackhawk's multinational group fights outside the rules of established warfare and
employs trickery, it is always for the good. (The operations of Sir Francis Drake
and other English privateers during the sixteenth century are somewhat analogous.) The Blackhawk group shows a propensity to fight "dirty," a common
theme with characters of the subversive type. By contrast, Captain America
attempts to fight in an honorable way. Nevertheless, sometimes when an honorable person cannot defeat evil, a dirty fighter can. Blackhawk demonstrates
the theme of conversion (to American ideals), complicated by his subversive
approach to winning.

Most superheroes were, to one degree or another, such conversion characters,
although their civilian personas often had the less desirable traits that May identified as subversive.[40] One such civilian character, Robert Gibson, is a rich young
man who deliberately exploits his flat feet to gain 4-F draft status. His apparent lack
of resolve and unwillingness to fight make him seem unpatriotic on the surface.
However, in the guise of Shock Gibson, as featured in *Speed Comics,* he menaces
the Axis powers.[41] Regardless of how these characters reach the decision to fight
on behalf of the patriots of the United States, their place in the realm of heroes is
established.[42] Most characters use their ambivalent, selfish, or even subversive public personae as cover for their true patriotic commitment. Ultimately these comic
book characters want to fight for the country, not for their own goals.

Since these characters proved commercially viable, more emerged over the
course of the war—each a champion of patriotic duty and usually with an explicitly patriotic costume. One of the lesser-known comic book superheroes from this
time was Uncle Sam (appearing in *National Comics,* published by Quality Comics). As the name implies, he looked exactly like his namesake on recruitment
posters and fought on the home front, as along with police, air raid wardens, and
average civilians. *Boy Commandos* was another comic book from Joe Simon and
Jack Kirby, the creators of Captain America. Nominally similar to Boy Scouts, the
Boy Commandos fought the same enemies as adult superheroes, except with guns.
Another Simon–Kirby collaboration was the Fin, a naval officer who wears a black
wetsuit with a large dorsal fin, and Citizen V (for Victory), who looks like a bellhop
with a large "V" on his chest and fights spies. The Sub-Mariner is a prince from
the undersea kingdom of Atlantis who defends the East Coast of the United States
from attacks by German U-boats. The Patriot is a descendant of Revolutionary War
heroes; when he invokes his ancestors, they grant him supernatural powers to fight

the country's enemies. Similarly Mister—later Major—Liberty summons ghosts from America's historical past to fight the enemies of the 1940s.[43] Another peculiar superhero of this era is the Human Torch, who (despite his name) is not human, but a kind of robot. Most of these characters came and went, not lasting more than a few issues. Exceptions include the Human Torch and the Sub-Mariner, who were given their own titles once their popularity was established.[44]

As artists often changed studios, similar characters were developed in parallel, with creators often borrowing features of a popular superhero, tweaking the details, and repackaging them for another publisher (Captain America mirrors the Shield, for example). Characters from competing companies sometimes resembled each other to a remarkable extent, occasionally leading to lawsuits. Captain America had to change his shield from a traditional lozenge/diamond shape when the publishers of *The Shield*, whose main character's costume includes a shield of this shape, sued for copyright infringement. In this case, the result was a marked aesthetic improvement, as Captain America's redesigned round shield became an iconic part of the character's kit.

Even nonmilitary comic book characters became involved in the war effort. The writers had to walk a fine line to avoid undermining the seriousness of the real war effort with make-believe. Like any red-blooded American male, Clark Kent desperately wanted to enter the service following the attack on Pearl Harbor. However, the writers were worried that children might expect Superman, with his incredible powers, to resolve the conflict by himself. To avoid this, they devised a clever "escape clause" to keep Superman out of the military. When Kent goes for his Army induction physical, he is so anxious to pass that—using his X-ray vision—he accidently reads the eye chart in the next room. Concluding that the bespectacled Kent is blind as a bat, the examining doctor declares him physically unfit for military service. This 4-F designation means that Kent (and Superman) has to fight for the war effort on the home front.[45]

Embracing his role, Superman demonstrates that all civilians, as well as military support units, play important parts in the war effort. In an issue from early 1943, Kent goes undercover to an Army Air Forces technical training facility. Throughout the story, the key theme is that the war is everyone's affair. For example, for each bomber crew member in the air, there are twenty men back at the base making sure that the planes can fly, the weather conditions, and that the intelligence is correct.[46] By showing the importance appear favorable to plan the mission of maintenance personnel, weather staff, and munitions makers, the comic explains the concept of a "total war" affecting all aspects of life. In reality, of the millions of men and women in the armed forces during World War II, only a relatively small percentage engaged in significant combat. In general, the comics and other media had people believing that the war was everywhere and that everyone was a combatant, but this obviously was not true.

Female Superheroes

Comic book females were either variations of the Betty Grable pinup (often designed to attract pubescent males) or avatars of the women and girls left behind (like the notionally realistic women in Norman Rockwell prints, who represented what American men fought for). According to the conventions of the androcentric cartoons of the day, these attractive comic book women played the part of victims for brutal Axis men, only to be rescued by virtuous Allied men. Of course, sultry vixens and villainesses were also common.

There were, however, two characters specifically written to appeal to girls: *Miss Fury* and *Wonder Woman*. They were also somewhat subversive characters by World War II standards, as they flouted traditional gender norms. Women were expected to help the war effort in the home and even in the factory, but they were not supposed to fight on the front lines. That role was reserved for men, according to the American values of the time (and still prevails, according to U.S. military regulations).

Tarpe Mills wrote and drew *Miss Fury* in April 1941. As a woman, Mills was a rarity in the male-dominated field. Her comic character, Miss Fury, fought Nazi spies around the globe. Her chief nemesis was Baroness Elsa von Kampf, a German aristocrat with a swastika branded on her forehead. The baroness was a striking blonde, but—lest readers be overly attracted—the swastika showed her true allegiance. This was reinforced by the baroness's name: *Kampf* is German for struggle and by extension war.[47] (The name no doubt also evoked Hitler's manifesto, *Mein Kampf*.) Mills also used the character to challenge German concepts of titled nobility. The baroness was evil, in part because of her unearned status, while Miss Fury was portrayed as a typical "classless" American.

The much more famous Wonder Woman was created by William Marston and artist Harry G. Peter in December 1941, with the typical patriotic symbols incorporated into her costume (including a star-spangled skirt). Nevertheless, her attempts to take on the Nazis or Japanese were surprisingly limited. Wonder Woman mostly deals with domestic criminals and spies, rather than engaging in combat directly with America's enemies overseas. At the time, the possibility of women in combat, even in comic books, was difficult for readers to accept. Some historians believe that Wonder Woman was significant feminist advance, since she was the first major female character in what had been a boy's medium. (The more critical assessment is that Wonder Woman is an extension of male sexual fantasy, a sort of dominatrix, tying up men with her magic lasso.) For the war effort, however, she encouraged both boys and girls to do their part—collect scrap metal, be vigilant, and so forth—as did all the other comic heroes.[48]

The Use of Children in Combat

The least complicated or controversial way for superheroes to assist in the fighting was to round up spies and let the "real heroes" in the military take care of the fighting overseas. Therefore, many story lines used the spy threat as the primary way to connect with the overall war theme. While the actual fighting was overseas, enemies of the Allies could be anywhere. The spy threat, hugely exaggerated, engaged the adolescent reader excluded from combat by age. By keeping a vigilant eye toward those of questionable background (presumably people with Axis-country origins) or suspicious behavior, the reader could count himself a soldier in the war. Given that so many men were in the armed forces overseas and adults were preoccupied with war production at home, the message was that it fell upon the young reader to prevent espionage through vigilance. They were expected to be dutiful, conforming watchdogs of democracy.

A Simon–Kirby collaboration that gained great popularity was DC Comics' *Boy Commandos,* which led Marvel to fire the two creators from the *Captain America* series. The characters are pre- and young-adolescent "dead-end kids" like the *Young Allies,* but in this case the characters originate from different countries, setting up the familiar conversion narrative.[49] They consist of Daniel "Brooklyn" Turpin, the scrappy American who retains a semi-civilian look with his bowler, Jan Haansan from the Netherlands, André Chavard of France, and Alfie Twidgett from England (naturally).[50] Captain Rip Carter nominally led them, but the kids were the real stars. What seems disturbing, at least according to today's values, is that the boys are regularly depicted in combat, guns blazing. This was not as far-fetched as it might seem: some American youths either had parental permission if only sixteen or seventeen or forged their birth certificates to join the armed forces.[51] The perception was that they fought together for a cause, even if the united front was merely for display and not a reality. The image was good for the home front, like Glenn Miller's swing band, which featured musicians from all parts of the United States, yet included no players of color.[52] Even more disturbing were the reports of German units comprising members of the organization Hitler Youth (Hitler-Jugend). Some of these boys, who had been indoctrinated into Nazi ideology from the ages of ten to fourteen, went on to serve as some of the German military's most fanatical units. In fact, Canadian units fighting against the Twelfth SS Panzer Division Hitlerjugend reported that it committed higher rates of atrocities.[53]

While there was no American equivalent to the Hitler Youth, the concept of youth in active combat was explored in the comic book *Girl Commandos,* an all-girl team that took on the Axis in various forms. The Girl Commandos some-times used machine guns on their enemies, but they mostly used hand-to-hand combat skills like their male counterparts, the Young Allies.[54] Like the Blackhawk group, the women in the Girl Commandos emphasized the need for everyone to work together to defeat the common threat. In this case, the implicit threat was that if the women were captured, they might be violated. This theme was a varia-tion of the famous World War I poster in which a mad beast ravaged Columbia.

The Girl Commandos consisted of a cross-section of "free nations" women. They included Pat Parker, who had flowing dark hair and wore a nurse's cap that extended down over her eyes to make a mask; the exotic Tanya, presumably Rus-sian or French, with a vampy dark-haired look; Chinese Mei Ling (think Madame Chiang Kai-Shek); Penny Kirk, who seems to be English; and the heavy-set Ellen Billings, there perhaps so more ordinary girls could feel included. Obviously, these characters were not aimed only at women and girls; as exotic females they also were there to titillate male readers. In one episode, the Girl Commandos take on a Norwegian spy working with the Nazis. Eventually the quisling realizes the error of his ways and switches sides to the Allies. While the Girl Commandos are shown playing a role in winning the war, they are nevertheless expected to return to their traditional roles afterward, such as teacher, nurse, or homemaker.[55]

Government Involvement in Comics and Cartoons

The U.S. Army was fully aware that comics could serve its purposes well. The first example of comics discussing the gripes of servicemen was in *Yank: The Army Weekly,* which began publication on June 6, 1942.[56] The Office of Morale Services created *Yank* with a staff partially made up of former *Stars and Stripes* writers. One reason for its popularity was its reporting staff—made up entirely of non-commis-sioned officers. The "Mail Call" and "What's Your Gripe?" sections allowed enlisted men to complain about Army life and vent about other issues. The best example was Sgt. George Baker's creation of the character Sad Sack (from the phrase "a sad sack of shit"). He has to put up with the problems that any enlisted man might go through: KP (mess duty), newly commissioned young officers whose inexpe-rience does not command respect, and the other daily privations endured by the citizen-soldier. "Sad Sack" was very popular, and the strip recurred through the entire publishing run of *Yank.* In fact, the character was so successful that Harvey Comics picked it up for commercial distribution in 1949.[57]

The characters who most embodied the conditions of the average foot sol-dier were Willie and Joe, created by illustrator Bill Mauldin and featured in the cartoon *Up Front,* which appeared in *Stars and Stripes.* Mauldin drew these one-panel vignettes of life in combat while he was in the Italian the-ater (during the 1943 invasions of Sicily and Salerno, as well as at Anzio in

1944). His characters suffer through the fighting and often display gallows humor about their situation (for example, asking merely for aspirin after being wounded). Mauldin's cartoons tell of the monotony of garrison life and the troubles soldiers encounter in their new employment: conducting maneuvers with fake guns, limited gas for vehicles, and the WWI-vintage materiel they were expected to use.[58] The difference with Mauldin's work is that he drew one-panel pictures, conveying information in a small space, rather than in a multi-panel format like a strip or comic book.

America's vast military buildup forced many famous comic book creators into the armed forces, where many pursued illustration or writing in some capacity. Some were allowed to continue their full-time work while doing their duty. For example, Will Eisner was sent to the Army's education and information branch, where he wrote material to help GIs learn different tasks. One strip that was adapted to this larger role was "Joe Dope," which showed the hapless hero learning what to do—and what *not* to do—in the field. Eisner was also a driving force in the illustrated manual *Army Motors,* which was produced to assist in proper vehicle maintenance at the Aberdeen Proving Ground in Maryland. It eventually became *PS: The Preventative Maintenance Monthly* ("PS" meaning "preventive service") and is discussed in chapter 3.[59]

Milton Caniff's success with *Terry and the Pirates* before and during the war gained him access to military aircraft. The result: Terry's flight-training experience is depicted as realistically as possible. Caniff's artwork is meticulously accurate, which was not always the case for military uniforms, materiel, and weapons in comic books. Eventually called up for military service, Caniff was allowed to continue his profession, finding his niche as an Army illustrator on such publications as the *Pocket Guide to China.* He illustrated a section that describes the differences between the Chinese (ally) and the Japanese (enemy). While the description was decidedly racist, its goal was also one of information. It debunked the silly idea that Japanese had widely spaced toes due to their *tabi* footware, and it taught that the two nationalities have different quirks in their pronunciation of English words.[60]

Joe Simon, one of the creators of *Captain America* and *Boy Commandos,* also served stateside, initially with the Coast Guard. He worked on *True Comics,* a syndicated weekly comic strip that told the stories of various heroic individuals.[61] At the same time, Simon served with the Combat Art Corps, which produced comics, strips, and other illustrated features for the U.S. military. (Successful artists such as Simon and Eisner could work on both civilian and military comics and cartoons during the war.) Later on, Simon was commissioned to do a one-shot comic book titled *Adventure Is My Career* for the Coast Guard.[62] It tells the story of how the Coast Guard was created and describes its duties, especially in times of war. Like *True Comics, Real Heroes,* and *Heroic* Comics, it served to tell of the real exploits of the armed services. As such, it was as much a recruitment aid and a form of propaganda as a source of information.

Some comic book creators actually saw combat. Jack Kirby, Simon's partner, was assigned to the Eleventh Regiment, Fifth Infantry Division, which was part of Lt. Gen. George S. Patton's Third Army. Consequently, he participated in the fighting in northwestern Europe and had real combat experiences, unlike comic creators who served stateside or in overseas support units. A senior officer recognized him as Jack Kirby the comic book artist and got him drawing materials. Kirby thought he might be asked to do officer portraits. Instead, he was made an infantry scout and ordered to make drawings of roads, buildings, and other items of military importance (a dangerous assignment).[63] Kirby rarely talked about these experiences but did use them as material for *Foxhole,* his short-lived war comic series of the 1950s (discussed in chapter 3).

Another propagandistic comic was *True Stories.* In one issue, the writers reject the concept of a master race and instead focus on how the Nazis pushed the athletic, tall, and blond paragon, while their leaders deviated considerably from this ideal. (Field Marshal Hermann Goering weighed three hundred pounds; Minister of Information Josef Goebbels was five feet, six inches tall, with a clubfoot; and Adolf Hitler's dark hair and eyes belied the Aryan ideal.)[64] There is some irony, therefore, in that *Übermensch* literally means "Superman."

This particular issue of *True Comics* was also significant because it merged *Real Heroes, True Comics,* and *Funny Book* into one oversized fifty-four-page comic. This conserved paper yet still gave children informative stories that (while patriotic) were a bit less propagandistic in tone.[65] The comic's editorial board comprised several famous members of the media, as well as historians to attest to accuracy (as it was seen in the 1940s). Other "advisors" included child stars Roddy McDowell and Shirley Temple. Presumably the child stars were window dressing, although in theory they helped determine what other children might wish to read.[66]

As part of their propaganda effort, the comics celebrated the sacrifices made by people outside of the armed forces. *Real Heroes,* published by the Parents Magazine Institute, depicts the tales of various people who made a difference in the war effort. For example, the first issue featured the personal profiles and stories of such historical figures as Franklin Roosevelt and World War I fighter ace Eddie Rickenbacker, among others. The Revolutionary War story of Molly Pitcher was told to attract female readers. The series, which ran throughout the war and later discussed the exploits of Medal of Honor recipients and even politicians, was unusual for a comic book, however, because it boasted an editorial board that included such prominent people as Eleanor Roosevelt, publishing magnate George Hecht, George Gallup of the Gallup Institute, and historians from Columbia University. As a group, they were responsible for determining the historically significant stories to tell as well as providing heft to the publishing effort. Beyond them, there was even a representative board of show-business children such as Roddy McDowell, Judy Garland, and Liz Cantor (entertainer Eddie Cantor's daughter), which suggests that children had some sort of input into in the story lines.[67]

Comic book imagery varied depending on the artist or the intended audience. Some artists who worked under tight deadlines did minimal background or detail work while others, such as Eisner, slaved over the smallest details. For those who attended to minutiae, the stories were often more complex as a result. Other artists, especially George Baker, Bill Mauldin, and Dave Breger, told stories of life in uniform, but their viewpoints varied. Baker, who drew "Sad Sack" for *Yank Magazine,* took a lighthearted look at the conscripted citizen soldier, often focusing on the transition to military life. Mauldin's stories for *Up Front* and later *Willie and Joe* featured combat and conditions encountered by soldiers in the field. Mauldin described the horrible conditions foot soldiers encountered in the European theater of operations, specifically his own unit, the Forty-Fifth Infantry Division. Mauldin drew his figures as unshaven, muddy, and otherwise miserable. His depictions were, and still are, indicative of life for combat troops on the line. Many World War II veterans wrote letters to Mauldin stating that his drawings were accurate and gave them a sense of commiseration that other comics did not. He understood their suffering.[68] Mauldin's depictions of Italy, military discipline, and the brutality of combat were so realistic that at one point General Patton wanted to discipline him. In Patton's opinion, Mauldin was undermining authority by creating cartoons that depicted sloppiness, poor mental attitude, and disrespect toward officers. For other commanders, such as Maj. Gen. Lucian Truscott Jr., commander of the Third Infantry Division, the cartoons were a welcome way for the enlisted man to vent without compromising combat operations.[69]

Depictions of the Enemy

A fear of spies on American soil contributed to many comic book story lines, even before the United States entered the war. Historically spies have been depicted as underhanded, treacherous, and ubiquitous (hence cautionary posters during the war, such as "Loose Lips Sink Ships"). While the level of espionage in the United States was not nearly as widespread as the popular press made out, the threat was useful to writers who wanted to show action against the enemy within the United States. Not all Americans were isolationists, and some comic book creators realized that war might very well be necessary, so comics were written to persuade the reader of this. One book looked at the organizational makeup of the U.S. armed forces. Titled *USA Is Ready,* it was published several months before American entry into the war. The comic reflected the American government's attitude that Germany was the biggest threat to the country; Japan was almost an afterthought.

For example, a section on the U.S. Marine Corps shows an interesting image of them fighting off a German seaborne attack on a presumably American beach.[70] In actuality, the Germans never conducted a naval landing of any significance, unlike the Japanese, who were certainly more accustomed to amphibious operations. Throughout the book, the armed forces are presented as having excellent equipment and materiel needed to fend off any attack. The impression given is that the United States was ready for all eventualities, which was disproven disastrously by the attack on Pearl Harbor. The American armed forces were not ready at all. As noted by many historians, arms were in such short supply in the fall of 1941 that the U.S. Army was training with wooden weapons and with civilian vehicles identified by signs as "tanks."[71]

How the enemies of the United States were depicted in propaganda, including comic books, is especially revealing. Traditionally, comic book bad guys fit into preexisting stereotypes. Criminals in comics often had scars or wore shabby clothes. African Americans were easily duped into fighting against the Allies until shown the error of their ways. Even "good Asians," such as Chinese nationalists under the leadership of Chiang Kai-Shek, followed predictable speech patterns and took subservient roles. During the war, the enemy was depicted as dishonest, underhanded, immoral, or evil. However, while the Germans were ridiculed, they were depicted as people. As noted, they were usually caricatures of aristocratic Prussian officers, with monocles or dueling scars, and they spoke with great arrogance. Nevertheless, it was specifically Nazis and their heinous ideology who were identified as inimical to the United States, not Germans per se. So, the villains that the major comic book characters fought were usually based on actual Nazi leaders of the Reich.

By contrast, all of Japanese society was painted with the same intolerant brush. During the 1930s and into 1940s, little distinction had been made between different Asiatic peoples. *Captain America* #6 introduces a sinister enemy known as Fang: Arch-Fiend of the Orient. Although the artwork shows many of these Asians as Chinese—with queues, skullcaps, and flowing red robes—the subtext was that all Asians were in collusion to dominate the East, if not the entire world.[72] Such stereotyped Asian villains were relatively rare, appearing in story lines only three times during the first thirty-five issues of *Captain America*. However, as World War II progressed and the fighting in the Pacific became deadlier, both the viciousness and the specificity of the Asian stereotypes increased.

Once the war began, little distinction was made between ordinary Japanese soldiers and Japan's leadership, including the emperor. However, greater efforts were made to distinguish the Japanese from the Chinese. The depictions of the Japanese were only partially comical and rarely distinct. All were shown as fanatical, violent, and unfeeling. The Japanese were usually portrayed as monsters, not men. This made it easier to kill the enemy: they were animals, not rational human beings. American writers' ignorance about Asian culture and preconceived stereotypes about the Japanese (reinforced by the sneak attack on Pearl Harbor) led comic books artist to draw all Japanese with an evil appearance.[73] The Japanese were portrayed with buckteeth, thick glasses, rat-like facial features, and postures that suggested underlying treachery. For instance, in *Captain America* #5 the reader is introduced to Captain Okada, the Oriental Master of Evil. He is refined in his manners, perhaps educated in the West, as was Adm. Isoroku Yamamoto, responsible for planning the Pearl Harbor attack. At the same time, Okada is more than willing to employ torture, including on innocent women (in this particular case, the daughter of a captured U.S. Navy commander). The story line is replete with references to evil ("sinister-looking Orientals" and such diabolical comments as "This is mild compared to the other tortures in store for her.")[74] This imagery never softened during the war.

As the war wound down and more servicemen returned to the United States, the popularity of certain characters waned. Those created specifically for the war went through multiple creative team changes, and most were quietly retired after hostilities ended. Even Captain America was not immune, and his appearances were slowly pared back. His nemesis, the Red Skull, kept his Nazi origins but became a criminal mastermind who controlled a vast empire around the world. As characters were not held to any consistent continuity, the Red Skull was reinvented more than once, until he was transformed into a tool of "Red Communism." The Boy Commandos even fought in space. *True Comics* and similar titles still published war stories but increasingly incorporated other historical and educational themes. Regardless, as the enemies of freedom changed, so did comic book villains. The characterization of the enemy evolved in war-themed comics during the late 1940s and early 1950s. As the Cold War took hold, the "Red Scare" of the Chinese and Soviet Communists replaced the Japanese "Yellow Peril." The Soviets and their underhanded ways were substituted for the Nazis of World War II. With the blacklist, loyalty oaths, and the Comics Code, comic books and the war genre changed substantially.

3   The Cold War Erupts, and Comics— Mostly—Toe the Line (1945–62)

Cartoonists, film-strip animators and comic-strip artists who, before the war, sought only to entertain were set to work to drive home the lessons that were to save American lives in battle and lead to victory. Cartoons were created to teach the skills of war, from dive-bombing and aerial combat to bayoneting. Rules and regulations of each branch of the service were humorously pointed up to help newcomers in the Armed Forces become well-adjusted, disciplined servicemen.

—FRANK BRANDT, *Cartoons for Fighters*

Following the end of World War II, comic books returned to familiar patterns of life along with the rest of American society. The comics, which had focused on fighting the enemies of the United States and building morale, reverted to more lighthearted entertainment, as well as taking on more ominous Cold War themes. Some comics still dealt with war or current geopolitical events, but characters closely associated with the war, such as Captain America, the Shield, and Uncle Sam, began to undergo a transformation. *Captain America* and many other titles—including such stalwarts as *Superman* and *Batman*—saw postwar sales decrease. By the end of the 1940s, although the comic book industry was still making money and gaining readership overall, it began phasing out or altering war characters. *Captain America* was pulled from shelves in 1947 (though he returned a few years later), the Boy Commandos were launched into outer space by the end of 1940s, and the surviving war comics generally shifted into Cold War mode.

The Post–World War II Years

During the war, comic book artists helped create support for the government and for the troops overseas. As the nation shifted from World War II to Cold War intrigue, so did the comics. Many characters received new assignments, such as corralling maniacal dictators or fighting the scourge of Communism around the world. Captain America, for example, left his Army career to become a social studies teacher.[1] This civic responsibility allowed him to fight the tyranny of Communism while simultaneously teaching its evils through patriotic explanation of the tenets of democracy.[2] The superheroes' return to relatively mundane occupations (by their standards, at least) mirrored that of actual veterans. One veteran and comic book writer, Jack Kirby, came back from war to resume illustrating comics. Exemplifying this shift, Kirby and Joe Simon, his old collaborator, reestablished themselves in the postwar comics' field by creating *Young Romance* #1, one of the first romance comics, in 1947. The romance comics comprised story lines that involved young love and relationships, akin to romance novels. These comics were created to appeal to a wider, specifically female audience.[3]

Fears of Communists' undermining of America were in the air, especially in connection with a possible nuclear war. One of the first comics to address this preoccupation was *Atom-Age Combat*. It emphasized how "Godless Commies" surrounded the United States on all sides, particularly after the detonation of a Soviet atomic bomb in 1949. As the push for scientific development prevailed in wartime comic books, Cold War comics championed American military victory through new technology developed by scientists liberated from Fascism. Most of all, Communism would be thwarted by American moral resolve to promote democracy.[4] America's idea of democracy was evident in many late 1940s comics, even if the reality of "democracy" often meant supporting anti-Communist dictators such as Anastasio Somoza in Nicaragua, Ferdinand Marcos in the Philippines, and Fulgencio Batista in Cuba.

Stories in *Atom-Age Combat* and similar titles often depicted futuristic combat involving rocket packs, atomic grenades, and atomic rifles. Battles were often set in areas containing strategic goods such as uranium. One 1952 story, "Assault on Target UR 238," shows Soviet air commandos, led by Air Marshal Boris "Butcher" Kasilov, exploiting an unnamed African tribe near a uranium site. The Soviets are depicted as overt imperialists, helping themselves to whatever they want. They aim to foment unrest within the country, so they can take it over; with its uranium in their control, they might dominate the world. To emphasize this portrayal, the Soviets' oddly shaped "air commando" helmets strikingly resemble those of Roman centurions. The story shows how the United States defeats the Soviets, with the help of the African guerrillas (and even actual gorillas!). One line foreshadows Greenpeace: "Allied forces deplore destruction of wildlife."[5] Young readers were supposed to identify these ideas as good for America and, thus, self-evidently good for the whole world.

The anti-Communist comic assumed special prominence after 1949 when the USSR exploded its first nuclear bomb. Suddenly, it seemed at the time, the Communists ruled a huge portion of the world's population and possessed nuclear weapons that threatened capitalist countries around the globe. After the Communists took over China in October 1949, the Soviets had to yield to this new version of the Yellow Peril as the number-one comic book villains. In these new war comics, American and allied forces most often find themselves fighting the Chinese or their North Korean allies. The portrayal of these Asian Communists rivals the depiction of the duplicitous and treacherous Japanese of World War II comics. The story lines warn that Communist subterfuge and attacks on "freedom" could come from the most unexpected corners. *Atom-Age Combat* #4 improbably involves a Mongolian officer in charge of a submarine in the Arctic Ocean.[6] Most prominent was *Is This Tomorrow?* produced by the Cachtical League of America, 1947. In this, comic books, like the rest of American popular culture and the press, found the threat of Communism everywhere. Comic books were important players in developing this theme.

A common story idea imagines Communists, or even the Soviets themselves, taking over the United States. Supposedly, the enemies of America have secretly infiltrated society through business or the media—the same basic premise that underpinned the House Un-American Activities Committee (HUAC).[7] The Catechetical Guild Educational Society of America, a Catholic organization, sponsored *Is This Tomorrow: America under Communism!,* a one-shot comic that discusses the invasion issue and the general undermining of society. The initial story concerns a small town first wracked by subversion from "concerned citizens," then subjected to a Communist invasion. In another section, the Communists explain that part of their plan is to incite race riots and use this unrest to weaken American society.[8] It also describes other supposed Communist plans to undermine the United States by abusing freedom of speech, taking control of the media, and activating "moles" within the government. The ensuing chaos is to be prelude to a Communist coup.[9] The back page of the comic provides readers with a "Ten Commandments of Democracy," modeled on the constitutional amendments but stressing good citizenship. These include knowing about the government, being active in politics, reading newspapers and magazines critically, practicing one's religion, and being tolerant of other religions and ethnicities. The message: if readers are sufficiently vigilant, the Communists will be unable to take over American institutions.[10]

This fear of Communism and atomic warfare also revived spy scares in the United States. As in patriotic comic books during World War II, espionage and intrigue made their way into Cold War comics, with story lines about the betrayal of American ideals. One comic book from the *Classics Illustrated* series deals with the history of spies.[11] In some comic book stories, towns stage fake Communist takeovers—to warn of the threats and to emphasize the rights Americans enjoy.[12] The comic books were successful in illustrating the fears of a Communist takeover to a broad population, especially as they only cost a dime (and were occasionally distributed for free). *Treasure Chest of Fun and Fact,* published from 1947 to 1969, was another comic book of this type; it emphasized how proper morals and Christianity would prevent Communists from expanding.[13] In short, regardless of their particular faiths or political convictions, comic book creators supported basic American ideals, including freedom of worship and confidence in capitalism. Perhaps the most emphatic story line in *Treasure Chest* was the story of Father (later Bishop) James Walsh, a missionary in China during the tumultuous years of Japanese control, civil war, and the Communist takeover. Throughout the serialized story, Walsh never wavers in his faith or his mission to convert the Chinese to Christianity.[14] Like *Heroic Comics* and *True Comics, Treasure Chest* also told stories of American heroes, such as the ones about the technical expertise of Orville and Wilbur Wright and the military success of Gen. Douglas MacArthur.

Of more immediate concern was the highly political question of how the Soviets obtained the information to build an atomic bomb and how they might use this weapon in the divided Germany. This worry fit established tropes of the comic book genre. One title that tied Soviet attacks to the larger issue of nuclear warfare was *Atomic War,* which published four issues in 1952 and 1953. The first issue's opening page notes that nuclear war would be a defeat for all, "the just and un-just alike."[15] The assumption was always that the United States would not start a war without provocation. Instead, the comic posits a scenario of Soviet-initiated nuclear war that would engulf Europe. It centers on Germany, where many military leaders speculated a war might begin. Other attacks occur in Asia and Africa, and Communist subversion threatens various countries in the Western Hemisphere. Some of the comic's vignettes were later used as plots in several movies of the 1970s and 1980s.[16] The story details the expected scenario step by step. The Communists fabricate an event to provoke war and the invasion of the United States.[17] This prompts an outpouring of support and vengeance from those who left Eastern Europe,[18] as well as struggle within the Eastern European countries. The Soviets kill anyone who speaks or questions the need for war.[19] As with many futuristic comics, the details are sometimes fantastic (such as atomic grenades) or arcane (references to the Office of Special Services [OSS], which had become the Central Intelligence Agency [CIA] by the time of the comic's release). Like many of the comic books from the 1930s and 1940s, creators were often uncredited, making it even easier for the companies to take the lion's share of the profits, as usual.

Historical Comics of the Cold War and Korea

Some comics illustrated the historical background of contemporary topics. However, this history could be problematically simplistic or selective, frequently recounting events to glorify their subjects rather than offer objective analysis. Such misleading historical material appeared in comic books such as *True Comics, Real Comics,* and some biographical stories in *Classics Illustrated.* As time went on, however, the comics partially changed course. They concentrated on stories of scientific progress or heroism against the elements, rather than the gung-ho military adventures that had initially dominated the stories. A *True Comics*–style title, *General Douglas MacArthur,* tells the story of the five-star general's life and military prowess. As with other biographical comics, this one highlights MacArthur's role in shaping the world and making it safe for democracy. It focuses on his triumphant return to the Philippines in October 1944 and his daring amphibious landing at Inchon, Korea, in September 1951. Despite its release after his dismissal by President Truman, it portrays MacArthur as a patriotic icon. The story glosses over his serious late-career missteps, such as his call to use atomic bombs on the Chinese, and his open opposition to Truman's war strategy and politics. As with most comics in this vein, it offers a starting point for further study, but the biographical and historical information is pared down to the basics.[20]

Another comic book of this type was *Heroic Comics*. While it had originally featured superheroes, in January 1943 the title switched to a war comics format, concentrating on heroism on the home front during World War II.[21] By the early 1950s, many issues centered on military personnel in Korea, such as the story of war hero Paul Wheeler. He had single-handedly held off a Chinese attack in 1950, for which he was awarded the Bronze Star with an oak leaf cluster.[22] Another issue, "G.I. Jap: American Hero!," memorialized Corp. Yoshiharu Aoyama, who earned a posthumous Silver Star for gallantry. He had attempted to rescue a fallen comrade despite taking severe shrapnel injuries to both legs, which led to their amputation and his eventual death.[23] Other stories told of civilians who saved others from injury or death, such as Roy Cadwell and Jack Jones, who rescued a woman and her children from a burning car in Los Angeles.[24] The series ended in 1955, when competition from other media, especially the rising medium of television, reduced the demand for comic books.

The U.S. government directly sponsored some post–World War II comics, largely for recruitment purposes. In *Li'l Abner Joins the Navy* (1950), the yokel's cousin McEasel joins the Navy to avoid marriage to Lana Turnip (a play on the name of "blonde bombshell" actress Lana Turner). When local bullies threaten McEasel, they are beaten in turn by Navy lads protecting their own; the bullies then join up with a spy from Slobovia (an imaginary, and presumably Communist, country). The comic book forthrightly presents what the Navy promises: a sense of purpose, self-discipline, and skills for a subsequent career outside of the Navy. Even better, the character (and by implication, the reader or potential recruit) might make a career in the Navy, rather than quickly rejoining the civilian population. The comic notes that only upstanding citizens get into the Navy—they need character references and can have no criminal record. At the end of the story, Li'l Abner sees the success of his cousin and enlists as well.[25] While circulation and sales figures have not survived, the comic seems to have been a successful attempt to use popular characters as window dressing for military propaganda.

The Navy followed up with a series about its history. The four-part series *Navy: History and Tradition* chronicled the early years of the Service or the force (the late 1700s), the Navy of the 1800s, the creation of the Great White Fleet (the early 1900s), and finally ended with the Navy during World War II. The comics tell the stories of famous naval officers such as Stephen Decatur, John Paul Jones, and William "Bull" Halsey, as well as recent Medal of Honor recipient Edward "Butch" O'Hare Jr. In all, these comics served to both inform and glorify the lives of those in the U.S. Navy.[26]

Over the course of the 1940s and 1950s, the characters most associated with World War II were either retired or readapted to changing times. The Shield finally bowed out in 1954.[27] Captain America's popularity waned following the end of World War II; thereafter he mainly fought Communist spies within the United States. At first, Cap fought alone after Bucky, his adolescent sidekick, was killed off in 1945. Bucky's death was intended to symbolize the loss and sacrifice occasioned by the war, but it also allowed Captain America to team up with other superheroes, in the hope of attracting a wider readership. Captain America even took on a new sidekick while working as a high school civics teacher (incognito, of course).

Regardless of these efforts to vary the story lines, Captain America's popularity slowly faded. Given his flagging fan base by the late 1940s, it is not surprising that Captain America never fought in Korea. The character was finally mothballed in 1954 (but briefly revived in the early 1960s). Around the same time, his original creators, Joe Simon and Jack Kirby, introduced Fighting American through Mainline Comics, their own publishing company.[28] *Fighting American* came too late for Korea and only lasted seven issues, from 1955 until 1955. (Neither hero participated in the Vietnam War; the role of defending America had changed too much by that time.)

Nonetheless, the war comic came into its own as a genre in the early 1950s. The plots usually revolved around acts of hand-to-hand combat and valor, regardless of its cost to the man or men at the center of the action. Sometimes the characters also spoke in moralistic tones about how the fight was necessary and good. The fears expressed in the news and civil society often emerged in comic book story lines, either in the guise of subversive Soviet spies or Communists aiming to dominate the world with their superior systems of government and economics. The anti-Communist witch hunts led by Sen. Joe McCarthy were regularly exploited by comic books and their characters. If a comic challenged this accepted norm, it was usually met with open derision as un-American or, at the minimum, failed to sell comic books in any number. This fear of going against American values was later demonstrated with the American Legion opposing comics that showed American servicemen as weak.

In the wake of the American-led UN intervention in South Korea in June 1950, following its invasion by Communist North Korea, the industry immediately increased the number of war-themed comics. After the "Red Chinese" came into the war on the North Korean side, the comics reemphasized the need to push back the Communist horde, along with the usual wartime themes of redemption, valor, and sacrifice for the greater good. Nevertheless, not all comics were one-sidedly patriotic. The treatment of domestic subversion had been nearly unanimous, but comic books had a bit more wiggle room regarding the Korean War. Of course, the majority of war comics—especially in the early stages of the war—showed American soldiers achieving miraculous victories against overwhelming odds. Yet two of the most substantial war comic titles to appear in the 1950s, *Frontline Combat* and *Two-Fisted Tales,* were among the most antiwar.

The main comic book publishers—Dell, DC, Charlton, and Marvel—went with traditional war comic story lines. These often focused on a single soldier who fights against long odds to win the day, not unlike the plots of classic superhero comic books. Other stories portrayed the conversion of dubious or wavering soldiers from possible subversive tendencies to proper American ideals. Educational Comics (EC) went against the grain, publishing comic book stories that were sui generis at the time. Publisher William Gaines, son of comic book pioneer Max Gaines, wanted to make EC an exception to its established competitors. Bill had no initial desire to run the comics business, but he changed his mind following the elder Gaines' death. The company shifted its focus, with a new name to reflect that change: Educational Comics became Entertaining Comics.[29] Still, EC's goal was not merely to entertain readers, but also make them think.

The driving force behind two of EC's most notable war comic books, *Two-Fisted Tales* and *Frontline Combat,* was artist Jack Davis (who made important contributions to many EC titles, from *Mad* to *SuperStories*). Davis approached the genre from a military veteran's standpoint, but this was true of many comic book creators. What made his work distinctive was its brutal depiction of combat. Artists such as John Severin, who had seen vicious fighting in the Pacific, drew and wrote many of the most graphic (or realistic) stories published. A "Meet the Editors" section in *Frontline Combat* noted that most of its contributors had served in the armed forces during World War II and partly based their story lines on what they had witnessed or heard in the war.[30]

Story lines treated current American fighting and largely avoided glorifying war, instead emphasizing the waste of humanity that actually results from it. *Two-Fisted Tales* and *Frontline Combat* were published from 1950 to 1952, during the height of the Korean War. American soldiers were often depicted as unwilling or unable to stop the Communist threat from North Korea, China, or the Soviet Union—and usually much more interested in preserving their own lives. Unlike previous war comics that had shown unwilling combatants converted to the cause, these stories were sympathetic to soldiers who questioned the morality or necessity of war. Some even considered in a sympathetic way what the enemy might be thinking. Because the stories emphasized fear and indecision rather than steely resolve, many members of the establishment, such as publishers, media executives, and government officials, considered them subversive and anti-American. To some, stories featuring such soldiers were tantamount to treason.

Davis took the shock value that had worked so well for EC's *Crime SuperStories* and applied it to the war genre. The story lines had two defining features. First, they were timely. Of *Frontline Combat's* fifteen issues, all but two dealt with the Korean War, which was unfolding as the comics were written. The comic books got many letters from servicemen who expressed their thoughts about how the war or the enemy was depicted. Many liked the currency of the stories, as well as their realistic depictions of combat. Second, the story lines avoided moralizing. Rather than retailing the glories of war or combat heroics, they dealt instead with the realities of combat: the brutal weather conditions, the shocking violence, and the horror of seeing friends die. These story lines were diametrically opposed to what military and political leaders were saying, which most popular culture outlets echoed uncritically. While EC's war comics were not actually anti-American, they were a sharp break with the mass media's typical propagandistic tone. It was almost taken for granted that antiwar sentiments would be suppressed until after war was over. Comics that showed wavering American soldiers, unsure why they were fighting, could be read as suggesting the United States itself was weak. Even so, EC was only exploiting the weakness of the Korean War's rationale. As with Vietnam and Iraq many years later, the original justification for American intervention in Korea seemed questionable as time went on and casualties mounted. In many media outlets the necessity of the war in Korea was not clearly identified, nor were the outcomes cogently developed.

Two story lines from *Two-Fisted Tales* illustrated the moralist's point of view. One, "Corpse on the Imjin," opens with the corpse of a Chinese soldier floating down the titular river.[31] As the story unfolds, the reader learns more about the dead man. After hand-to-hand combat, he had been drowned by an American soldier. While not bloody, the death is presented in a violent way, and the reader is led to identify with the killer by the use of the second person: "You feel him struggle." The reader is asked to experience killing in a primal sense, rather than shooting at a distance. While many comics dealt with hand-to-hand combat, it was usually shown as quick, heroic action. For readers at the time, "He kicks to stay up, but you are heavier and you press him under!" must have been a shock to the system. Finally, the writer notes, "You're tired. . . . Your body is gasping and shaking weak . . . and you're ashamed!"[32]

The second story tells of a Korean farmer and the building of his house. It compares the process to homesteading on the American frontier. As the man finishes and looks forward to raising a family, the war erupts. The house is destroyed, its occupants killed. The final image is the same as the opening panel:

a large American artillery piece shooting at a distant target. The reader is suddenly aware that the gun emplacement has been constructed on the remains of the farmer's house.[33]

Many of the tales treat how men may buckle under the stress of combat. Examples range from an American tank driver who surrenders after his fellow tankers are rescued by a helicopter, to a German paratrooper who cracks under the pressure of constant enemy bombardment. This sort of humane treatment ran opposite a goal of military training, which was to see the enemy not as a human but as an object that must be removed by whatever means necessary (forcing his retreat, capturing him, or killing him).[34]

Jack Davis and his crew on *Frontline Combat* and *Two-Fisted Tales* strove to present an accurate picture of warfare and even of the specifics of a particular battlefield. For example, when they wrote a series on the fighting in Korea, they used the location's correct name, the Changjin Reservoir, not the Chosin Reservoir, as was more common in American reports at the time.[35] While these details may seem minor, the writers considered it important to accurately depict current events in their proper context.[36] EC Comics was not alone when it came to the verisimilitude of events portrayed on the pages of their comics. They did, however, stand out when it came to its depictions of the harsh realities of combat and the moral ambiguity of war. Characters even grappled with the emotions of fear and cowardice. All of these stories entertained revenge fantasies or imagined the "adventure" of combat. Heroics were commonly written into the story lines. Many of the popular comics took the approach of "fighting for the good cause." For example, in the story lines from *Combat Casey,* the Red Chinese are depicted in the way the Japanese had been during World War II. Slanted eyes are meant to reveal shiftiness and treachery, and the Chinese use trickery and deceit to kill Americans. Even their guns look "evil."

The *Combat Casey* series from Atlas (now Marvel) ran for thirty-four issues, attempting to work a comic around a specific, non-superhero character. Casey is depicted as a "man's man," always in the thick of the fighting. Like a superhero, he cannot be kept down because he fights on the "right" side. The story lines are often convoluted: they seemingly show him fighting in both the European and Pacific theaters of World War II and in the Korean War—simultaneously! Furthermore, the way the character is rendered, with a prominent red beard and a wild look in his eyes, at times makes him appear psychotic. Casey's exaggerated bravado is balanced by a suitably intellectual sidekick, Penny P. Pennington (who wears glasses, so we know he reads books). Pennington's early experiences in the Army are used to convey what basic training is like. The stories even explain how and why certain military procedures were invented and drilled into soldiers. In this regard, at least, the story is a form of indoctrination into military service.[37]

Unlike in most comic book depictions of the Germans or the Japanese, the uniforms and equipment of enemy soldiers during the Korean War are portrayed with some degree of verisimilitude. Uniforms are presented with proper insignia, and the weapons look like what the armies actually used, rather than fantastic representations. Comic book publishers had learned from their earlier World War II comics that soldiers who read the comics cared about such accuracy. If the artwork was not realistic, soldiers or other knowledgeable readers would complain or, worse, possibly stop buying the comic books. The men fighting in Korea often were the boys who had read the World War II comics. Comic reading had become part of their leisure time as boys, and when they went to war themselves they took comics with them. This may have necessitated the move to more mature themes as the comic readership aged , so that a wider audience could be reached.

However, this veracity operated only on a micro level. Although the enemy was sometimes treated in a realistic way and with a degree of sympathy, the North Korean Communists were depicted as if emulating the worst atrocities of World War II, such as the Japanese "Rape of Nanking."

In the Korean War comics, two themes prevail. First, combat on the tiny peninsula was close quartered and incredibly deadly. Americans and their allies fought and died there in obscurity and in great numbers. Unlike the hallowed sites scattered across Europe and the Pacific, Korean battlegrounds were (and still are) places no one knew about and very soon forgot about in large part because the justification for the conflict was more abstract than it had been in 1941. War-themed comics of the 1950s captured this popular attitude. Unlike comics of the 1940s that showed the loss of life as a necessary sacrifice, the justification for combat losses in the Korean War comics, however, were far more ambiguous. On their pages, troops often die simply because of the indecision of incompetent officers or frightened enlisted personnel. Second, the North Koreans had learned from their Soviet and Chinese masters: they manipulate American sentimentality by playing on sympathy for the downtrodden or weak. While Americans believe in helping the underdog, this is also seen as a potential weakness that might be exploited by its enemies. For instance, if a comic book shows an orphan, a lost animal, or an attractive woman, the commies are certain to use them as bait to ensnare and destroy Americans.[38] The Korean War lacked the clear-cut morality of World War II, and the comics posited different and evolving reasons for the stalemate, much like the politicians and generals. Technically a UN "police action," the war's purpose remained in doubt. Was it to stop Communism at the 38th parallel, to reunify Korea, or to take on newly Communist China? Years later, the American interventions in Vietnam and Iraq were explained by a similar pattern of shifting rationales.

Dr. Wertham and the Comics Code

In 1954 the renowned psychologist Dr. Frederic Wertham published *Seduction of the Innocent,* a book that explicitly linked comic books to juvenile delinquency.

Wertham was the key figure denouncing comic books' negative influence on American youth and American society. His background was in clinical psychology, and while working on juvenile violence, he observed that comic books were read by many youths in his care (often of subpar intelligence). He used this to claim that youthful criminals learned from comic books. True or not, this charge catalyzed a societal debate about the supposed degeneracy of the medium. Wertham also tied youth violence to the impending Communist threat to the United States. In his book he noted that even American military authorities found some comics too violent to sell at their posts but handed them out to troops going into combat to ramp up aggression.[39] He also believed that the United States should not export such comics to other countries, as they depict Americans as bloodthirsty and violent.[40] During the anti-Communist paranoia of the 1950s, such charges were enough; many in Congress concluded comic book regulation was a subject worthy of investigation.[41]

Wertham blamed many of society's ills on the widespread popularity of comic books, especially those from the EC line run by *Mad* magazine publisher William Gaines. These arguments and those from many other like-minded critics eventually led to congressional hearings on the influence and deviance of comic books. Wertham was an expert witness for the government when the Senate Subcommittee on Juvenile Delinquency convened its "Comic Book Hearings" in April 1954. Headed by Sen. Estes Kefauver, the panel concentrated on the violent nature of horror and crime comics and their possible connection to violence in American youth. During his testimony before the panel, Wertham noted that many of the troubled youngsters interviewed had read comic books. While the committee did not single out war comics for equally harsh treatment, they were affected by the new rules that the hearings spawned.

Authorities such as Wertham were also concerned that comics depicting the moral ambiguities of the war undermined the fighting spirit of American servicemen. To the authorities—Congress, psychologists, and pundits such as Philip Wylie, author of *A Generation of Vipers*—the comics showed soldiers as soft or effeminate. Real men fought the battles with grit and determination and won the day regardless of their internal doubts. (That this completely contradicted the charge that comic books were making American children too violent did not seem to trouble the critics, logic not being their strong suit.) Not only the Communists but also American women were responsible for the supposed weakness of American troops in Korea. By coddling the soldiers when they were younger, their parents—especially mothers—had made them open to Communist manipulation. Indulged as children, they had lost their "killer instinct."[42]

In response to this broad range of criticism, especially the contentious congressional investigations, a consortium of comic book publishers created the Comics Magazines Association of America (CMAA), which in 1954 issued the Comics Code Authority (CCA)—informally known as the Comics Code.

Publishing companies agreed to adhere to its regulations; in exchange, the CMAA issued an official CCA seal to certify that they conformed to the new standards of decency. To earn this seal, comic books could not depict drug use, excessive violence, or disrespect toward the government (civil or military officials in particular). The code also prohibited the use of salacious sexual imagery or details about the commission of crime, to prevent details provided by comic book creators from influencing impressionable young readers. Finally, certain kinds of advertising—as for pellet guns, knives, or "art models"—were also banned.[43] Comic book publishers were expected to self-police their storylines, and companies that did not conform were forced out of business. Advertisers and newsstands usually shunned comics without the CCA seal for fear of the economic ramifications. In the end, the pressure became too much even for Gaines, who had publicly sparred with Wertham during the hearings. He abandoned all his other EC Comics titles in favor of *Mad*. These attacks convinced many people at the time that comic books corrupted children's values—even more than rock and roll music or the new medium of television.[44]

War and Patriotic Comics under the Code

By the mid-1950s, comic book companies were in a difficult position. First, they had to follow the Comics Code or lose access to many potential readers. At the same time, while its strictures made it harder to attract readers and keep their interest, ignoring it risked the same fate as EC's abandoned titles. The result was that eighteen publishing companies exited the market, and none entered it, between 1954 and 1956.[45] Second, after the creation and proliferation of hydrogen bombs by the Soviets and the rise of Red China, fears of Communist encroachment around the world dominated the political climate during the late 1950s. Publishers were not about to produce comics that questioned government authority or could be accused—however absurdly—of sympathy with the Communist cause. Third, as they were earlier, comic books were commonly passed from reader to reader, thus reducing total sales.[46] These conditions favored the largest comic book publishers, who could create safe, yet popular, titles that appealed to the widest possible audience. Fourth, the competition for children's attention from new forms of entertainment such as television and rock and roll music made the comic book a second-tier medium.

The publishers had to adapt or perish. Many simply quit publishing or merged with other comic book publishers. For Charlton, Dell, DC, and Marvel, the war comic still had a market. The remaining companies redesigned their story lines to keep them topical yet entertaining. Their comics had to deliver exciting action and adventure, as the code now made it difficult to publish anything that appeared critical of the war. In the new era of code-driven stories, comic creators still tried to interject satiric humor and comments into their ostensibly patriotic stories while conforming to the new guidelines.

Jack Kirby expanded on his ideas about presenting realistic combat with *Foxhole,* put out by Mainline Studios, which operated from 1954 to 1957. As with *True Stories,* Kirby emphasized that this new World War II comic was produced by actual veterans of that war and reflected their real combat experiences. The cover of the first issue of *Foxhole,* titled "A Day at the Beach," shows a wounded American soldier, bandages covering most of his face, writing to his mother about how combat is "a day at the beach." The cover was derived from Joseph Hirsch's painting *High Visibility Wrap,* part of the Army art program that conveyed the violence and horror of war.[47] The cover underscored the realism Kirby hoped to achieve. Despite a favorable reception, *Foxhole* only lasted seven issues, from 1954 to 1956.[48]

Kirby and Simon also decided to create a new patriotically themed superhero, partly because they had never received any residual earnings from the popular *Captain America* series. (Marvel owned the rights to all their work during that time.) *Fighting American,* featuring the titular superhero and his sidekick Speedy, debuted in 1954. There were immediate problems, however. First, although Kirby and Simon had originally envisioned the character as a straightforward anti-Communist, poor initial sales caused them to modify this concept. While the motivations of Johnny Flagg, Fighting American's alter ego, remained unchanged, the stories morphed into a parody of the form of "Americanism" then reaching its climax. The same year *Fighting American* appeared, Congress inserted the words "under God" into the Pledge of Allegiance, and the Army-McCarthy hearings came to a head.

Senator McCarthy was openly challenged by Col. Joseph Welch during a televised hearing of the Permanent Subcommittee on Investigations (the Senate equivalent of HUAC). The senator's bullying tactics had played badly on television, and after Welch asked him "Have you left no sense of decency?" McCarthy's popularity declined, and far more quickly than had Captain America's. This began a change in the public's attitude toward anti-Communist witch hunts more generally, which indirectly altered the comic book as well.

Therefore, starting in its second issue, *Fighting American* evolved into a satire of American society, including the most absurd kind of red-baiting. Thereafter, the superhero is ranged against overtly silly villains, such as Poison Ivan, Hotski Trotski, Count Uscha Liffso, and Rhode Island Red. These evil Communist characters are always shown as very ugly. In "The League of the Handsome Devils" in *Fighting American* #2, a gang of well-mannered, polished, and handsome gentlemen are involved in various crimes. It is only revealed later that they wore masks to disguise their ugliness. Their goal: to bring down society so that the ugly may rule (an amusing, if preposterous, take on the façade of normality adopted by Communist spies such as Alger Hiss and Julius and Ethel Rosenberg).[49]

In another story, "Stranger from Paradise," a small Russian boy writes to Speedy, Fighting American's "capitalistic" sidekick, to tell of the wonders of Communism: seeing Lenin's body, the fun of watching torture, and the excitement of all things Russian. The story ends with Fighting American and Speedy taking the lad's entire family to America. In the final dialogue, Speedy asks why he wrote such a letter, as it is obvious that he and his family did not like life in Russia. The boy responds that it was so that he could speak his mind.[50] By praising life in the Soviet Union so extravagantly that no one in the West could believe him, the young Russian was actually hinting that he really believed the opposite. Again, even though the comic was written as a satire, it still exemplified the American assumption that all Russians wanted to escape an oppressive regime. If Simon and Kirby's new strategy was too subtle for its intended audience, they never got a chance to find out. The overall downturn in the comic book business had placed too great a financial burden on them. Without the resources to sustain the operation until it could turn a profit, Mainline Comics collapsed. *Fighting American* only lasted for seven issues, like *Foxhole* before it.[51]

While Mainline and EC took on the horrors of combat or satirized the "international Communist conspiracy," Dell Comics (DC) treated war themes differently. Its comic books stuck to variations of traditional formulas, using either historical or adventure points of view. Unlike Mainline, Dell was one of the most substantial comic book publishing companies of the era, having been a powerhouse in the comics market since its beginnings in the late 1930s. Its war comics tried to be informative yet entertaining, presenting World War II to appeal to historically minded people as well as more typical comic book readers. Many employed the "true tales" format DC had used successfully since the 1940s. This approach made Dell's comics seem more like history lessons with pictures than sensational entertainment. Given the backlash from the Comic Book hearings, this educational content was a much-needed selling point that showed its commitment to Dr. Wertham's thinking.

Although DC produced many different war-themed comic books in almost all subgenres, *Combat* was perhaps the most successful. The writers of *Combat* tried to utilize actual people, units, and actions to give realism to the story that many other comic creators sought to avoid. *Combat* was published quarterly from 1962 to 1973, a period virtually coterminous with the Vietnam War.[52] As the role of American advisors in Vietnam expanded into a major military commitment, the growing unpopularity of the war made it a poor setting for the heroic actions Dell wished to relate (and, presumably, the Dell Comics' readership would pay to see). As an alternative to this contentious contemporary reality, *Combat* presented World War II, as readers could more readily identify with its seemingly simple morality and the goal of unconditional victory.[53]

For example, one issue narrated the Allied attack on Monte Cassino, where the abbey, a religious and cultural icon dating back to the seventh century, was destroyed during one of the bloodiest and most controversial battles of the European campaign. The issue focused on the four assaults on the monastery that took place between January and May 1944.[54] Even then, controversy surrounded the decision to shell and bomb the strategically important monastery despite reports that German forces were using it as an observation post that provided a commanding view of the entire Liri River valley leading into Rome. Even now, debate surrounding the veracity of the claims that provided the justification of the destruction of the abbey continues. Compared with the political uncertainties in the Middle East after the Suez Crisis, in Eastern Europe after the aborted Hungarian Revolution of 1956, and in Asia after the unresolved division of Korea, however, even Monte Cassino represented an era of understandable moral values.

Unlike the contemporary political issues that seemed to elude satisfactory resolutions, stories of World War II depicted a clear goal, a clear enemy, and a clear victory. Moreover, comic book readers, like Americans in general, often did not know the difference between North Korea and South Korea. Given the pervasive racism of the time, many readers found it difficult to identify with the "inscrutable" and "exotic" Asians. It was much easier to portray stereotypical Asian villains than to persuade Americans that Koreans truly shared their desire for freedom or at least to escape Communism. Europe was far more familiar, geographically and culturally, to the average reader. For all these reasons, the European theater of World War II became fodder for many mainstream comic books during this period.

Dell's Influence on War Comics

Dell Comics set the tone for the war genre for the next two decades. Another of its important titles was *Our Army at War,* published from 1952 to 1977. The successful series featured conventional stories of combat and individual valor. It became an even bigger hit after the appearance in 1958 of Sgt. Frank Rock, a character created by Robert Kanigher and drawn by Joe Kubert.[55] This creative team was responsible for many popular DC war titles in addition to *Sgt. Rock,* such as *Enemy Ace, Unknown Soldier,* and *G.I. Combat.* Unlike *Combat,* however, Kanigher's stories emphasized the action of the story, often giving no indication of where or when the combat takes place.[56] Kanigher had served in the military, and Kubert was stationed in Germany during the Korean War, but neither had combat experience.[57] (As a teenager, Kubert had cut his professional teeth drawing Hawkman and other characters for DC before joining the Army in World War II.)[58] Despite this apparent handicap, their work was an important part of the wave of war comic characters that solidified DC as a comic book powerhouse. Kubert's characters, such as Sgt. Rock, had to meet the standards of the Comic Code. Nevertheless, DC war comics remained immensely popular with readers. The characters were exciting and brave, and the stories still glorified combat, at least combat involving American soldiers. However, anything that might be even accused of subversion was disallowed.

Sgt. Rock's introduction in *Our Army at War* counterbalanced the uncertain or cynical soldiers of Korea depicted in other comics. Rock is the pinnacle of the "tough guy" sergeant. His backstory is one of hardship: with both parents killed during the Depression, Rock must leave school to work in a steel mill. There he demonstrates his physical prowess, and he becomes a boxer who can stay standing through sheer determination. He is not a man with moral doubts, nor is he easily shaken. Although Rock fights in the Pacific on occasion, his exploits are mostly against the Germans in Europe or Africa. If Rock has any reservations about the war, he does not voice them. Instead, he relentlessly pushes forward, doing what it takes to keep his men safe. Always the tip of the spear in combat, Rock carries out great acts of heroism in the face of German tanks or other threats. His exploits exceed even those of the most active American special operations units during the war, such as the pathfinders of the 82nd and 101st Airborne Divisions and the Navy's underwater demolition teams. Rock exemplifies the fantasy of the American warrior, superior to any other on the planet.

The stories of Sgt. Rock and his Easy Company infantry unit were the first of three major comic book titles from DC that achieved lasting fame. The second, *Haunted Tank,* concerned an American M3 "Stuart" tank crew haunted by the spirit of Maj. Gen. J. E. B. Stuart himself. The story line combines the idea of a spiritual life (in this case the guiding hand of the Confederate general), American technological advantages, and the can-do spirit of those who do not doubt the cause for which they fight. *Haunted Tank* became a mainstay of another multistory war comic, DC's *G.I. Combat.* Originally published by Quality Comic Books, DC took over *G.I. Combat* after issue #44, and *Haunted Tank* became one of its most a popular stories. Eventually DC expanded it into a stand-alone title.

Haunted Tank is similar to *Sgt. Rock* in that it seldom refers to a particular battle or other specifics. A number of stories, however, use the desert as a background, explicitly referring to the first American landings in North Africa in late 1942. More notable was how Kubert drew the stories. While he was not the first artist to draw its characters, he was the most frequent artist on both titles. His drawings of weapons, vehicles, and uniforms are quite detailed—with the exception of the German military, whose uniforms and vehicles are often inaccurate or miscolored. The stories also frequently show the M3 Stuart, a lightly armed and armored tank, up against the formidable German Panzer Mark VI. Military historians consider the German tank, commonly referred to as the

Tiger, as one of the best in World War II. It was far superior to even the main American battle tank, the M4 "Sherman," and could have easily disabled or destroyed an M3 in actual combat. In the *Haunted Tank* stories, however, the Stuart's crew often has spiritual assistance. As a result, the crew's war record is impressive: this single tank is a virtual one-vehicle wrecking crew against the Axis. Between its introduction in *G.I. Combat* #87 and when the crew switches to a larger tank in issue #150, the little Stuart destroys 115 Tigers, 24 Messerschmitt aircraft, 2 submarines, and assorted other German military assets.[59] If only all tanks in the U.S. Army had done as well!

The third of Kanigher and Kubert's war-themed comics was *Enemy Ace,* first featured in *Our Army at War* #151. Hans von Hammer, the comic's protagonist, was based on German World War I flying ace Manfred von Richthofen. Unlike other DC characters, he is wracked by guilt over the horrors of the war. While he keeps winning dogfights, he becomes increasingly aloof from his men. His sole companion is a wolf he finds in the Black Forest. Unlike most DC characters, Hammer is often conflicted as he struggles to balance the inevitable killing war entails and his obligation to defend Germany from its enemies. Obviously the comic presents von Hammer in a sympathetic way— though an enemy, he is the title character. This is rare in the often black-and-white world of comic books, although more understandable by the late 1950s when the West Germans had become a part of the North Atlantic Treaty Organization. Von Hammer's enemies now take the role of villains, especially the French pilot known as the Hangman. Otherwise unnamed and faceless, this enemy is remorseless in combat. He is simply a killing machine. Naturally, by comparison, von Hammer attracts the reader's sympathy.

In another change, many of DC's comics introduced quasi-love interests for their heroes. A certain nurse often helps von Hammer recuperate; in some later issues, the Hangman's aristocratic sister replaces the nurse. Sgt. Rock, the crew of the Haunted Tank, and Johnny Cloud—a Navajo Indian who becomes an Army Air Forces P-51 pilot—share a love object: Mademoiselle Marie, a member of the French Resistance. By adding these ethnic characters and erotic attachments, comic creators tried to widen their audience base and broaden the existing conversion ethos already in war comics. Women could assist in combat and serve as a reason to fight, yet continue to represent normalcy away from the front line.

Science fiction comics began selling better during this period. In an attempt to tap this market, DC merged some war comics with tales of the unknown. The series *The War That Time Forgot* introduced this seemingly odd combination to the public under the *Star Spangled War Stories* umbrella. As with other features, the stories were relatively short. Instead of tales with some connection—however tenuous—to reality, in these American forces fight dinosaurs on isolated South Pacific islands. Set during World War II, the nominal enemy is the Japanese military, but the stories concentrate instead on the saurian menace. These volumes are more like Japanese monster movies than typical war comics. As in *Godzilla,* the monsters are metaphors for the horrors of an atomic attack and radiation poisoning or of scientific monstrosities yet unknown.

While DC was the sales leader, putting out the major titles mentioned above, Charlton Comics Group actually published the most titles in the war genre. While not known for high sales or pay parity for its staff, Charlton produced over two dozen war-themed titles, mostly before 1968.[60] The company had several notable characters, including Shotgun Harker and the Iron Corporal. At one point, World War II veteran and renowned war comic book illustrator Sam Glanzman drew both. The vast majority of Charlton's comics were set during World War II, although they sometimes covered other conflicts. Many of the titles only produced fifteen thousand issues in monthly sales but still had runs of several years.[61] After the late 1970s, the company often reprinted older comic books, which it sold until Charlton Comics ceased publication in 1986.[62] In many ways, Charlton typified early comic book companies, grinding out sensational titles of varying quality to make a quick profit. Given its longevity, it seems to have succeeded.

Comics Produced for the U.S. Military

War comics were not simply a commercial business. The U.S. military also saw the benefit of suiting comic books or similar material for training purposes as well as entertainment. Working off the success of *Joe Dope* comics from World War II, the Army contacted Will Eisner to work again on military publications. The idea: military personnel would better remember basic field discipline and maintenance rules if the material was presented in visual form and with humor. To that end, Eisner started work on *PS: The Preventive Maintenance Monthly* in 1951. A small, pocket-sized publication, it gave the soldier a chance to read up on varied maintenance tasks. Over the years, *PS* articles addressed such topics as the inner workings of the air filters on an M113 armored personnel carrier and the need for proper maintenance of the new M-16. *PS* was an immediate success, and Eisner edited it for many years. After his role began to diminish, the Army brought in Kubert, who served as an illustrator and editor on the magazine for some time. *PS* is still published today, and its comics continue to inform and entertain.[63]

Another Army-produced comic was *Five Years Later . . . Where Will You Be?,* which began in 1962. It looked at the lives of people in an unidentified small town in the United States. While its main purpose was to encourage a stint in the Army, it also strongly encouraged education. A ne'er-do-well who wants to drop out of high school is one of the main characters. When a friend comes back to town with stories of how the Army provides not only discipline and a practical education but the opportunity to travel, the story's protagonist realizes that the Army is a better option than nothing.[64] This story was similar to *Li'l Abner Joins the Navy*. The key difference was that characters in *Five Years Later* were generic, so more readers could identify with them.

Social Issues in War Comics

During the early 1960s, some war comic books started to delve into the major social issues of the day, the role of minority troops in particular. As the civil rights movement picked up speed, DC's major titles began to revamp their cast of characters to include minorities. *Sgt. Rock* added Jackie Johnson (an African American) and Little Sure Shot (a Native American) to his squad, while *Haunted Tank* introduced minorities in various story lines. Many comics developed into the "squad" or "platoon" story lines favored in such movies as *Guadalcanal Diary, Battleground,* and *A Walk in the Sun.*[65] Since readers got to know these characters very well, the war took on a personal aspect. *Sgt. Rock*'s "Battle-Happy Joes of Easy Company" is a typical example. Despite many replacements over time, the core members all have nicknames reflecting their roles in the unit. As the comic introduced new characters here or there, many who resonated with fans later became regulars.

Rock's right hand is Bulldozer, a mountain man who can single-handedly carry and fire a machine gun, yet show tenderness toward others.[66] Wildman is a temperamental Jewish former high school history teacher who sometimes goes berserk in combat (understandable, considering the Nazi enemy).[67] Ice Cream Soldier's unflappability under fire makes him an effective killer.[68] Little Sure Shot has deadly accuracy with a rifle (no doubt from all his practice with bow and arrow). He has left the "old ways" behind, yet still talks of his life on the reservation.[69] Jackie Johnson voices the need for racial equality.[70] As one of the first African American characters to play more than a supporting role in comic books, Johnson was the fictional equivalent of baseball's Jackie Robinson. Although the U.S. armed forces had been officially integrated in 1948, the new policy's practical implementation took some time. It took even longer for comic books, where the sight of a minority soldier was rare until the early 1960s and limited even then.[71] Gays will necessarily be "integrated" into the military faster; after all, they are already present in nearly every capacity. But, following the earlier pattern, war comics have lagged this development.[72] The multiethnic platoons eventually favored by movies and comics implied the need for greater inclusion of minorities—and the conversion of those opposed to it within the United States. Many saw the military—in actuality as well in as popular culture—as a means to unify people behind a common cause. As Richard Slotkin notes, however, the multiethnic patrol was an idealized image of American society, not the reality.[73]

In mainstream comics, many superheroes started to deal with topics such as civil rights in various ways.[74] One seemingly patriotic and war-themed super-hero comic was created during this time. *Tales of Suspense* #39 from Marvel introduced readers to a character named Iron Man. "Iron Man Is Born!" was written by Stan Lee and his cousin Larry Leiber, with art by Don Heck. Iron Man is the nom de guerre of Tony Stark, a brilliant scientist and arms mer-chant. He attempts to use transistorized electromagnets to lighten weapons, increasing their portability in the jungles of Vietnam, where American advi-sors are operating, even before official American combat action in 1964.

While testing out the equipment, Stark is badly wounded by a Vietcong (VC) booby-trap. He is then captured by Wong-Chu, a diabolical Communist warlord. Chu forces him to work with Dr. Yinsen, a physicist from Timbetpal (a fictional country apparently based on Tibet and Nepal), to create new weap-ons for the Vietnamese. As Stark's wound could eventually kill him, Yinsen and Stark create the Iron Man suit, which saves his life and imbues him with the superpowers he needs to fight for freedom. Yinsen sacrifices himself to give Stark enough time to power up the suit, which he then uses to defeat the warlord. Iron Man is never involved in Vietnam afterwards, but it is interesting that the story premiered in March 1963, before Vietnam had attracted much attention in the United States.[75]

By the mid-1960s, both mainstream and lesser-known comics started to work in some genuine details from the war; the tunnels utilized by the VC had become a popular subject. Even Dell began to reflect the vicious reality of combat—up to a point. Some stories started to show dissension within the ranks, a topic that had been more or less taboo. Nevertheless, the overwhelm-ing majority of war comics before 1965 did not question American policies or motives. Despite the escalating conflict in Vietnam, they continued to portray combat in traditionally valorous terms. Although the crises and conflicts of the 1950s and 1960s—such as the Suez Crisis in Egypt in 1956, the Ameri-can intervention in Haiti in 1959, and the Cuban Missile Crisis in 1962—were generally ignored, there was enough material for comic books as the increased intensity of the Vietnam War and the rising age of readers caused a growing cynicism about American culture and politics, which became a defining char-acteristic of the comics by the late 1960s.

4 War Comics in a Time of Upheaval (1962–91)

The glorification of war, which we do with our young, is a bad
thing, very bad. It's only good if a person has to defend
their country. There're very few instances like that.

—JAMES WARREN, in *Blazing Combat Collection*

For a new generation of American youths who avidly consumed the war comics and films of World War II, the Cold War, and the Korean War, the Vietnam War might have seemed their chance to experience the storied glory of a "good war." As the war intensified, however, increased reporting led the public to pay greater attention, forcing comic books to deal with the conflict. Trying not to alienate readers with differing views about the war, comics publishers sometimes dodged the issue with a warped "fun-house" view of military life, distorting its incidents, ideals, and problems. But as the war dragged on, the difficulty of being all things to all people led even mainstream war comics to adopt a neutral or antiwar stance. After the Vietnam War ended, comics creators tried to bury the war by returning to tried and true World War II gallantry. The 1980s saw a rise of patriotism, tied to President Ronald Reagan's call for increased military expenditures. Comic books such as Marvel's *G.I. Joe: A Real American Hero* reflected this.[1] Other comics took Reagan and his ideals and wrapped them in anti-American forms. Either way, as the 1980s ended, war comics routinely used Vietnam as a theme.

Prowar Comics

For publishers such as Charlton, the Vietnam conflict was simply an extension of the heroics of World War II. Charlton's July 1967 issue of *Army War Heroes* is typical of the series (and the publisher's expectations). Its four vignettes deal with World War II in Europe, World War II in the Pacific (with Japanese soldiers who looked surprisingly like North Vietnamese Army

[NVA] soldiers), artillery in general, and Vietcong tunnels. The stories contain all the standard war comic elements: sneaky enemy traps to prevent the advance of honest American soldiers, a squad member hit in the open where no one can reach him, the shooting of American wounded in violation of the Geneva Conventions, and the hero's extraordinary acts to save his comrades. At the end of "Terror in a Viet Cong Tunnel," as the hero is in hand-to-hand combat with a VC, he fends off his attacker and hits him hard on the jaw to "hear the bone break."[2]

Charlton editors even reprinted *Army Digest* articles in their comics. "Terror in a Viet Cong Tunnel" is printed directly across the page from an *Army Digest* article ("Here Isn't There") on research and development in various environments. The article acknowledges that war is far more chaotic than it could possibly be portrayed in comics—or for that matter in films or on television. According to the author, the way American forces are shown defending strategic hamlets in South Vietnam recalls Hollywood westerns, where a fort is surrounded by "savages" keen to defeat "civilization."[3]

Some comic book publishers used the struggles of Vietnam to create sympathy and support for the war. They focused on the new conditions of conflict: guerrilla tactics, vicious fighting, and an uncertain front line. Dell, which had offered war tales since the beginning of the comic book form, introduced several titles to promote the war during the early 1960s. *Jungle War Stories,* which ran from 1963 to 1965 and then retitled as *Guerrilla War* through 1966, portrayed the war in Vietnam from the perspective of American advisors early in the conflict. Its story lines depicted the low-intensity conflicts that dominated headlines of the time.[4]

In the Dell war series *Tales of the Green Beret* (published from 1967 to 1968), the newly organized U.S. Army Special Forces—the Green Berets founded at the behest of President John F. Kennedy—were put to the test in the first major conflict to utilize their unconventional skills. Many story lines reflected the American military's official stated goals of winning hearts and minds. The idea was to defeat the enemy in part by providing the South Vietnamese with modern services, such as medical care, sewage and water treatment, and access to education through the construction of schools. The original purpose of the Green Berets was to be a force multiplier, supplementing these efforts. Instead of fighting independently, they would be more effective training Vietnamese civilians to fight for themselves long after the Americans left.

Another pro-war comic, *Tod Holton, Super Green Beret,* showed the war in unambiguous terms: the United States versus the Communist hordes. In the creation story, a politically astute teenager gets his uncle's magical green beret.

When worn by someone of virtue, it gives the wearer superhuman strength and abilities, such as invisibility, heightened intelligence, teleportation powers, and superior military skills. (This works only for virtuous Americans, of course—not for the duplicitous VC who wears it in one story line.[5]) The racist depictions of the enemy recall the "Japanazis" of World War II. The VC and North Vietnamese are bucktoothed and use immoral guerrilla tactics—shooting from concealment, attacking civilians rather than soldiers—with a general lack of respect for life. Many of the comics feature the VC terrorizing civilians and torturing Americans to achieve their goals (or even as a savage form of amusement). (The comics downplayed or suppressed atrocities committed by American and South Vietnamese forces.) The first issue mostly centers on Vietnam, although in one story Holton goes back in time to prevent Hitler's escape from Germany on April 30, 1945.[6]

The second issue goes even further afield. In one story, Tod rescues Peace Corps volunteers from a small African nation under the control of an Oxford-educated local who exploits indigenous myths to rule the population.[7] Given that the Peace Corps was meant to counter the image of Americans as an occupying army, it is an odd story device, even as a response to the antiwar movement. Tod also dons the green beret to travel in time once more, to fight the British during the Revolutionary War.[8] However, were not the Americans in Vietnam comparable to the eighteenth-century British in the American colonies? Perhaps the message was simpler: ideals might be nice, but to get something done, a good military (or a man in a magic hat) is necessary. The ideological confusion of the time is evident, which may have been the reason the series sold poorly, ending after two issues.

The Green Berets also appeared in a comic strip. "Tales of the Green Berets" (the same name as the comic book), illustrated by Joe Kubert and written by Robin Moore, ran in the *Chicago Tribune* from 1966 to 1968 and was syndicated throughout the United States.[9] The stories focus on two themes. The first describes how Chris Tower, a reporter with Green Beret training, becomes a staunch supporter of the Special Forces and sometimes even actively participates in their missions, experiences similar to that of Moore, a journalist who trained with the Green Berets despite being a civilian. The second purpose of the comic was to illustrate the variety of jobs that Green Berets performed, to show the many areas where they served. One series of stories was set in Central America; another involved the escape of an East German scientist's family through "Checkpoint Charlie" into West Berlin. The series ran for two years but was retired following the Tet Offensive in July 1968, Kubert having other obligations, such as his work at DC.[10] Nevertheless, the comic book remains popular, and a number of companies have since offered reprints in compilations.[11]

By the time of Vietnam, Sgt. Rock was dealing with his demons and the stress of combat within the popular series, so Kubert created another character for the DC stable. Introduced in *Star-Spangled War Stories* #151 (June 1970), *The Unknown Soldier* advanced the premise that one man (at the right place and time) could make a difference in a war. Disfigured while fighting along-side his brother and haunted by his past, a soldier becomes a chameleon to infiltrate and defeat the enemies of the United States. Again, the stories ignore the contemporary Vietnam conflict, celebrating instead the heroic exploits of World War II. The Unknown Soldier's full disfigurement and identity are never revealed, so his deeds become a cipher for all the righteous soldiers of that honorable war. In the early stories he is a French Resistance leader of African origin with the code name Chat Noir (Black Cat; his real name is never given). The story "Invasion Game" reveals that Chat Noir had been a high-ranking U.S. Army sergeant until court-martialed for a crime he did not commit. He then goes AWOL before sentence and escapes to France, where he fights for the Maquis. He rescues the Unknown Soldier on D-Day. The story's last panel shows him back in uniform with full stripes at Arlington's Tomb of the Unknowns (along with the Unknown Soldier character).[12] Later on, Chat Noir returns as a frequent companion of the Unknown Soldier; the publishers hoped to attract more African American readers.

As in Kanigher's series (*Sgt. Rock, Enemy Ace*, and even *The Haunted Tank*), the *Unknown Soldier* tales jump from place to place, often crossing time lines. Unlike Sgt. Rock, the Unknown Soldier often takes part in the Pacific cam-paign. In the Unknown Soldier's flashback origin story, the reader learns that a Japanese grenade disfigured him and killed his brother, and war became a vendetta. The Unknown Soldier was another version of May's conversion hero. The soldier was fighting for the idea of America and the equality of all Americans. He takes on Chat Noir as an equal, which segregation had obvi-ously made impossible for most American troops in World War II. Even as the series ended, the Unknown Soldier stands for the ideals of America. How-ever, in later iterations—two miniseries in the 1990s and the current series, launched in 2008—the Unknown Soldier changes into a tool of the govern-ment, specifically the CIA.

Some artists tried to split the difference, taking a stance that acknowledges both the antiwar movement and the more conservative elements that sup-ported the war effort. One such artist was Sam Glanzman, another stalwart of the industry. Like Jack Kirby, Glanzman was a combat veteran of World War II. For writers like Glanzman, who served in the Navy, the war served as a means of traditional action-and-adventure storytelling; his war became a vendetta. His work spans the 1950s through the present day, with his most memorable creations rooted in various war comics (especially titles from the

Charlton Comics group). Glanzman translated his wartime naval experience into tales of valor and triumph. His comic Battlefield Action was the story of Shotgun Harker, a hard-boiled, cigar-chomping, shotgun-toting Marine sergeant in Vietnam.13 His bumbling, longhaired sidekick, Chicken Smith, has a peacenik attitude of "make love, not war." With doubts about the identity of "the real enemy," Smith is an unwilling draftee—complete with flowers in his hair. Despite this caricature, in *Battlefield Action*, Glanzman tried to accommodate antiwar sentiment into a mainstream comic book.

Antiwar Comics

Warren Publishing's *Blazing Combat* series, which ran from 1965 to 1966, comprised essentially antiwar comics, in the manner of EC's *Frontline Combat* and *Two-Fisted Tales* (and quite unlike DC's *Sgt. Rock,* which glorified the heroic individual). In fact, James Warren and Archie Goodwin—the publisher and principal writer, respectively—both credited Harvey Kurtzman's EC war comics as their inspiration. Like those EC series, *Blazing Combat* met fierce resistance from the Pentagon, the American Legion, and other groups that viewed it as subversive. Their concern was that comic books might influence American servicemen by showing how divided the country had become over Vietnam. While *Blazing Combat* only lasted four issues, the series had an impact on other comic book creators and helped change the war comics genre.[14] The comic was published quarterly, in black and white, and in magazine format. These distinctions are important. First, as a quarterly, it had more pages and stories, with a longer "shelf life," giving the company more time to make a profit. Second, black-and-white publication reduced publishing costs—allowing Warren, who had to put up his own money, to meet his publication schedule. Third, the magazine format allowed *Blazing Combat,* like EC's *Mad* magazine, to skirt the Comics Code and run material that might otherwise have been censored.[15]

One of the most important issues treated by Korean or Vietnam war comics was the treatment of the local population and enemy soldiers. The story "Viet Cong," appearing in *Blazing Combat* #1, discusses the torture of enemy soldiers by a member of the Army of the Republic of South Vietnam (ARVN). It was written by Archie Goodwin and drawn by Joe Orlando, who actually witnessed the torture of a VC as a Green Beret advisor in Vietnam. His fictionalized counterpart believes the torture unnecessary to obtain information, but he recognizes that ARVN soldiers use different methods from the United States (a distinction that has since been lost).[16] This story appeared in 1965 when American involvement in the conflict was in its early active combat stage, although advisors had been present in Vietnam since the second Eisenhower administration.

Other stories looked at how the local population in Vietnam tried to stay out of the war and its politics, to simply survive. In "Landscape," a farmer attempts to grow rice while avoiding the violence inflicted on his small hamlet by both sides. The old man watches as various family members die from torture, starvation, or combat, yet he still hopes for peace. Nevertheless, at the end of the story—just as he is lamenting that the battle has destroyed his entire family, crop, and home—he is killed in the crossfire between the Vietcong and South Vietnamese soldiers. As American helicopters land to disgorge more troops, the reader sees the farmer's hand sinking into the rice paddy.[17] The story resembles those in *Two-Fisted Tales* that centered on Korean civilian casualties, as in the story "Rubble" noted in chapter 3.

These *Blazing Combat* issues came out around the time of the first "underground comix" (the idiosyncratic spelling indicated the break from the mainstream) and the first organized antiwar protests at the University of California–Berkeley in late 1965 and early 1966. The founders of the underground comix movement tackled subjects that the Comics Code did not allow, such as sex, drug use, and direct challenges to authority. However, at this time both underground and mainstream comics were adapting to the increasing age of readers (many were in high school or college). Marvel was the first mainstream publisher to attempt to reach this older audience. Its *Spider-Man, Fantastic Four,* and *X-Men* titles all dealt with the anxiety and other issues facing teenagers and young adults.

At first Vietnam comics mirrored those produced during the Korean conflict. Most were prowar, often relying on crude stereotypes: the Asian as the Other and therefore a threat to the American way of life. In the Chinese, they found an enemy who merged the new fears of Communism with the preexisting threat of the "Yellow Peril." In the Korean War, however, *Two-Fisted Tales* and *Frontline Combat* had been the only significant antiwar comics, and they had died off by the time the war ended. By contrast, as the Vietnam conflict dragged on, the antiwar comics that began with *Blazing Combat* spurred even more antiwar and antiestablishment mainstream and underground comics. While the majority of comics remained either prowar or neutral, a significant number took a stand against the war. The difference can be largely explained by two interrelated trends. First, the Vietnam War went on much longer than the Korean War. By 1968, when the country tipped to majority antiwar sentiment, the conflict had lasted longer than the entire Korean War, with no end in sight (despite the Pyrrhic American victory during Tet that year). Second, larger changes in the culture, driven by the baby boom generation as it reached college age, led to a broader questioning of authority. This combination fundamentally shifted the very premises of public opinion in a way never seen during the Korean War, even though that conflict had eventually become just as misunderstood in its ramifications and divisive in its conclusions.

This changed environment made possible the commercial success of the underground comix movement, which was far more political and confrontational in style. An early example was Julian Bond's 1967 *Vietnam: An Antiwar Comic Book,* which made the case that the war was being used to hurt or punish African Americans. Bond was an influential voice of the civil rights movement and as a member of the Georgia state legislature, he had openly opposed the war in 1965. Rather than escape into fantasy, readers were encouraged to think of the serious issues at hand. The story, only sixteen pages in length, utilized standard comic book techniques: pictures with written descriptions either above or below the artwork. However, it was clearly written with a teenager or young adult in mind. *Vietnam*'s format was evocative, and while it never achieved the distribution or sales of mainstream comics, it accurately represented the contemporary issues from a dissenting viewpoint. In the opening panels, Bond drew from current politics, noting famous African Americans who opposed the war, including Martin Luther King Jr., Malcolm X, members of the Southern Christian Leadership Conference, and others.[18]

Bond's point was that the war in Vietnam was no glorious fight but a tyrannical war that should prompt blacks—who had few rights back home—to question its necessity. He also gave an alternative history of the war, using photographs as a basis for the illustrations. Especially effective were the drawings based on iconic images of those African American leaders. Bond symbolically linked the struggle of the Vietnamese against colonial domination to the fight for civil rights in the United States. The comic noted that minorities were fighting in proportionally larger numbers than whites, despite having little to gain from the war. While the comic was not pacifist as such, it was very much against the Vietnam War and strongly challenged the value of the sacrifices made in it by African Americans.[19]

Such underground comix reflected the newfound freedom of expression that altered many forms of media from that era. They experimented with alternative forms of drawing, with stories that reflected the time's uncertainty, the sexual revolution, and the antiwar movement. Robert Crumb is considered the most substantial of the underground comix artists, but many lesser-known comix creators also sought to capture the images and emotions associated with the time. Early artists who later gained notoriety from their comix include "Spain" Rodriguez and S. Clay Wilson. Some major publishers also sought commercial advantage by catching this wave. For instance, Marvel Comics often dealt with aspects of society that DC would not touch. From the 1960s onward, its publications amassed a large following through alienated characters who were disdained merely for being different. The mutant powers of the X-Men excite society's hatred and set them apart (like the Jews in Nazi Germany). The teenage angst of Peter Parker/Spider-Man and the family dysfunction of the Fantastic Four resonated with readers with their own problems. These societal issues entered into the story lines of cutting-edge comics, with underground comix taking these to the far extreme. In either case, the goal was the same: to develop characters for an older and more sophisticated readership, one receptive to political satire and cultural and societal critiques.

One underground comic book that dealt with the war from this subversive perspective was *The Legion of Charlies* (written by Tom Veitch and drawn by Greg Irons). It compared the murderous rampage of the Manson Family in Southern California to the actions of American soldiers in Vietnam, specifically the My Lai Massacre led by Lt. William Calley in March 1968. This polemical comparison was unreasonable, however. Given the Vietcong's attack modes—on soft targets such as movie theaters, pubs, and other public places—no one could be sure where or when an attack might come, and any civilian might be the attacker. In the view of Veitch and Irons, this meant that some soldiers were akin to Manson's random killers. Regardless, the idea that all Vietnam veterans were bloodthirsty murderers was necessarily untrue. Whatever one thinks about the actions of American combat troops, the majority of servicemen in Vietnam were support troops who never engaged in combat. *The Legion of Charlies* also made the case that Lieutenant Calley's actions differed only slightly from what political leaders in Washington expected from all servicemen.[20] By extension, in the comic's view Manson was no different from President Richard Nixon, except in the scale of their crimes: both slaughtered innocent people according to their deity-like whims.[21]

Hydrogen Bomb and Biochemical Warfare Funnies, an underground collection of vignettes from several artists, directly took on the immorality of war. Like most underground war comix, it purported to shock readers with the futility of armed conflict. Greg Irons drew one of its tales, "Raw War Comics," which starts like many traditional war movies and comic books: "Our story begins somewhere in the no-mans-land created by men at war!" The soldiers have iconic military paraphernalia from World War II: a Thompson submachine gun (not often used by Americans in Vietnam) and the Lucky Strike cigarettes coveted by men on the front during the 1940s. The protagonists reflect nostalgically about daily life back home, but the story quickly turns violent as they are shot and killed. Despite the story's black-and-white images, the soldiers' deaths are quite graphic, and it suggests, "This isn't what's supposed to happen!"[22] The issue intends to show the actual brutality of combat, making typical comic books seem stupid glorifiers of war. The images are crudely drawn, but they make their point: war is not neat or pleasant, and people die in awful, grotesque manners.

In "The Last Laugh," war is "a political whorehouse," and nuclear war is a response to sexual frustration. The soldiers are drawn with their penises in hand, portraying combat as a form of sexual release. The military official who pushes the button to start a nuclear war sees it as a letdown (he also fondles himself while fantasizing about sexually uninhibited hippie women). He notes that he feels cheated by the technology—he wants to "bust, maim, squeeze, twist, mash, gorge, and kill." In the end, all is meaningless, as everyone dies in the atomic blast.[23]

Mainstream Comic Books Respond to Vietnam

DC Comics was the publisher most likely to introduce new characters and story lines. With the success of *Sgt. Rock, The Haunted Tank,* and *Enemy Ace,* it created other characters that approached combat from a mental, rather than physical, dimension. One can read these stories and sense the tension arising from the troublesome perception of the military in the Vietnam era. The comics mirrored the reception of American soldiers returning from Vietnam, including the disgust that some World War II veterans had toward their Vietnam-era counterparts. One comic book character who bridges this World War II–Vietnam veteran gap is Capt. Phil Hunter, featured in DC's *Our Fighting Forces.* In many early story lines, he fights the duplicitous Vietcong and their guerrilla combat tactics. By the 1970s, however, the character reflects the contempt often shown by the media toward the military.

As *Our Fighting Forces* continued into the 1970s, its emphasis shifted to the exploits of Lt. Ben Hunter, Phil's father. During World War II, Lieutenant Hunter leads the Hellcats, a team of soldiers openly resentful of his authority.[24] The Hellcats are criminals and ne'er-do-wells, depicted in a manner that crosses the antiheroes of *The Dirty Dozen* (a 1967 World War II action film in which criminals are trained as commandos) with characters from the era of *Blackhawk.*[25] (Both groups are natural fighters who disdain Army discipline.) The series was published in 1968 when morale on the home front shifted from majority support of the war to a majority who agreed with the news media's increasingly pessimistic judgment that the war was, at best, a stalemate. The characters often reflect the draftee military and the seeming futility of the war. Although some comics still showed the war in positive terms, overall the comics were shifting from the glory of combat to alternative views of warfare.

Unsurprisingly, the successful concepts of one comic book publisher were borrowed by others. For instance, *The Dirty Dozen*–type unit, in some form or other, was employed by most companies. It was also a standard scenario in many war movies of the period. A group of soldiers—punished for lack of discipline, military decorum, or even deviant or sociopathic traits—volunteers for an "impossible mission." The inducement is a pardon for their crimes—in the unlikely event that they return alive. Marvel came out with two short-lived examples of this subgenre. The first was *Combat Kelly and the Deadly Dozen,* loosely adapted from the movie *Kelly's Heroes* (a 1970 Clint Eastwood vehicle that was itself a send-up of the original *Dirty Dozen*).[26] To attract a wider audience, it incorporated two characters from the popular *Sgt. Fury and His Howling Commandos* series, and it included a woman in the group.[27] Although that series only lasted nine issues, *G.I. Joe: A Real American Hero* revived the idea of including a woman as an integral part of a team in the 1980s. The second of Marvel's attempts in this vein features a single soldier trying to redeem himself in combat. The main character of *Sgt. Stryker's Death Squad* is in a Sergeant York–style predicament: in spite of his superb military skills, his moral objections to killing make him an inefficient warrior.[28] His attitude changes only after the death of his superior/mentor. He finally realizes his warrior potential after involvement with four deviants who, naturally, are offered their freedom if they carry out a nearly hopeless mission. The series is set in the North African desert during the first American combat against the Germans in World War II and lasted just three issues.[29]

By the 1980s, the cartoon-like fantasies of refighting the Vietnam War came into existence, with *Rambo* (1985) and *Missing in Action* (1984) highly influential on the culture. The films were revenge fantasies to be sure, but they were also subversive of traditional authority. The government cannot be trusted: it is lying to the people about MIAs, and it betrays the heroism of American fighting men. While the government was dishonest concerning the facts of Vietnam, it is important to note that the stories that were presented in the 1980s featured soldiers who were brave and not just the stereotype of the disgruntled draftee.

Post-Vietnam and the Role of Minorities in War Comics

In the 1960s and 1970s, racial explosions tore apart the fabric of society, and the antiwar movement challenged the legitimacy of the American political and military system. Somehow comic book creators had to address these new issues. The comics needed new ideas to attract readers, and they experimented with new formulas. Some stories addressed drug use; others tackled the race issue directly. Expanding on the World War II movie version of the integrated platoon, war comics began to create self-sufficient minority characters able to carry their own comic titles. Due to the overwhelmingly white readership, however, these characters found only limited success. African Americans, although nominally integrated into the United States military since 1947, did not fully participate in integrated combat until Korea. War comics of the time echoed this development and tried to address racism in the military by introducing more African American characters, at first only in secondary parts. They became increasingly prominent in various subplots, which led to an African American title character for DC comics in the 1970s. The character was codenamed "Gravedigger" and was featured in a twenty-six-issue series titled *Men of War,* which ran from 1977 to 1980.[30]

In the Haunted Tank story "Let Me Live, Let Me Die," from the spring of 1970, an unnamed African American soldier tires of his work as a supply depot loader during World War II (when blacks were usually relegated to such support roles). He longs to see combat and not just on the receiving end. The Germans destroy his supply dump, and he's not happy about it: "[They] laughed at us! Errand boys . . . we had nothing to fight back with. . . . I heard 'em laughin' . . . over the machine guns! I . . . can still . . . hear them laughing!" Throughout the story, the soldier expresses his will to fight and, if need be, to die like a man. Even though the crew of the "rebel" tank argues against taking the man on, commander Jeb Stuart ignores them, giving the man a gun. Two remarkable things occur in this issue: the ghostly guardian of the Haunted Tank does not appear (due to attitudes toward slavery, we assume), except in a small role at the beginning of the story. More important, Jeb embraces the dying man for saving the crew of the tank.[31]

African American soldiers were still uncommon in comics when DC introduced its *Men of War* title. In this comic, also set during World War II, African American sergeant Ulysses Hazard starts out in a graves registration unit, only to become a single commando on "suicide missions."[32] Hazard takes on many high-risk/low-survivability missions involving such tasks as protecting President Roosevelt and defeating enemy saboteurs on American soil. Gravedigger's responsibilities resemble those of the early Captain America. In *Men of War* #16, Nazi soldiers horribly scar his face, recalling the scars of slaves in the antebellum American South (and perhaps the traditional dueling scars of Prussian officers).

One important feature of the *Men of War* series is the Germans' behavior around those they consider *Untermenschen.* They are the most fanatical Nazis imaginable, and they thoroughly enjoy inflicting physical and psychological torture on civilians and soldiers alike. One sadistic German major, presumably SS, even guillotines POWs.[33] However, the story line also suggests that not all Germans are inherently immoral. In "Berkstaten," the Gravedigger convinces a German soldier of the wrongness of the Nazism. At the end of the story, the soldier "does the right thing" and protects a concentration camp Jew by shooting the SS's evil Dr. Krugger (a Dr. Mengele manqué). Granted, he then kills himself over his guilt for betraying Germany.[34]

Vietnam War Comics and Analysis, Twenty Years Later

Many studies of culture and society demonstrate how current events and their artistic representations regularly influence each other.[35] This was, indeed, true in the aftermath of Vietnam. Objections to the conduct of the war and mistrust of national leaders permeated Hollywood and literature in the wake of the American withdrawal in 1975. While Tim O'Brien, Phillip Caputo, and Larry Heinemann drove the war home to Americans through their memoirs and fiction, films such as *The Deer Hunter* (1978), directed by Michael Cimino, and *Apocalypse Now* (1979), by Francis Ford Coppola, gained considerable recognition. Each overshadowed Ted Post's less provocative 1978 film, *Go Tell the Spartans*. The same cynicism that fueled Cimino and Coppola reverberated in Hollywood fantasies throughout the early eighties when fictional heroes Jason Rhodes, James Braddock, and John Rambo, all soldiers or Marines who served honorably in a war they were prevented from winning, returned to the jungle to rescue those left in POW camps, simultaneously saving the day and restoring lost honor. By the mid-1980s, however, popular perceptions of the war in Vietnam—and the military in general—began to shift, and more personalized, autobiographical accounts of the conflict began to appear in film, literature, and comics.

When the December issue of the comic *The 'Nam* hit the stands in October 1986, it coincided with a renewed interest in the actual war itself and was part an ongoing wave of Vietnam-themed novels, memoirs, movies, and comics that flooded American culture for more than a decade. Two months after readers were introduced to Pvt. Edward Marks, *Platoon* opened to rave reviews on screens across the country. Oliver Stone's semiautobiographical film based on his own Vietnam experiences captivated audiences. Stone's film was wrapped in a layer of verisimilitude largely absent from theatrical portrayals of the war since *Go Tell the Spartans* debuted. Several other movies and television shows followed on the heels of *Platoon*. Like *The 'Nam* and then-contemporary memoirs, each tried to depict the conflict in Vietnam not in heroic or comedic terms, but as a multifaceted contest seen through different points of view. Each had an impact. *The Short-Timers,* a novel based on author Gustav Hasford's experience in Vietnam, later became the basis for Stanley Kubrick's *Full Metal Jacket* (1987). The same story later became a miniseries from DC Comics' Vertigo imprint, titled *The Other Side* (2006). The writer of the comic book, Jason Aaron, was inspired by Hasford, who was his cousin.

The push to make these films, television shows, and comics was often noted as a way to show the brutality and confusion of the war while taking away some of the false heroics that had permeated many of the depictions of World War II or general war movies. Though not explicitly stated, it is quite probable that the success of television shows such as *China Beach* inspired specific story lines within the comics. One issue of *The 'Nam* (#23, from October 1988) noted the importance of medical staffs, who were essential to keeping wounded soldiers alive once evacuated from the field. Even a later miniseries of *The 'Nam* (#49–51) dealt with a nurse and her husband both in a combat zone and in danger. Because comic books, movies, and television are all visual storytelling media, this cross-pollination can be quite extensive. In 1986 *Platoon*'s commercial success inspired television, movies, and comic books to return to that conflict for potential stories. Earlier Vietnam comic books had enjoyed only limited popularity, and sales had been disappointing. In the mid-1980s, however, Marvel was trying to expand the appeal of its comics to meet the adult readership that *Heavy Metal* and Warren Publications titles had successfully tapped. Marvel's entry was *Savage Tales,* named from an earlier comic on the same theme, and it was produced in magazine format in black and white. Again, by producing the comics as a magazine, Marvel was able to avoid the restrictions of the Comics Code, still enforced at that time. *Savage Tales* contained many stories of war and action, including one Vietnam story, "5th of the 1st," written by Doug Murray and inspired by his time as a combatant in Vietnam.[36]

Savage Tales only lasted for nine issues, but Marvel recognized the possibilities of Murray's work. The publisher followed up with the creation of *The 'Nam,* a full-color traditional comic intent on showing the Vietnam conflict in a quasi-historical way. In an interview, Murray recalled that the story covered the war from the buildup of troops in the early 1960s to the fall of Saigon in 1975, a novel concept.[37] One of the few Marvel characters featured in *The 'Nam* as well as his own series was Vietnam veteran Frank Castle, aka the Punisher.[38] *The 'Nam* was a hit for Marvel, running for eighty-four issues. Its skilled storytelling and its peculiar perspective led to its popularity. For example, one story arc describes the death of soldiers not from fighting, but from heroin use. Another depicts the infamous My Lai Massacre from the viewpoint of the Vietnamese. These stories were unusually realistic for comic books and offered readers something different from *G.I. Joe* and any other DC war comics.

The 'Nam was a long-lasting series, and if the letters to its editors are representative, it resonated with Vietnam veterans as well as their children. The first thirteen issues followed one specific soldier, Ed Marks, as he proceeds to his tour in Vietnam. Murray, the primary writer for the series, based the comics on his experience as a sergeant in Vietnam. The character Marks arrives in Vietnam and serves from 1966 to 1967. The plot advanced on a monthly basis, paralleling the pace of real events as they originally occurred—and the comic's publication schedule. One arc, issues #24 to #26, discussed the different images of the Tet Offensive in January 1968. Issues #25 and #26 dealt with the U.S. Marines in Hue and the vicious fighting that took several weeks to end.

The cover of *The 'Nam* #24 demonstrates how art can (literally) reframe history. It imagines an alternative version of Eddie Adams' iconic photograph in which Vietnamese police chief Nguyen Ngoc Loan shoots a suspected VC prisoner during Tet. The illustration makes it appear as if the viewer is right there, just past the general and his victim as Adams takes his picture. The result is that Adams seems to be photographing the viewer, just behind the execution, as well. It makes the viewer feel present, and possibly even complicit, in the event.

Unlike *G.I. Joe* already quite successful, *The 'Nam* at first tried to remain realistic to combat conditions—although many noted that its characters saw more combat than most actual soldiers did. However, *G.I. Joe* did sometimes incorporate Vietnam story lines. One of its most popular characters, the mysterious ninja-commando Snake Eyes, is originally a member of a Special Forces team in Vietnam. Wayne Vansant, the primary artist for most of the series, was a major contributor to *The 'Nam*'s success. He had been in the Navy and had considerable practice drawing military equipment before his stint on *The 'Nam*.[39] He was later instrumental in other military-themed comics, such as *Days of Darkness, Days of Wrath,* and *Battle Group Peiper* (see chapter 5).

Another Vietnam comic produced in the late 1980s, Apple Comics' *Vietnam Journal* series, centers on the struggles of Scott "Journal" Neithammer. Drawn in black and white, its carefully researched stories are based (in part) on creator Don Lomax's own Vietnam experiences. While many traditional war comics depict warfare as noble or at least necessary, *Vietnam Journal* followed the precedent of *Two-Fisted Tales* and examined all of the war's horrors, violence, and meaninglessness and the troops' confusion. It also examines the serious, practical problems that plagued soldiers, such as the replacement of the reliable M-14 rifle with the initially flawed M-16, rampant drug use, and instances of "fragging"—assassinating military superiors. *Vietnam Journal* was more "realistic" than *The 'Nam* because Lomax refused to ignore these issues. Unlike Murray and Vansant in *The 'Nam*, he did not have to follow the Comics Code. In interviews, Murray discussed how the code restricted him: vulgar language was minimized, drug use eliminated or only obliquely referenced, and racial conflicts downplayed. Marvel enforced the code to reach the widest possible audience.[40]

When the war was still ongoing, some criticized comic creators whose superhero characters did *not* fight. For example, Captain America goes to Vietnam only once and for a limited purpose. To readers who grew up with Simon and Kirby's characters fighting the good fight against the enemies of the United States, this was a letdown.[41] Instead, most superhero characters stayed at home during the Vietnam conflict, fighting society's ills. In short, their role was no different than it had been before World War II. The public had become more skeptical, not just of America's foreign adventures, but of the true-blue superheroes who had dominated comics in the pre-Vietnam era.

By the early 1990s, however, the public mood had shifted again, and comic book publishers had more confidence that readers might accept a broader role for these now "classic" characters. Circulation slipped after changes that made *The 'Nam* available only by direct sale from comic book shops or by subscription, but not on regular newsstands. To gain more readers, Marvel's editorial staff introduced superheroes into the mix. In one issue, *The 'Nam* #41, Captain America, Iron Man, and Thor all fight alongside the American military. Readers universally derided the use of these fantasy figures in a "reality-based" comic book.[42] Despite such complaints, at least Marvel met its monthly schedule. By comparison, Apple Comics' informal deadlines led to erratic publication dates and confusion about when the next issue would be available; readership dropped precipitously. From 1987 to 1990, Lomax only managed to publish sixteen issues of *Vietnam Journal*.[43] While now considered one of the best Vietnam comic books, with thought-provoking stories and superior art, many potential readers never saw it, and sales were too low to continue production. However, *Vietnam Journal* spawned three sequels of sorts. The first, titled *Tet '68,* comprised a six-issue story line set during the Tet Offensive. The second series, titled *Khe Sanh,* was a four-part series inspired by the battle of that name, also in 1968. A projected four-issue follow-up, *Valley of Death,* would have focused on the fighting after Khe Sanh. However, only one issue made it to the stands before the cancellation of the series.

Lomax approached the Vietnam conflict from varying perspectives, discussing some lesser-known aspects of the war. His final four-part series, "*High Shining Brass,*" does not tie into the others. It tells the true story of Bob Durand, who served with distinction as part of a Special Forces A-Team. He fought alongside CIA operatives and various units comprising natives such as Nungs and Montagnards in clashes with NVA regulars during classified missions in North Vietnam. Together with a Nung guerrilla group, Durand's team harassed the NVA as it moved supplies over the Ho Chi Minh Trail along the Laotian border; he also helped a Vietnamese family defect from the North. The end of the comic mentions that Durand had significant problems readjusting to life in the United States, largely a reaction to various drugs he was given in Southeast Asia.[44] The comics that came out of the late and post-Vietnam era were significant in their portrait of war as brutal and inglorious. While some, such as the early *Sgt. Rock* and *G.I. Joe,* treated warfare almost as sport, the dominant approach was now one of somber reflection.

War Comics in the Reagan Era

The election of Ronald Reagan in 1980 led to significant changes in the political ideology, as well as the popular culture, of the United States. In the public perception, at least, Reagan was the antithesis of Jimmy Carter, his predecessor.

Carter encountered many political issues not of his own creation, such as the taking of American hostages by Iran in 1979 and the Soviet Union's invasion of Afghanistan. These struggles made him appear weak. By contrast, Reagan presented himself as a politician who took the initiative to decisively correct things—not unlike comic book superheroes. His willingness to build up the military (and, sometimes, use it against threats to American interests) made him appear strong. He also used his political pulpit to reassert the traditional image of the United States, banishing the political doubts and cultural uncertainties that were a legacy of Vietnam. While some of the most propagandistic comics appeared during Reagan's term in the 1980s, occasionally interesting attempts countered his attitudes.

As already noted, the U.S. government recognized that comic books and other visual media could be useful tools for indoctrination. To that end, in the 1980s government-produced comics helped to train irregular troops (for example, guerrillas), to educate readers about the Communist threat, and to entertain (that is, distract) the troops. Even the CIA created several quasi-comic books to demonstrate the need for American intervention around the world—to forestall Communism or protect U.S. interests. The first, *The Freedom Fighters Manual,* had neither a traditional format nor a sequential narrative. An illustrated book, it explained how to carry out acts of sabotage and domestic terrorism against the Sandinista government of Nicaragua. Some of the recommended tactics are almost comical, including breaking light bulbs and throwing tools into sewers, although they would have more impact in this very poor country than in the United States. Another suggestion, to threaten party bosses with anonymous phone calls, was more potent, especially in the era before caller ID. The idea was that, fearing possible attacks, the leadership would be less effective. Still, such tactics hardly seem sufficient to terrorize the Sandinistas into relinquishing power.[45]

A more comprehensive comic book, *Grenada,* utilized propaganda to justify the American invasion of that country, by describing the rise of Communist forces there and how their presence demanded military intervention.[46] It deploys many of the Reagan administration's justifications for the invasion: the oppression and torture of the inhabitants, threats to American medical students on the island, and a potential "domino effect" leading to more Communist regimes in the Caribbean. One of the unusual aspects of *Grenada* is the degree of its brutality. One panel, for example, shows Grenadians and their Cuban allies beating Antonio Langdon (the comic's author) with rifle butts. The next page depicts the insurrection's leaders as greedy opportunists, not true Communists, who use the situation to line their own pockets. What's more, the black Grenadians are depicted in stereotypical ways, almost recalling Jim Crow caricatures from the late nineteenth century. The most shocking image is a panel at the bottom of page 12 that shows a Grenadian soldier being shot in the head by a Cuban soldier. The artwork takes the extreme violence that Greg Irons had used in his anti-Vietnam underground comix and uses it for the exact opposite purpose. At the very end of the comic book, the American troops are lauded as liberators and guarantors of freedom.[47]

Following the film industry's lead, comic books shifted to celebrate the now more powerful and popular military establishment. By the early 1980s, the DC comics that had ended with the axiom "Make War No More" were gone. In 1982 Marvel introduced the comic *G.I. Joe: A Real American Hero,* which allowed the U.S. military to shine again, conveniently tied to a line of new Hasbro toys. Created by Larry Hama, a Vietnam veteran, its over-the-top story lines sought to give young readers a sense of pride in America. The comic book's basic group of characters consists of combat veterans specifically chosen for their Vietnam service. Their enemy is not the traditional Soviet bloc, but instead a shadowy terrorist group, COBRA. As the series progressed, both the G.I. Joe squad and COBRA took on larger and more diverse groups of characters. For the Joes, these new characters allow the reader to see combat's aftermath. One, the mysterious Snake Eyes, cannot talk, and his face is never seen. It develops that he is a Vietnam veteran of the venerable long-range reconnaissance patrols, who has lost several friends on an unspecified mission.[48] Later on, readers discover that Snake Eyes was disfigured during the Iranian hostage rescue mission of 1980 when his team's chopper hit a refueling tanker. In typical war-story fashion, Snake Eyes rescues a teammate, suffering horrible scars in the process.[49] He also closely resembles the typical Hollywood "revenge fantasy" character, such as Rambo or Dirty Harry, who says little but punishes those who threaten American society.

COBRA also expanded to admit additional nefarious characters. These included mercenaries such as Major Blood, Destro, an international arms merchant, and the Baroness—representing upper-class Germans seeking a fashionable leftist cause (like those who joined the Red Army Faction, aka the Baader-Meinhof Gang). Another possibility is that she represented the old ways of war (the European idea of fighting as native attribute). At the same time, these figures mock social classes; their wealth-induced ennui helps explain their evil actions. The official military community considered mercenaries (or "mercs") a danger: for a better price, a merc might switch allegiance at any moment. Such dishonor resembles the Asian war tactics depicted in World War II comic books. Later on, the character Zartan (a master of disguise) and his mayhem-making associates, the Drednoks (an Australian motorcycle gang), were introduced.

Over time, the series increasingly emphasized the threat from COBRA rather than the Soviets. The Joes even work with the Red Guard, their Soviet equivalents.

Perestroika and glasnost led to a genuine thaw in American-Soviet relations, making such cooperation more palatable to readers and opening the way for new enemies such as terrorists. They also recalled the World War II era, when the United States and the Soviets fought a common enemy. Moreover, *G.I. Joe*'s writing teams incorporated historical events into their story lines. *G.I. Joe Special Missions* #1 tells the story of a Soviet ship commandeered by COBRA. As the Baroness and Firefly, another mercenary, come aboard, he asks if it will be difficult to take control of the ship. The Baroness assures him that Soviet ships carry a limited number of small arms, to prevent mutiny (like that on the battleship *Potemkin* following the 1905 workers' uprising in Odessa).[50]

In *G.I. Joe* #39, the Joes attack a group of mercenaries holding an American scientist hostage at their base in a fictional South American country. As the mercenary military officers—their names and uniforms suggest that they are Cuban or Russian—regard the carnage, one says that the Americans did their job well. Asked how he knows it was Americans, he replies that the British SAS (Special Air Service) would have killed everyone; had the Israelis conducted the raid, no one would know it had happened; and that no other Western countries had a sufficiently well trained team to do the job.[51] Many *G.I. Joe* issues took the time to explain basic military terms and procedures to their young civilian readers.

The concept of patriotic superheroes pursuing political and military goals came to an apex in 1987 with *Reagan's Raiders*. In this series, which satirized the gung-ho Americanism of the era, the president must fight the "World Terrorist Organization." He turns himself and his cabinet volunteers into superheroes using the "Alpha Soldier" generation effect: a super-soldier process similar to the one that transformed Steven Rogers into Captain America. It was never explained why superheroes needed guns to fight terrorists or piloted antique World War II bombers. Naturally, the *Reagan's Raiders* costumes are drenched in patriotic symbolism: entirely red, white, and blue.[52] The comic's writers make plenty of satirical points, as well as Hollywood insider's remarks, about Reagan's political and film career. Although envisioned as a continuing series, *Reagan's Raiders* did not last long, running for just three issues. Perhaps its absurdity, even by comic book standards, doomed the series. The Iran-Contra affair (alluded to in the final issue) also put the concept in a negative light.

The Bastardization of the Patriotic Hero

By the 1980s, the comparison (and combination) of Captain America with his antithesis, the Punisher, was popular within Marvel's fictional world. While this theme became pervasive in the 1990s (see chapter 5), the first comparisons occur in the early 1980s, when comics were exploring post-Vietnam patriotism and exacting vengeance on America's enemies. The two characters first met in January 1980.[53] In this episode, as Captain America combats gangsters terrorizing New York in his usual above-board way, the Punisher goes after them like a vigilante. The struggle climaxes as the Punisher seizes Cap's shield, a moment immortalized on Frank Miller's cover. Even at this early stage, the duality of the characters is already apparent. The ultimate goal of both is a just society, but they approach it with very different methodologies. Captain America wishes to eliminate enemies to society through legal means, while the Punisher is willing to use unrestricted violence, especially against those who act violently themselves. (The Punisher is not very different from Dirty Harry or the Charles Bronson character in *Death Wish*.[54]) The Punisher even aims a gun at Cap but does not shoot. The confrontation ends with an outcome acceptable to both: the bad guys are halted.

By this time, Captain America lives in New York, where he battles rampant street crime. When the Punisher visits wearing his black outfit, Anna Kappelbaum, a holocaust survivor and Cap's neighbor, thinks he is a member of the SS.[55] This first issue establishes many pointed comparisons between the characters. Both possess superior reflexes. (When Cap throws his shield, the Punisher deflects and steps on it. Cap replies, "Not one man in a thousand could stop my shield like that."[56]) Later in the issue, the two unite against the Mob. When the Punisher gains the upper hand and is about to kill gangsters, Cap lectures the Punisher on the need for due process and the law. Yet in the late 1970s and early 1980s, when crime rates skyrocketed all over the country, many in the reading public may have wanted the Punisher's form of justice.

Captain America appeals to the Punisher: they must take the moral high ground, even in war, lest American soldiers stoop to the level of the Other—whether the sadistic Nazis or Japanese of World War II, the Vietcong during the Vietnam conflict, America criminals, or (after 9/11) terrorists.[57] Finally, foreshadowing conflicts to come, Cap tells the Punisher, "I've handled a few guns in my career, but I've never willingly taken a life, and I never will."[58] As the two heroes part, however, Cap makes the explicit comparison himself: "We're very much alike . . . the Punisher and I. . . . Each of us is fighting a very personal war."[59] Again, regardless of the surface tension, the characters complement each other.

Antiwar Comics and Realism

By the late 1980s, the media were reporting stories of the CIA's involvement in illegal arms and drugs sales. Eclipse Comics used these "untold" stories to counter the propaganda of comics such as *G.I. Joe* and movies such as *Top Gun*.[60] Its first graphic novel, *Brought to Light,* comprised two self-contained stories. The reader simply flipped the book over to read each story. The first,

"Shadowplay: The Secret Team," told the history of the CIA and specifically linked it to the Iran-Contra scandal that marred the Reagan administration. The second story, "Flashpoint: The La Penca Bombing," told of an attack that killed several journalists researching the American connection to the Nicaraguan rebels known as the Contras. The center-spread map shows American covert actions since Fidel Castro's takeover of Cuba in 1959. It showed how pervasive American intelligence agencies were and how successful they were in coercing foreign governments or groups to do America's bidding. Both stories and the map drew on the work of the Christic Institute, whose civil lawsuit against various CIA officers, using the Freedom of Information Act, disclosed many relevant government documents. Detailed bibliographies even appeared at the end of each story.[61]

Eclipse also produced *Real War Stories,* which in 1987 took a critical look at the American military, with a second issue in 1991. Both were made in conjunction with the Coordinating Committee of Conscientious Objectors, originally created in the 1960s. The comics are a direct tie to the underground comix of the 1960s—part investigative journalism and part oral history.[62]

The period of the 1960s through the 1980s saw monumental upheaval in most areas of American society. The Vietnam War and subsequent foreign incursions influenced American culture as well. Media outlets used these news stories to play off myths of conflict and to reflect how people felt about war in general. Vietnam was the dominant narrative in this period. By the early 1990s, when the Gulf War was in full effect, the media attempted to rehabilitate the U.S. military from the stain of Vietnam. Comics started to reassess the need for an "enemy." As the Soviet Union collapsed and the threat of Communism abated, the comics looked for new enemies to remain relevant while still showing the glory of combat.

5 The Resurgence of Superheroes after the Fall of Communism (1991–2001)

It was a matter of either you take some steps against the enemy or he was going to shoot you in the back. So you have a job to do, and you can't afford to be a "jolly good fellow." Like a lot of American attitudes about being hale and hearty, chin up, school colors, and all the rest of this crap people put out, or about being cold blooded; you just think about getting the job done. You go from A to B and, if there's something between A and B, you get rid of it. So the name of the game is, you go from A to B and you get very impersonal.

—WORLD WAR II VETERAN BOB MILLER,
in Patrick O'Donnell's *Beyond Valor*

As the 1990s began, the war stories depicted in most media, including films, books, and comics, moved away from the horrors and uncertainties of Vietnam and started to embrace more traditional narratives once again. The fall of the Soviet Union, the end of the Cold War, and 1991's short and successful Gulf War with Iraq led to a renewed American triumphalism. The United States was described as the world's sole hyperpower—and even the putative "end of history" was optimistically speculated, by Francis Fukuyama.[1] The fiftieth anniversaries of major World War II events encouraged this trend, by reminding the public of the clarity of the fight against Fascism and Imperial Japan. Compared to the instability of the post–Cold War world, the apparent moral certainties of the Cold War and especially "the good war" looked very appealing. In this new environment, some comic book creators, like some historians, challenged the conventional perceptions of war and the military. But rather than adapt to new threats, most preferred traditional story lines, enemies, and formats.

The war comics of the 1990s attempted a return to the clear-cut depictions of right and wrong that prevailed before the moral traumas of Vietnam. These comics debuted at a time when the Republican Party was recouping its losses from the George H. W. Bush era. While Bush had served as Reagan's vice president, he was not perceived to match Reagan's strength. Moreover, while he won the Gulf War, he lost the presidency to a candidate—Bill Clinton—who some saw as representing the counterculture and indecisiveness of the Vietnam era. This conservative reaction in the comic book story lines paralleled the political movement to reestablish the Republicans in Congress: 1994's Contract with America.

Despite such nostalgia and the related political agenda, by the end of the decade the war comic had turned to realism and introspection. The opening quotation from Bob Miller illustrates how abstract concepts of morality and fair fighting rarely figure in authentic accounts of combat. The heroic depictions of combat in comics, television, and film usually do not accord with this reality. Yet the idealistic perception of combat, as disseminated by the media, the military, and the government, tends to persist in the public's consciousness. In the 1990s, comic book creators sought to capture more of the chaos of combat as experienced in such recent conflicts as Vietnam and the Gulf War. Older antiwar comics, such as *Two-Fisted Tales, Frontline Combat,* and *Blazing Combat* (first published in the 1950s and 1960s), were reissued in the 1990s for a new generation of readers.

Over the decades, the median age of readers had shifted up. Most were now in their late teens or early twenties—old enough to be in the military, as many were. Compared to earlier comic book audiences, these young people had viewed graphic violence in movies and on television, and they expected it in comics as well. Comic book publishers ramped up violence and swearing and even experimented with new imprints specifically designed for this market, interjecting more adult themes to lure older readers. By treating moral dilemmas that encouraged their readers to think about the long-term impact of violent action, they tried to show the horror, as well as the glory, of war.

As the United States turned away from its traditional Cold War enemies, war comics also shifted their focus. Traditional-style comics, generally about World War II or Vietnam, were still published or reissued, but they now aimed for greater accuracy about the realities of war. There were three reasons for this shift. First, although the Gulf War was the last traditional land war the United States has fought—with significant ground units fighting each other—it ended sooner than most people had envisioned. The American government feared that the Iraqi army (the world's fifth largest, with years of recent military experience) would pose a substantial threat to the United States and its interests. The war might have turned even deadlier if Saddam Hussein used the weapons of mass destruction that he still possessed. Not generally understood was that Saddam's army, weakened and demoralized after eight years of brutal war with Iran, would quickly collapse when faced with massive coalition firepower.

The second reason for the shift in war comics was that by the end of 1991 the Soviet Union had formally ceased to exist. With even right-wing American extremists forced to rethink their Cold War worldview, traditional comic book villains moved away from the USSR. The villains eventually merged into other

(more nebulous but equally sinister) enemies, such as drug lords or Middle Eastern terrorists. Stories reverted to the time-honored, albeit strange, tradition of
substituting regular troops with armies of the undead. Although the Communists—the dominant threat to the United States for over four decades—had been
effectively vanquished, these supernatural monsters could strike from anywhere
and at any time. While the USSR had posed a genuine existential risk, psychologically these new enemies seemed even more sinister. Like post-9/11 terrorists,
such monsters served as a catchall representation of Americans' fears.

The third reason for the search for new enemies was that the warm reception
given to returning Gulf War troops prompted new efforts to recognize Vietnam-era
veterans for their sacrifices.[2] Some comic book creators rewrote their traditional
World War II stories, adding a "deeper meaning" to the war's violence and confusion that had not previously been presented at any length. Others issued Vietnam
stories that allowed for some cathartic release, if not a justification of the fighting
itself. One approach was to expand the backstories of the traditional characters.
Garth Ennis, using such characters as Enemy Ace, Nick Fury, and the Unknown
Soldier, revisited older war tales with a 1990s slant. Another method was to use
comics to relate historical events, as Marvel's Doug Murray did in *The 'Nam*. The
distance from the end of these wars, plus the political reality that there was no
significant threat to the United States at the time, meant that the comic book
companies often merely revised or republished old titles.

Regardless of the specifics of such war stories, the simple fact is that these comics
attempt to insert a dose of reality into a realm usually associated with fantasy. In
some cases, the tales are almost apocalyptic in tone, centering on atomic warfare
and its horrible aftermath. Stories revolving around fear of terrorists using stolen
nuclear weapons were not uncommon; large threats always make for good readership. Other comics engaged people politically by incorporating contemporaneous
affairs into the narrative. During the Gulf War, Saddam was demonized as a new
Hitler. Two notable attempts to narrate his evil deeds were Innovation Comics'
Desert Storm: Send Hussein to Hell and *Elementals* #17, in which superheroes literally beat up Saddam. The *Desert Storm* issue is intriguing because, though dated
April 1991 (after the war ended), it was written as the real war was unfolding. The
comic was created to support the troops (and was read by some of them), yet the
war itself was over before the issue hit the stands. Instead, editor David Campiti
notes, the comic was dedicated to the troops who had fought the war and would
now return (it was hoped) to a successful, quiet life.

Desert Storm: Send Hussein to Hell treats only one actual war story; the
remaining vignettes feature other Innovation Comics characters with little
connection to patriotism or the fighting. The comic's lead story, "Overkill,"
concerns a pilot who ejects from his plane while flying over Iraq. It retails
the very stories the media was relaying to the American people: chemical and

nuclear weapons, suicidal fanatics, and the dangers behind enemy lines. Yet when the pilot comes face to face with Iraqi soldiers, he actually sees them as "dehydrated, sick, lice-ridden, [men with] burst eardrums. Home but so very far from home."[3] The tale attempts to show the reality of the conflict as the very opposite of the media's reports. It also harkens back to the *Two-Fisted Tales* approach of presenting enemy soldiers as human, rather than stereotypical brutes. The next vignette is a one-page political satire depicting the adventures of "Iraqi and Abdulwinkle." An homage to the "Rocky and Bullwinkle" television cartoons,[4] the characters recreate the old "rabbit out of the hat trick," but instead of a white bunny, they pull out "Stormin' Norman" (the nickname of Gen. Norman Schwarzkopf, the head of coalition forces). The story ends with the question, "With friends like you, Abdulwinkle, who needs a Great Satan?"[5]

Gulf War Journal reprises the character of Scott "Journal" Neithammer—the focal point of *Vietnam Journal*. Don Lomax, its creator, made sure that this new iteration widened its focus. For instance, Journal's daughter lives with her husband, an Israeli national, in Tel Aviv, where they suffer a direct attack. (Saddam's forces did in fact fire Scud missiles at major Israeli population centers, as well as some Saudi cities.) To extend this attention to the war's immediate victims, Lomax also adds a new character: Journal's young aide, a Kuwaiti witness to Iraqi brutality following the invasion of his country on August 2, 1990. By comparison, American civilians were not directly affected by the war. What's more, the government did everything it could to shield them from certain unpleasant realities—such as seeing dead soldiers on the field or flag-draped coffins arriving at Dover Air Force Base. This policy, with occasional exceptions, had been in effect since Vietnam. As in World War II, official propaganda—controlled by the government and funneled through the media—dominated war reporting. Ironically, post-Vietnam comics often depicted the realities of war in a more "adult" way than either the government or the mainstream media.

The protagonist's identity as a combat reporter was effective for several reasons. Gulf War journalists not only reported the news but also occasionally became news themselves. When Iraqi forces captured Bob Simon and his CBS News crew, it became a major story in a war where the coverage focused on high-technology warfare rather than the human element. A reporter is close to the action, yet with a degree of detachment and knowledge about the overall situation, which the ordinary soldier may not possess. Unlike the story lines from *Frontline Combat* (often told in the second person), *Gulf War Journal's* quasi-journalistic approach made the tale seem more informative and objective. Lomax presented the brutal facts, including depictions of burnt Iraqi soldiers, such as those killed on the "Highway of Death" as the Iraqis retreated.

Apple Comics, which rereleased *Vietnam Journal* and introduced *Gulf War Journal*, even resurrected *Blazing Combat*, the classic war comic originally released by Warren Publishing Company. The revived series incorporated several stories from the original 1960s issues, as well newer ones. Like the original series, the new stories depicted the violent nature of combat. Several Lomax *Vietnam Journal* vignettes were reprinted, and other artists contributed, such as Larry Hama and Wayne Vansant from Marvel's *The 'Nam*. The revived *Blazing Combat* series was split to accommodate the World Wars in one subseries while covering Korea and Vietnam in the other. As in the original comic books, this Apple series only lasted four issues—two from each category.[6] There was some interest in the older series but not enough to spur further purchases of the comic books, and Apple Comics Publishing collapsed. Apple's various titles presented Vietnam and other wars in a realistic and humanistic way, similar to the antiwar comics of the 1950s and 1960s. Along with many critically acclaimed comics that attempted to capture the reality of war, Apple's fell victim to the sales war.

Changes to *The 'Nam*

The evolution of the American attitude toward the military led to changes in war comics as well. With the victory over Iraq and the bitter taste of Vietnam at least diminished, comic book creators found ways to retroactively justify that latter war—sometimes going so far as introducing characters who would have allowed the United States to win. The Marvel series *The 'Nam* started to shift its attitude even before the Gulf War officially began, during the 1990 build-up of coalition troops in the Saudi Arabian desert. In one attempt to attract more readers, Doug Murray, despite considerable reservations, introduced three of Marvel's best-known superheroes to refight the war in Vietnam.[7] While a significant number of readers considered the issue a failure, it attempted to use the medium to give its audience exactly what the audience wanted: a satisfying outcome to a war many had not understood.[8]

The story begins with a soldier reading comics (which had belonged to a dead comrade) as he prepares to rotate back to the United States. The tale then explores what superheroes might have done to prevent or shorten the war. In this story-within-a-story, Captain America, Iron Man, and Thor defeat the Communist Vietnamese forces—at one point capturing Ho Chi Minh and bringing him to trial for crimes against humanity.[9] The scenario recalls a two-page *Look* magazine spread about Superman capturing Hitler and Stalin and taking them for trial.[10] The fantasy is a common one: Captain America punches out Hitler on Jack Kirby's cover for *Captain America*'s debut issue in late 1940. Both images were published before America's involvement in World War II. Other comics depict conspiracies of those who stand to profit from the war or, worse, its loss. In addition to corruption, a major theme is a hatred of all things governmental, which has played a large role in turning a significant part of the American middle class against a liberal tradition of progressive government. This suspicion of authority underlies many later *'Nam* issues, reflecting the writers' own struggles to understand their Vietnam experiences. While the comic books do not implicate American government as such, in these conspiracies the war's shifting goals and the overlapping agendas of different agencies make its role appear convoluted at best.

"Creep" in *The 'Nam* #66 describes a soldier who has been repeatedly wronged by the government throughout his early life.[11] After being drafted into the Marine Corps and showing prowess with a rifle, he is made a sniper. His mission is to kill the Vietcong tax collectors, and his skill at this gains him notoriety.[12] Eventually, he finds out that he will rotate back to the United States as a reward for his success. However, the media—unspecified, but presumably the domestic American news outlets—spin his actions as the unnecessary killing of civilians. When told of his mission's discontinuation, he becomes enraged, deciding to strike out on his own and continue waging war in his own violent way.

"Creep" was followed by a three-issue story line featuring Frank Castle— aka the Punisher—and his need to "go it alone" against military and government officials who would not allow the United States to actually win the war (#67–69, April–June 1992). The writers never directly accuse the American government of deliberately losing the war, but they do suggest that those who make the key decisions have ulterior motives (such as personal profit) or, at best, have no conception of how their decisions affect the fighting in the field. Although the projected run had called for ninety-six issues taking the story to the fall of Saigon in April 1975, the series ran into problems, and it was cancelled in 1993 at #84.[13]

The last story of the series is *The Punisher Invades the 'Nam*. In this graphic novel, the Punisher character from the Marvel universe gets an expanded role. The story utilizes a revenge scenario,[14] as the Punisher and his Montagnard warriors liberate a camp where a Chinese physician, known only as the Death Doctor, and Cuban mercenaries conduct medical experiments on American POWs.[15] In addition to the POW/MIA issues written into the story, it also describes the CIA's involvement in various aspects of the war.[16] While the Punisher is shown avenging the loss in Vietnam, he also appears in other comics to reaffirm and justify America's belief system. In a way, *The Punisher Invades the 'Nam* was another attempt by Lomax to allow the Americans some "closure" about prisoners of war, while simultaneously destroying the people who won the war. It is an extension of the Vietnam revenge fantasies peddled by Hollywood in the 1980s, perhaps best exemplified by the series of films starring Sylvester Stallone as John Rambo, a disaffected Vietnam veteran on a rampage.[17]

Punisher vs. Captain America

The superhero has always represented a fantasy persona with whom a reader can identify. These characters embody readers' wishes: flight, superhuman strength, X-ray vision, and other powers that could allow them to triumph over tormentors. How the characters act out readers' impulses and desires, however, is morally much more complicated. For the most part, the protagonists employ their powers for positive ends: stamping out injustice, fighting for the weak, punishing those who threaten the readers or other communities, or simply preventing the bad guys' villainous plans. However, it is also possible to exploit these powers to act out less noble desires: dominating others, spying and eavesdropping without detection, or wreaking disproportionate vengeance on real or suspected enemies. Sometimes, in fact, readers even identify with the stories' antagonists to indulge such fantasies. Comic book creators recognize and capitalize on these desires by creating morally ambiguous superheroes, combining both good and bad impulses. Thus while two comic book superheroes may share certain abilities and ultimate values, they often operate under quite different personal moral codes, as expressed by their different fighting styles.

A comparison of two of Marvel Comics' most famous characters demonstrates how convictions and motivations can overlap and differ. One defines the best of America, while the other manifests darker revenge fantasies (especially punishing those seen to have embarrassed or humiliated the United States). These characters are, respectively, Captain America and the Punisher. In certain respects, each embodies different aspects of actual American policies. Captain America defends the highest ideals of the United States and democratic societies worldwide but within the law and without undue force. The Punisher represents the promilitary aspects of American policy: maintaining the strongest possible armed forces and punishing anyone who threatens American society or interests—as quickly as possible, to deter possible further resistance. To paraphrase Theodore Roosevelt, Captain America speaks softly; the Punisher carries a big stick.

Clad in his red, white, and blue uniform, Captain America is one of Marvel Comics' most enduring characters. His creation dates from just before the United States entered World War II, when the country began to move away from isolationism but was not yet militarily engaged around the globe. A symbolic incarnation of the United States, he stands for an aggressive defense of our values and interests. Cap and his alter ego Steve Rogers represent the ideal American spirit: moral strength fighting for equality while following the law and only using deadly force as a last resort. The cover of the very first *Captain America* portrays these values in a simple and direct way: an American citizen ridding the world of its biggest threat, Adolf Hitler.[18] What better way to demonstrate that hope than by having a superhero, literally dressed in the colors of the United States, deliver the punch? While Cap keeps his gloves clean whenever possible, his junior partner Bucky is far more willing to kill. Bucky's comparative ruthlessness is demonstrated in *All Winners #7*, where he uses a rifle to shoot—in the back no less!—an escaping Japanese soldier.[19] He has no compunction about killing evildoers. Even in his later incarnation as a cold warrior, Captain America maintained the mythos of the righteous, moral America associated with Ronald Reagan. As a duo, they exemplified how public policy operated in the Cold War: Cap represented America the moral leader, while Bucky used violence behind the scenes to achieve the government's aims. Bucky's reliance on expediency and less disciplined methods anticipated the Punisher's even more lawless methods.

In the early 1990s, Captain America started to change, as did the very nature of American foreign policy in the post-USSR world. U.S. forces around the world were realigned, and important American bases in foreign countries were closed, including Clark Air Force Base and U.S. Naval Base Subic Bay (both in the Philippines). The fight against terrorism—which, while important to Reagan, had hardly been top on his list—became a more important issue in foreign policy. Terrorists are the ultimate subversive enemy, as they blend into the population, strike disproportionate fear in the public, and defy detection (racial profiling and body scanners notwithstanding). Typically the comics echoed this real-life shift to a new enemy.

Captain America's evolution had to stay within certain bounds, however, or he would no longer stand for the same ideals. Instead, this shift called for the Punisher, a new type of superhero with fewer scruples than Cap. Even more than Bucky, the Punisher exemplifies a darker part of the American psyche. He is willing to do anything necessary to rid the world of dangerous people, and he easily compromises his values and ethics (such as they are) for the "greater good." Conceived in 1974, after the American withdrawal from Vietnam but before the fall of Saigon, the Punisher was as a minor antagonist of Marvel's Spider-Man. He quickly grew in importance, switching sides to work with Spidey against various evildoers. Frank Castle, clad in the Punisher's black uniform with a huge skull on his chest, appeared in several different comic book titles. An increasingly successful character spawning a number of graphic novels and "guest spots" in other comic books, Castle has a popularity due in no small part to his role as avenger, brutally destroying any and all threats to America. Castle typifies an attitude that pervades comics of the 1970s and 1980s: no more deference to aspects of the law that allow criminals to escape justice. Instead, Castle just makes it happen, usually in a violent, almost biblical, way. Over time, he develops into the antithesis of Captain America.

Despite their differences, Cap and the Punisher team up whenever the situation is undeniably bad and the forces arrayed against them are indisputably evil—

such as terrorists bent on releasing what later became known as weapons of mass destruction (WMDs). However, what is the greater good in these cases? Does the desired end of a safe and secure America justify the Punisher's willingness to kill or his cavalier attitude toward due process and civil liberties? Alternatively, is Captain America's lawful brand of retaliation, as the United States was then embracing under President Clinton, the better response? When Clinton met the 1998 terrorist bombings of American embassies in Africa with limited and ultimately ineffective cruise missile strikes, some people, especially those who feared the erosion of American power abroad, wanted greater action. In the same way, comic book readers no longer wished their superheroes to negotiate, preferring them to use any means necessary to punish those who threatened "the American ideal." As will be shown in chapter 7, while the two characters sometimes worked together, the death of Captain America elevated the Punisher's importance and altered his symbolic role: now America's primary protector was willing to go to extremes.[20]

During the 1980s and 1990s, Marvel started to experiment with various superhero backstories, and the similarities of the two characters' origins increased, whether intentionally or not. The Punisher character relies more on his military training, and Frank Castle becomes a captain in the Marine Corps. For this role, he needs the intellect to handle men in the field and the social skills to function as a team player. This contrasts with his earlier series, when he is an enlisted man in the Marines or the Special Forces, whose operatives work independently or in very small groups. Steve Rogers takes on the "Captain" moniker only in costume; otherwise, he is a mere Army private. Both characters deal with the loss of family members. Rogers loses his parents to illness before World War II, while the Mob kills Castle's family after they witness a hit. Despite these parallels, Captain America and the Punisher display their contrasting methods for dealing with injustice and rectifying society's problems even when they work together. While Captain America often injures combatants, he rarely kills them; his hand-to-hand fighting style follows traditional notions of honor. The Punisher is far more willing to use technology to kill, not disable, and he frequently does so by stealth and from a distance. Yet the combination of the two characters and their different approaches to political and military action proved successful with readers.

The characters' interaction culminates in "What If the Punisher Became Captain America?" in *What If?* #51. The *What If?* series developed alternate and parallel iterations of existing story lines. For example, Red Skull defeats Captain America, and Frank Castle turns down the opportunity to replace him. Those who subsequently take up the role conspicuously fail to live up to its demands. Only after Castle's family is killed does he agree to assume Cap's mantle, but for a different reason: to seek revenge.[21] His vengeance culminates in a typical Punisher conclusion: the violent death of his and society's enemies. Many people in the 1990s believed that the United States needed to be tough on violent crime at home and on violent enemies abroad. As someone who sees things in black and white and is uninterested in the constraints and ambiguities of the law, the Punisher fits easily into this agenda. As the story ends, however, and Castle must decide whether to kill a mobster in cold blood, another "Captain America" interrupts him (this Cap figure is an android doppelgünger, presumably built by the government). After a lengthy discussion between the two about why Captain America must be a human being, Castle stops the execution and finally drops his Punisher persona. He takes on the Captain America moniker and adopts his ideals as well. This merging of the characters, while only a hypothetical variation, illustrates the concept of force tempered with justice, the very American ideals for which the original Captain America stood.

Another character, U.S. Agent (aka John Walker), was able to work with Captain America, even though Walker's politics are far more reactionary than Cap's (his combat methods are more akin to the Punisher's).[22] Yet despite their apparent similarity, the Punisher regards U.S. Agent as a weak imitation of Captain America and his ideals. In *Punisher: No Escape* he reveals his true feelings about U.S. Agent, telling him: "You're the jerk who tried to take over from Captain America when he was down and out. Guess you couldn't cut it. Cap's a boy scout, but a tough boot to fill. You aren't worth Jack."[23] While Castle hates Cap's naiveté, he is disdainful of anyone other than himself who might stand in for the original Captain America. He appears to feel that he somehow violates an American icon, even when his attitudes resemble his own.

Toward the end of the story, as both U.S. Agent and Punisher rescue people caught in a fire, the possibility that U.S. Agent might fill Cap's shoes is unmistakable. Castle notes, "He's relentless. Dedicated. Unquestioning. Shame he is the Commission's whipping boy."[24] (The Commission for Superhero Activities eventually demands the registration of all superheroes, leading to the Superhero Civil War in which Captain America dies.) But to Castle, U.S. Agent is a poor substitute for Captain America and easily manipulated for political ends. At the story's close, U.S. Agent tells the Commission that it is wrong to pursue Castle, regardless of his dubious tactics, because the Punisher is working for the best interests of the people.[25] After failing to capture the Punisher for the Commission, U.S. Agent supposedly assassinates him instead. With the Punisher seemingly "dead" to the world, Castle is able to continue his mission of hunting down enemies of the people. Despite this, U.S. Agent ultimately lacks the backbone to replace Cap, who always held his ground. Who is up to the task of portraying Captain America remains in doubt.

The United States was conflicted about heroic figures during the early 1990s. Captain America and the Punisher reflected this conflict, despite their radically different ideas about the proper use of American power. In the three-issue mini series *Punisher–Captain America: Blood and Glory* (1993) and *Punisher: No Escape* (1994), the Punisher was the extreme action hero who took no prisoners and no back talk. This mirrored Reagan's tough foreign policy stance toward the Soviet Union and, especially, against such supporters of terrorism as Libyan strongman Muammar el-Qaddafi. (George H. W. Bush continued this policy against Manuel Noriega, the drug-running dictator of Panama, among others.) In *Punisher: Empty Quarter* (1994), the Punisher pursued a ruthless terrorist into the Arabian Desert. The story also described a group of terrorists who trained together, holding a terrorist convention of sorts, a virtual a parody of the Commission for Superhero Activities.[26]

Captain America took the sort of legal, balanced actions generally considered justifiable when other forms of conflict resolution fail. He worked within the framework of international law, not unlike President Clinton's policy of negotiation. While the comic never referred to these political implications, the creators alluded to it in interviews. Captain America also served as an enforcer of democracy, punishing those who would lead their countries in an undemocratic direction. But what role did he have in this new "end of history" world? With most of the long-standing external threats to the United States seemingly removed, the political debate raged over what to do with a huge military establishment that no longer seemed necessary. These arguments about how to spend the "peace dividend" lacked the urgency of previous security debates, as did the parallel efforts of Captain America and the Punisher.

The first substantial look at the two characters after Desert Storm's successful conclusion was the *Punisher-Captain America: Blood and Glory* series (1991). The story line for the series was both novel and somewhat uninspired. It chronicled sales of American-made weapons by Mr. Slickster, a gunrunner to General Miguel Navatilas, dictator of the fictional Central American country of Medisuela. The story criticized American policy in Latin America, especially when Washington was propping up evil dictators simply because they were anti-Communist. This story line was significant, as it alluded to the Department of Defense procurement scandals of the late 1980s. It also recalled the origins of comic book villains pre–World War II during the 1930s (see chapter 1). As it turns out, the guns misfire and explode. The gunrunner knows the weapons are defective; Cap prevents their sale, having heard him confess as much to a colleague.

Gunrunning proves an effective way for the United States to conduct a proxy war throughout Central and South America, recalling America's constant interference in the region.[27] As the story progresses, the characters often reflect on how Americans feel about wars in the post–World War II era. Some believe that total victory is the only acceptable goal of any American intervention. Others take the position that immediate necessity justifies some wars, even if their ultimate outcome and their morality might be dubious. In this dialogue, Captain America states his ideals and morality again: "There is no such thing as a just war . . . unless maybe the one that made me what I am." He goes on to say that excessive use of force is not always worth the cost, as demonstrated by the atomic bombing of Hiroshima and Nagasaki. Many characters in the comic think that Captain America is too simple-minded for this new era of moral complexity, with its necessity of shifting friends and foes. Cap sees political issues as a clear case of "us" versus "them," while realpolitik dictates that the government of the United States must sometimes support dictators for what it believes is the greater good.

When the Punisher is introduced later in the same issue, the punitive nature of his persona is juxtaposed to Cap's tempered benevolence. The Punisher notes, "Civilians don't see the war for what it is. They see what a soldier has to do as no different, no better than the enemy. But those who see the world so black and white never stop to think that it's a gray light that reaches the floor of the jungle."[28] The American public had been taught by Hollywood to believe in a "good war"—that heroes fight and die in a moral, righteous manner; that the good guys never commit atrocities. According to such historians as Stephen Ambrose, Paul Fussell, and Peter Schrijvers, how American soldiers really thought and acted (even in World War II) was far less heroic than what Hollywood, or the comics, would have had us believe.[29] The Punisher's modus operandi in combat is simple: start the bleeding, stop the breathing, and promote shock—classic combat principles.[30] Unlike Cap, who aims to subdue the enemy, the Punisher simply eliminates him.

Despite this, from this point to the end of the miniseries, the two fight as a unit, not so much against evil foreign actors but to end corruption within the U.S. government. The premise of the first issue is that several government agencies are selling weapons to a friendly dictator who, in turn, sells drugs to America. The Machiavellian scheme calls for the United States to eventually use the drug issue as an excuse to invade Medisuela and dominate the surrounding countries. This story line is not surprising: the similarity with U.S. involvement with Noriega is obvious. (He is even mentioned by name, as an example of someone who opposes the United States in the region.) Many believed that (as a side effect of the Iran-Contra program) the CIA was deliberately selling drugs to lower-class citizens, especially blacks, to "keep them in their place." This story line also refers to the punitive policies that many politicians advocated against the drug violence permeating American cities in the 1980s and 1990s.

The story also returns to the theme of how some see conflicts in overly simplistic terms of peace and war. The Punisher often suggests that wars must be fought to win, not merely to keep the peace. One bit of dialogue is indicative. The Punisher sneers about Cap, "Eagle Scout thinks differently. Acts like it's still D-Day, charging up some beach to take the enemy head-on."[31] Castle's point is that one cannot go after all enemies head on. He believes that the best attack is through guile and misdirection, the hallmark of special operations. In other words, "Who Dares, Wins"—the motto of the British Special Air Service (SAS).

The series takes a disturbing view of what American agents will do for results, regardless of their individual political beliefs, when they are sometimes driven as much by personal demons as realpolitik. For example, Attorney General Roger Mollech's ruthless sacrifice of General Navatilas shows his bestial nature, consistent with his sexual and violent appetites. The larger story depicts members of the government abusing the system for their own benefit, rather than effectively fighting external enemies or defending American ideals. Angela Stone, Mollech's malevolent assistant, even tortures a woman with a drill to obtain information about Captain America and the Punisher.[32] By comparison, Cap carries no offensive weapons. This is a point of honor as the two superheroes enter the Medisuelan jungle to destroy cocaine labs and find the illicit weapons. Cap asks the Punisher what he is carrying. After the Punisher rattles off his various weapons, he asks Cap, "Let me guess. . . . You don't believe in weapons?" Cap replies, "Not that. I just don't need them."[33]

As the armed conflict continues, the Punisher shows his willingness to do what it takes to get things done, whether driving a knife into someone's shoulder and using him as a human shield or subjecting his enemies to other forms of torture. At the time these comic books appeared, most Americans recoiled at the use of torture, knowing that it violates the "rules of war." In a prescient description of what happened after 9/11, the comic book shows the American government, in great secrecy, condoning torture with little regard to lives lost.[34] In a further perversion, government officials also use torture for personal gain. The idea is startling for Cap, but not for the Punisher, who realizes that this conflict amounts to "the Stars and Stripes fighting a war with the tactics of the Nazis."[35]

Despite their different actions, the two characters share the same basic beliefs. Both are cynical about the government but fight for the country's underlying ideals. Both want justice, especially for people unable to obtain it for themselves. Both seem to carry residual guilt for failing to protect those closest to them. Both learn from each other and adopt parts of the other's fighting and judicial tenets. Most obviously, both are born of war—but how they adapt to war is what sets them apart.

Not surprisingly, the symbolic significance of the two characters is repeatedly demonstrated. The Punisher's black uniform and skull logo strongly echo the dress and symbols of the dreaded SS. As with the SS, the uniform shows the Punisher's power and induces fear in his enemies. Even within the comic book universe, this costume underlines that the Punisher's methods, if not his motives, are highly suspect. For example, the assassin Crossbones—a similarly black-clad villain— is part of the Red Skull's organization, the Skeleton Crew, and a major enemy of Captain America.[36] Through this overlap between good and evil, the stories employing both Captain America and the Punisher enact the internal struggle of many Americans about the country's role in the post–Cold War world. If the United States uses its power to intervene for human rights or to defeat tyrants, this is seen as imposing its will on the world, usually in a heavy-handed manner.

However, if the United States refrains from intervening, then Americans are perceived as self-centered and unwilling to do what is right. It is often a no-win situation. Even within the realm of popular culture, the question of what the United States should (or should not) do for other countries leads to much consternation and deliberation. Either way, an absolute victory, like the unconditional surrender of the Axis, is no longer possible. Here superheroes become instead a fantasy substitute for a much more ambiguous and unsatisfying reality.

The Mid-1990s and the New World Order in Comic Books

As the Cold War ended and the era of American unilateralism began, the comics experienced a renaissance of sorts. With an older audience—average readers were now in their early twenties—with more disposable income, comic book publishers tried to reach even more readers. Given the volatility of the stock market, some investors were attracted to the prices paid for such comic books as *Action Comics* #1 (Superman's first appearance), which sold for $1,500,000 in mint condition at Sotheby's Auction House in 2010.[37] This sort of frenzy spurred comic book publishers to reintroduce characters from the golden age of comics to protect the newly unstable, post–Cold War world. (As they usually owned the rights to the characters, this maximized potential profits.[38]) They played off their connections to World War II and traditional patriotism, evoking an era when wars and enemies seemed simpler, at least in memory. The Pacific wars from World War II through Vietnam were far more violent and morally questionable than realized in the United States. Yet these revived characters came from a time when the American military supposedly fought by moral rules. They were suddenly dropped into the combat style of the twenty-first century, where greater firepower is used. This implicitly underlined the government's openly heavy-handed and violent methods, as opposed to the 1940s and 1950s, when such brutality was largely concealed.

One attempt to revive a classic patriotic character was the Fighting American.[39] Originated by the famous team of Jack Kirby and Joe Simon, creators of Captain America, the reenvisioned *Fighting American* miniseries used a cynical humor more consistent with the United States of the mid-1990s. The character's real identity is Johnny Flagg, a war hero, former athlete, and TV talk show host. In 1985, after being gunned down by enemies of America, Flagg is placed in another supersoldier program, like the one originally used to create Captain America. Retooled as part of Reagan's increased defense budget during the 1980s, it has now been turned against the Communists. Unlike many other comics, in which the Super-Soldier Serum leads to immediate results, this transformation takes ten years, during which the Soviet Union collapses. (Between the end of the Communist threat and 9/11, the United

States apparently faced few external threats apart from relatively low-level terrorism.) Nevertheless, comic book superheroes, no less than governments, need threats to justify their actions. These can be manufactured if need be, so superhero comics develop enemies embodying perceived internal threats.

The primary enemy of the new Fighting American is Def Izzit (or deficit), who creates a serum to make people spend frivolously, "like the Pentagon."[40] Also making regular appearances in the comic is the Media Circus, a nuclear family purportedly representing the average middle-American household, whose members are regularly asked their opinions by the news media (not unlike the Nielsen ratings).[41] The media then manipulate these answers to mean whatever they want them to mean. Despite this environment, the Fighting American maintains his moral compass and fights for what he feels is right in the world, while the citizens are little more than easily led, materialistic sheep.[42] Even in DC's *Elseworld* series, the patriotically themed characters first created during World War II (and the golden age) come out of retirement for use by the government. One character is the Americommando, a superhero who fought valiantly in World War II and later runs for Congress in the series *The Golden Age.*[43] (The costume of Tex Thompson, the Americommando, is very similar to that of Howard Chaykin's character American Flagg.) The twist in this case is that the Americommando is actually a tool for the Red Hunters of the House Un-American Activities Committee. In an even more fantastic twist, unrepentant Nazis put Hitler's brain into the body of another superhero named Dynaman.[44]

Surprisingly enough, these characters still represented true-blue patriotism. Their creators, such as Howard Chaykin and Alex Ross, occasionally used them to convey a satirical view of heavy-handed American foreign policy.[45] While this concept has been around almost as long as the comic book medium, these modern satires were more directly political and geared toward readers with some knowledge of current events, primarily older teens or young adults. For example, characters' names echoed those of real people in the news, and the fictional countries where the events occured strongly suggested actual places (such as "Bezerestan" for Afghanistan). Their creators' implicit political views are clear to knowledgeable readers, yet the stories can also be enjoyed purely as entertainment.

American ideas of right and wrong were the focal point of the two-part miniseries *U.S.*[46] The comic suggested that while the country had broken or violated many of the premises on which it was founded, it could not escape its past, nor should it necessarily do so.[47] The title's acronym refers not just to the United States but also to its quasi-superhero character Uncle Sam (who has some limited powers, such as clairvoyance). He often sees specific historical events from the point of view of the underdog—the poor, the oppressed, or the vanquished. Shay's Rebellion, the lynching of African Americans, and the Blackhawk War of 1834 all figure in the story lines. As with the Media Gang, the comic addressed the issue of intense media manipulation. In one sequence, Uncle Sam battles his evil alter ego for "the soul of the American people."[48] In the end, Uncle Sam is proved to represent the best of America, but he must remain vigilant against those who would manipulate the United States to advance their own selfish purposes.

U.S. exemplified the idea that with Communism essentially vanquished, the world was perhaps a safer place. Now the United States could and should concentrate on unseen internal enemies. In the words of Walt Kelly's cartoon character Pogo, "We have met the enemy and he is us."[49] The characters often fight greedy industrialists who wish to exploit the United States, rather than external enemies who wish to bring the country down. As the enemies took on a different role, so did the ideology: superheroes express their patriotism in a quest for social justice rather than an existential defense of America.

The early 1990s saw the development of some new patriotic characters. Two of the more interesting are Agent Liberty and SuperPatriot. The first is an outgrowth of the *Superman* series; the second is part human, part cyborg, whose artificial arms morph into any weapon he can imagine (as long as they retain their original mass).[50] Both characters are ideologically motivated. Agent Liberty is part of the "Sons of Liberty," a group of ex-military men who look to "bring America back to its original values," as well as "seek the restoration of the spirit of the Constitution and the Bill of Rights."[51] The eponymous character, wearing a more muted version of the traditional red, white and blue, had been part of an advance reconnaissance team during the Iran hostage rescue attempt (Operation Eagle Claw) in 1980, only to be abandoned and officially forgotten in its aftermath.

SuperPatriot is a rare breed—a liberal superhero. Erik Larsen, the character's creator, classified himself as a "bleeding heart liberal," and his political leanings influenced SuperPatriot's creation. Larsen thought it "would be a nice change of pace to have a left-wing liberal that wrapped himself in the flag for a change."[52] One thing that readers seemed to take from the *SuperPatriot* comics was that genetic engineering could go awry.[53] Not everything about him relates to his ideological aims. When asked about why he completely obscured the character's face, Larsen's answer was that "it looked cool."[54]

Violence in War Comics

Not only did 1990s comics feature struggles about the country's response to new and barely defined enemies, they also contained brutally realistic depictions of combat. This was not entirely new; as has been shown, comics began to depict the violent nature of combat as early as the 1950s. Following the commercial and critical success of Steven Spielberg's 1998 movie *Saving Private Ryan,* however, comics took brutality to a completely new level.

The influence of contemporary films had started with another war movie, Oliver Stone's *Platoon.* As mentioned in chapter 4, it had partly inspired the more graphic depiction of Vietnam in comic books written by Don Lomax. Lomax worked on Marvel's *The 'Nam* and by the early 1990s had produced the sixteen-issue series *Vietnam Journal.*[55] The last two issues described the severe torture of American POWs by the North Vietnamese Army. Nevertheless, Lomax makes a point of showing neither side in black-and-white terms, instead putting the reader into the mind-set of the combatant, who often cannot clearly distinguish right from wrong in the heat of battle. His work entertains shades of gray, just like the morally complex issues of the war.

As the 1990s continued, the role of the United States in a world without serious threat of large-scale conventional or nuclear wars continued to spur comic book creators to reenvision many of the characters who had populated their childhoods. With the end of the Cold War, many thought the world would enjoy increased tolerance and peace. Not all comic book writers agreed, however. One dissenter was Garth Ennis. Originally from Northern Ireland, Ennis grew up on American and British comic books, specifically war comics.[56] In fact, he often noted that he had never liked the superhero genre. *Unknown Soldier,* an Ennis title from the mid-1990s, looked at battlefield morality and how it might reflect the tensions created when people believed in the values of American society but had to kill to preserve it.[57]

In this version, the Unknown Soldier is without his assistant Chat Noir, nor does he show much mental stability. Manipulated by the OSS and its successor the CIA, he has seen too many killings and too many people corrupted by power. The premise is that William Clyde, a former Special Forces officer who has become the CIA's main operative, is seen within the agency as a "boy scout," unwilling to implement a dirty war against America's enemies.[58] Lured into looking for a person code-named "the Unknown Soldier," he encounters several witnesses to this enigma's furious retributions around the world. At the end of the story, the Unknown Soldier—while seeking a successor to do what is right for the nation—confronts Clyde.[59] It is hinted that the old Unknown Soldier (and the United States, the initials of which he shares) "sold his [its] soul" when the United States was willing to overlook Auschwitz and other Nazi atrocities to obtain German weapon technology for the struggle against the Soviet Union. This betrayal causes a psychotic break in the Unknown Soldier, leaving him riddled with guilt. Many military personnel struggle emotionally when forced to reconcile following orders with doing what is "right."[60]

The story finally demonstrates the blurring of roles between uniformed military combatants and intelligence agents in civilian clothing. When one side disregards the Geneva Conventions, morality becomes confused: are those being executed civilians or terrorists? This violence against seeming noncombatants was more common in the comic books of the 1990s. The American people usually see themselves—and the actions of their military—

as honorable, not blurred. This self-perception is flattering; the reality is far more disconcerting.

Ennis described another case of lowered moral inhibitions in "Nosh and Barry and Eddie and Joe."[61] En route to a fishing expedition, SAS members reminisce about their mission in the Gulf War. Later on, a member of the team relates other secret actions. According to him, a squad mate had been part of a psychological operations team that was secretly drugged. This drug (naturally, put in their tea) gave them increased physical power and acuity, but it also removed their inhibitions toward violence. At the end of the mission, the soldiers were "asked" to continue fighting the good fight under the drug (which suppressed the memories of their actions) or retire with the full recollection of their actions (but without the drug, thus resulting in nightmares). This story, and all others that appear in *Weird War Stories Annual,* conjures not external ghosts or apparitions but the deeper horrors within each of us. This dilemma has been at the forefront of training in American military circles: the perception of how to train an efficient, robot-like soldier unwavering in combat, without moral qualms about killing an enemy. The story shows the popular concept of automated weaponry that will allow the military to place smaller numbers of troops in harm's way, yet still attain the military goals envisioned by political leaders toward automated weapon systems as a vital part of military doctrine in the post–Cold War world.

The artists illustrating these stories also made a major contribution, enhancing the human element as an essential part of the storytelling process. Wayne Vansant used his experience drawing *The 'Nam* as a springboard for other military-themed comics, including *Semper Fi,* a nine-issue series from Marvel. The focal point of *Semper Fi* is the Whittier family and its interaction with the U.S. Marine Corps through multiple generations.[62] Vansant puts this fictional family at the center of every major historical event in which the Marines took part, from the Revolutionary War to peacekeeping in Lebanon in 1983. The title also looks at the emotional difficulties of Dan Whittier as he returns from Vietnam, as well as his daughter's desire to become a Marine herself. The history of the Marine Corps is told in a reasonably objective manner, as the stories stick largely to historical facts, rather than merely presenting propaganda. The series is somewhat derivative, and the artwork's indebtedness to *The 'Nam* is evident and intentional.[63] It was expected that *Semper Fi* would be a hit as a spin-off from *The 'Nam.* However, it never attained the expected readership (even with a built-in Marine audience) and soon after ceased publication. While not a commercial success, it inspired two later series drawn by Vansant, *Days of Darkness* and *Days of Wrath,* from Caliber Comics.[64]

Like *Semper Fi,* these series try to give a human face to the home front as well as the battlefronts of World War II. Both involve the Cahill family of Maverick, Texas. *Days of Darkness* begins on December 7, 1941, with three sons posted in the Pacific as the family celebrates the matriarch's birthday. Two of the sons, Dan, a Marine, and Stewart, a naval aviator, experience the devastation of the attack on Pearl Harbor. A third brother, Sullivan, is serving with the Army in the Philippines, where the Japanese also attack his outpost. The six-issue arc was later republished as a trade paperback, and *Days of Wrath* was likewise slated to run for six issues. Here, Sullivan experiences the viciousness of Japanese attacks on the Philippine Islands, while his brothers fight during the first major U.S. offensive, on the island of Guadalcanal. Unfortunately, the series suffered from a common problem facing many publishers: a lack of money. Apple withered, and all its titles ended before their intended story arcs were complete. Vansant's *Days of Wrath* ended at four of six proposed issues. Lomax's *Vietnam Journal: Valley of Death* series stopped at issue #1 (of a proposed two). These also had only limited success, but were thematically interesting, as the intertwined military families gave them greater psychological depth.

Another company that wanted to continue the tradition of war comics with a realistic feel was New England Comics, run by Rod Ledwell. His series, titled *WW2*, often depicted particular battles from World War II or other historical events that are less well known. His comics, like those from Apple, were in black and white to reduce production costs. However, while Apple had highly talented artists, New England Comics did not. Many of the stories lacked the visual excitement that other comics frequently achieved. This is not to say that the *WW2* comic books were poor, but the artwork definitely discouraged readers accustomed to the glossy pages of more mainstream comics. Nevertheless, Bidwell tried to find his niche and succeeded to an extent. Like Dell Comics some twenty years earlier, he managed to tell stories of battles and events rarely seen in the genre.[65]

At the same time, a resurgence of reader interest in the original *Frontline Combat* and *Two-Fisted Tales* led to their rerelease in the 1990s. The hope was that, like their initial print runs, the republished original comics might excite sales among investors through the speculative collector market.[66] In addition to the above titles, buyers were reintroduced to such comics as *Aces High,* which had a run of only five issues in the 1950s; now interest was such that the complete run was reprinted as a slipcase set.[67] As with so many war-themed comics of the 1990s, however, these titles often hewed to tried-and-true story lines or adapted the monster theme to war stories. Epic, a Marvel offshoot, published a new series titled *Strange Combat Tales.* In this four-part series, necromancy causes the dead to rise. The narrative incorporates the destruction of New York by a major attack. For those who believe in the paranormal, the story is a premonition of the 1993 and 2001 World Trade Center attacks. *Strange Combat Tales* presents a madman (in this case the malevolent spirit of Oliver Cromwell) who must be defeated by the Knights Templar, joined by those of strong moral conviction.[68] The premise is odd, to say the least, but it does not venture upon uncharted waters.

General Douglas MacArthur. This comic came out not long after MacArthur was asked to step down from his role as commander in chief of Allied forces in the Korean Conflict. The story noted the major milestones of his life. (Fox Features, 1951, private collection of the author)

Spy Smasher #11. This comic and *Commando Yank* #12 were smaller digest-size comic books produced for soldiers overseas. The stories were the same as the regular size issued, just shrunk in size and done only in black and red ink to cut down on production costs. The idea here was that everyone could aid the government in fighting the Axis at home and abroad. The stories also encouraged readers to invest in war bonds and stamps. (Mighty Midget Comics, 1942, private collection of the author)

Commando Yank #12. This comic used the hero in more militaristic costume, but the enemies he fought were the same: spies and saboteurs at home. (Mighty Midget Comics, 1942, private collection of the author)

USA is Ready. This comic book was one produced in the early part of 1941, when the United States was still a neutral country. The stories often described U.S. military prowess and told of how these weapons would defeat any enemy. Note the interesting design of the tank on the right. (Dell, 1941, private collection of the author)

War Heroes #9. This comic used pictures and accounts of the vicious hand-to-hand combat in the Pacific against the Japanese as an enticement for readers. The stories were factual in origin, but simplified in form. (Dell, 1944, private collection of the author)

War Heroes #6 This cover, done in the summer of 1943 for publication in the fall of that year, was a way for readers to imagine the landings which had occurred in North Africa, Sicily, and many Pacific Islands by this time. (Dell, 1943, private collection of the author)

Remember Pearl Harbor. This comic featured written accounts of the attack as well as comic stories that showed accounts of valor. This comic, like the 9/11 comics produced soon after the attacks, was a way for artists and writers to reach a wide audience as well as stir up emotion. (Street and Smith, 1942, private collection of the author)

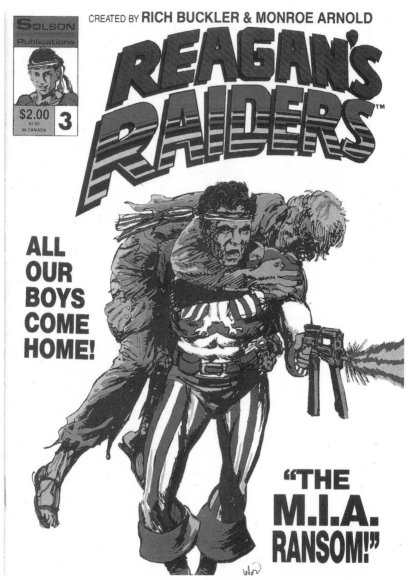

Reagan's Raiders #3. This comic book featured the then-president of the United States as a superhero, and in this particular story line, Reagan the hero went back to rescue POWs left in Vietnam. (Solson Comics, 1986, private collection of the author)

DC Comics also returned to the war genre by recreating their *Weird War Series*, an anthology title from the 1960s. This five-issue series (four regular issues and a special annual) gave the original concepts a new twist. Each issue was "hosted" by Death, a skeleton who wore a different military uniform in each issue. The artwork was well done, displaying Sam Glanzman's talents, particularly in a feature about Andersonville, the notorious Confederate prisoner-of-war camp. One inmate is actually a woman dressed as a Union soldier, who defends another soldier from marauding prisoners as well as disease. Eventually, after the soldier discovers her secret and they fall in love, the same marauders within the prison kill her.[69]

Other stories in *Weird War Tales* show ghoulish encounters, such as an American "tunnel rat" serving near Cu Chi in Vietnam who sees ghosts attack his fellow soldiers while underground.[70] Several stories deal with the demons within. One, "Looking Good, Feeling Great," follows a man who, despite his excellent shooting skills, cannot or will not join the military. Deranged by the tale's end, he is encouraged to "feel the burn" by a television exercise guru, so he shoots up the town.[71] *Weird War Tales* explores the unexamined costs of war in the form of deprivation, captivity, and psychosis. It certainly does not glorify war; rather, the series laments violence that serves no purpose beyond violence itself. Several of the creators, with or without connection to the military, wanted to emphasize the futility of fighting.

The key link of all these stories within this period was their focus on the stress and violence of combat. The stories were presented in a quasi-horror mode within military situations, but their overriding feature was the true chaos of combat. This critical look into the nature of war reflected the new realism in popular culture (even within a surreal or supernatural context). While comics have often tried to present combat realistically, the popularity of films that did the same made their production less shocking.

War Comics as "News"

The war comic is not new, nor is the idea of using a comic book to inform readers about conflicts around the globe. The violence of war has been a prominent feature in comics since their inception in the 1930s. As previously noted, Joe Kubert was one of the foremost war comics artists in the history of the comic book industry. Many of the comic books from the later 1990s tried not only to entertain but also to enliven history (with a decided slant toward personal reflection and emotion), as opposed to simply reciting the "facts." For example: Kubert's story on the human impact of the Bosnia crisis of the early 1990s, as told in *Fax from Sarajevo*.[72] Told in the first person through faxes from real life artist Ervin Rustemagic to Kubert, it is a compelling portrayal of one man's suffering and his attempt to reunite his family. As with Kubert's graphic novel

Yossel and Art Spiegelman's graphic novel *Maus,* the personal connection gives the book an intimacy never felt when reading a textbook on the same subject.[73]

In the field of historical comic books set during the conflicts of the 1990s, one name has the greatest prominence: Joe Sacco. Sacco's academic grounding in journalism allowed him to ask the right questions of the right people. His travels in Europe, Israel, Gaza, and the West Bank in the early and mid-1990s led him to create his signature works: *Palestine* (depicting the Israeli occupation of the West Bank), *Safe Area Goražde,* and *The Fixer* (the latter two set in a disintegrating Yugoslavia).[74] The books tell the story of the conflicts using personal interviews conducted by Sacco. He uses the comic book format to make in-depth journalistic report of the conflict. *Safe Area Goražde* expands on Kubert's *Fax from Sarajevo.* Sacco's tale is mostly set in the city of Goražde, located in a UN-declared "safe zone." However, as the reader soon learns, the area is anything but safe. Innocent people on all sides are brutalized, and encountering the wrong person can mean death. Sacco works in black and white, which creates a stark (metaphorical, moral) landscape. An introductory section on the historical politics in the Balkans gives readers some understanding about how these events had built over time.[75]

Sacco captures the frustration, sadness, and agony felt by those in the war zone. He describes the elaborate lengths that citizens of Goražde go to for even simple electrical service. By reading these two graphic novels, one gains an understanding of the origins of the conflict and perhaps even some idea about its possible resolution. While more of a human-interest piece, *The Fixer* is the sequel to *Safe Area Goražde* on two levels. First, it revisits the Bosnian crisis years later. Second, it follows the story of Neven (a part-Serb, part-Muslim man Sacco interviewed in the first book) and how he adapts to his new life. Neven is a "fixer," an intermediary between various factions during the anarchic days following the dissolution of the Republic of Yugoslavia. Sacco also includes a bibliography for follow-up reading, as do many other historical comics.

Dark Horse Comics also sought to revive the tales of real-life heroism that had permeated the comics of the 1950s. In 1994 it introduced a five-issue series about soldiers who were awarded the Medal of Honor. As with many other war comics, these were four- to seven-page vignettes created by various artists. One cover, *Medal of Honor Special Edition* #1, was actually drawn by the famous Kubert to lure in more readers.[76] While not as successful as the publishers had hoped, the cover was pure Kubert. In fact, the soldier holding a bandaged comrade-in-arms looks very similar to Kubert's work on *Sgt. Rock.*

Even Will Eisner came back to the war comics' fold with *Last Day in Vietnam.* Eisner wrote and illustrated this graphic novel based on his travels to Asia doing research for *PS* magazine. The graphic novel contains a variety of war-themed stories. The first, "The Last Day," is about a major who wanted to make it through the suddenly dangerous last day in Vietnam. Another, titled "True Love," tells of a soldier ambushed by a Vietnamese prostitute while on leave in Saigon. The final story, "The Transfer," is based on Eisner's personal recollection of a soldier in World War II who, when drunk, asked to transfer from a supply outfit to a combat unit. In the end, the soldier receives his transfer but dies shortly thereafter. Again, the stories relate the human element of combat and undermine the false bravado so often shown in war movies or war comics.[77] The use of personal war recollections as a basis for comic books gives the books a sense of legitimacy as well as education; using famous writers and illustrators ensures that they are good entertainment. These small stories are a good introduction to the basics of conflict before moving on to more detailed works.

A graphic novel about the development of the atomic bomb came out in early 2001, before 9/11. Written primarily by Jim Ottaviani, *Fallout* approaches the subject in a journalistic/historical mode. It follows the creation of the bomb by Leo Szilard (among others), through the fabrication of the weapon, and the aftermath, when the project's director, Robert Oppenheimer, loses his security clearance. Ottaviani is a niche creator, and his G.T. Labs continue to produce comic books geared toward people knowledgeable in science.[78] The books are drawn in black and white, with the support of several artists, who give each story a fresh but sometimes uneven feel. *Fallout* portrays the human side of the manufacture of the atomic bomb, as does Keiji Nakazawa's *I Saw It*.[79] In an interview, Ottaviani said that he took the same approach to his comics as Spiegelman, in that his books are a combination of historical fact and creative dialogue.[80]

The war comics of the 1990s often tried to capture the anxieties of Americans in the post–Cold War world. Not knowing what the future held, the violent superheroes often continued punishing the enemies of America, Reagan-style. As the decade wound down and the new millennium approached, some comic book creators used comic books for education and moral discussion, as well as entertainment. The comics allowed the United States to refight and "win" the Vietnam War. They also gave a sense of closure to that conflict by grappling with the issue of POWs. In addition, war comics of this time imagined new threats to the United States through the rise of terrorist mercenaries in various guises. Still, some would return to the reassuring and nostalgic depictions of "noble" combat. While the events of 9/11 pushed comic book creators to resurrect World War II propaganda concepts, they also incorporated the cultural sensitivities of the modern United States.

6 The Role of Comics after 9/11 (2001–3)

It doesn't matter where you thought you were going today. You're
part of the bomb now. And somewhere in the world a handful of men
with famished eyes sit around a radio or a telephone. Twenty minutes,
four thousand murders later, they praise God for the blood that stains
their hands. Oh God, how could this happen here? We've got to be
strong—stronger than we've ever been. If we lose hope here, bury
our faith in this darkness, then nothing else matters.

—JOHN NEY RIEBER AND JOHN CASSADAY, *Captain America* #1

L
ike films, television, and music over the last sixty years, comic books
became a more socially conscious forum for young people to learn about
adult ideas. This started in a major way during the 1960s. As the war in
Vietnam consumed more of America's political energy, comic book characters
had to respond somehow. For example, when Stan Lee and Steve Ditko introduced Spider-Man in 1964, he was soon dealing with drug-addicted veterans and
campus radicals.[1] Even so, until the 1990s comics remained largely apolitical, with
only a brief interruption during the Gulf War. Joe Sacco's *Palestine* and *Safe Area
Goražde* enjoyed only limited sales compared to bigger, less political titles, such as
Superman, Spider-Man, and *X-Men.* The idealized violence of such superheroes
replaced earlier attempts to inject political activism and combat realism.

This all changed after September 11, 2001, when terrorists crashed four high-
jacked airplanes into the World Trade Center, the Pentagon, and a field in rural
Pennsylvania. These events transfixed the United States, especially as images of
the destruction were constantly repeated on television. Even more than Pearl
Harbor sixty years earlier, 9/11 brought war home for most Americans. While
this affected everyone, comic creators had special reasons to respond. This was
due, largely, to three factors. First, as much of their readership consisted of young
people and children, they felt a responsibility to explain the events in an understandable way; second, most of them lived in New York City and experienced the
devastation firsthand; and third, their superheroes should have been able to stop
this sort of attack, in theory at least. This last issue created a conundrum, as story

100

lines could not merely continue as if 9/11 had never happened. Apart from a few symbolic gestures, superheroes had stayed out of previous wars. The mismatch between their amazing powers and the grim realities of war could be embarrassing, so their creators had largely confined them to fighting domestic villains. However, 9/11 effectively merged the battlefield with the home front.

Although comic books are usually created months in advance, the first comic book about the events of 9/11 came out less than three weeks later. *The Amazing Spider-Man* #36 featured an all-black cover portraying Americans' anger and frustration about the attack. People in the comic ask Spidey why he did not stop the terrorists. Spider-Man even asks the question of himself. The question was unanswerable, because fantasy hits its limits in the face of tragedy on that scale. (*Maus*, a fictionalized comic book treatment of the Holocaust, was possible but only after enough time had passed. But a fantasy superhero's prevention of the Holocaust would cross a boundary over which most readers would be unwilling to follow.[2]) This is why *Amazing Spider-Man* #36 and other 9/11 comics focused on the men and women of the New York City Fire and Police Departments, the "real life superheroes." The first comic books released in the immediate aftermath of the attacks (anthologies published jointly by DC, Marvel, and Dark Horse) helped raise funds for the Red Cross. Four of these featured firemen or other heroic people on their covers (*Heroes: A Moment of Silence*; *9/11: Emergency Relief*; and *9/11*, vols. 1 and 2). They reflect several different viewpoints of the events and address the emotions surrounding the attack, the television coverage, and the feelings and experiences of the writers and artists themselves.

In all these comics, the characters express the confusion of most Americans with the fact that the new enemy of the United States was not a powerful and highly armed country—like Germany or Japan in World War II or the Cold War's Soviet Union—but a superficially unimpressive group: terrorists with box cutters. This time, however, the comics were more even-handed than they had been in World War II, eschewing racial and cultural stereotyping of America's enemies.[3] For example, Captain America breaks up an attack on a Middle Eastern teenager, and he notes that particular criminal individuals, not a whole religion or race, were responsible.[4] The characters often call for tolerance of all ethnic groups in the United States, especially Arab Americans, reflecting the changed attitudes toward these minorities. The comics attempt to counteract the anti-Muslim hysteria that swept parts of the country, which even led to the deaths of people who simply "looked Arab." Vignettes from each of these *9/11* anthologies try to address the increased hatred in a rational way. For example, in *"A Burning Hate,"* a child criticizes an Arab kid for reading *Superman*, saying "Superman isn't one of yours. He's American." The Arab boy points out that Superman is also from another world, and he fights for the right of all immigrants to the United States to achieve the American dream.[5]

Comic book creators tried to show that terrorist groups were not all Arab, and not all Arabs were terrorists. An underlying frustration with, and even hatred of, religious zealots of *all* stripes and the need for greater tolerance were key to the story lines. Captain America, a character created to battle America's enemies, returned to his "original purpose." Cap was already scheduled to return in another volume, largely to fight typical "comic book" supervillains working for their own impure personal ends. The 9/11 attacks forced the creators of the new *Captain America* series to go back to the drawing board; they wrote a five-issue story arc that tied the attacks to a wider plot against the country. These terrorists are not traditional Marvel-style villains, who are far more sophisticated—with uniforms, cutting edge technology, and weapons in great numbers—than real terrorist groups that rely on theft of weapons and crime to finance operations. Instead, the new evildoers share only the real terrorists' Middle Eastern background and modus operandi.[6]

Depictions of the Attack

Because most major comic book publishers are located in downtown Manhattan, and because the terrorist attacks resonated so strongly with the American people, it is unsurprising that several graphic novels treat 9/11. Several are somewhat difficult to classify, however; they do not use the typical format of the graphic novel genre (that is, illustrated books interspersed with text). Alex Ross did several poignant renderings of exhausted New York firefighters. Will Eisner drew one picture in mostly black and white: a man staring at a television with a hole in the middle of the screen, while smoke pours out and a red stream, presumably blood, issues forth.[7] Frank Miller, in a comic published shortly after the attacks, notes that he is sick of both the terrorists *and* the mindless flag-waving.[8]

The two *9/11* volumes feature work by many of the leading comic book artists and writers. One story combines the famous World War I poem "In Flanders Field" with the visual imagery of the World Trade Center attacks.[9] In *9/11* vol. 2, two renowned war comic artists, Sam Glanzman and Ted Rall, wrote and drew vignettes that convey a sense of loss and the need for some sort of retribution. Glanzman wrote his story, "There Were Tears in Her Eyes," as a discussion between him and his grandson about the attacks and the possibility of a wider war. Glanzman mentions that he does not want to discuss his own war—World War II—or the carnage that he witnessed. Nevertheless, he specifically asks if the bombings of the two Japanese cities were a "necessary means to correct an injustice." His answer is that even the horrific atomic bombings of Hiroshima and Nagasaki ultimately worked for the betterment of all. As the bombings swiftly concluded the war, saving untold lives, these extraordinary means were justified.[10] He even notes that the terrorist attacks in New York were being called a crime rather than an act of war.[11] He points out that the World Trade Center and the Pentagon attacks were seen differently by different people. It is a thought-provoking statement that shows how different American citizens felt about the "event" and the eventual "response." Glanzman's vignette ends with a comparison of the Islamic extremists to the Nazis. When people do not stand up for what is right, they allow evil to occur. For more politicized artists, however, the attack and the war on terrorism provided an impetus for further consideration.

Ted Rall, a writer of both comic strips and graphic novels, gave his recollections in the vignette "The Day My Train Stood Still," where he explored the chaos of getting from New York City to the outlying suburbs following the attack. He showed how some looters, figuring the police were preoccupied with bigger issues, were shamed into leaving the stuff they had stolen. At the end of the story, he reports that some of the train's passengers wonder why the full story of the carnage is not being told by the news media.[12] After the United States began bombing Taliban positions in October 2001, Rall arranged to become the only "combat cartoonist" in Afghanistan. His work there was eventually compiled in *To Afghanistan and Back*, which—though not a graphic novel in the strict sense—artistically combines drawing and text to tell the story. Unlike other historically themed comic books, *To Afghanistan and Back* included several essays, in which Rall makes no attempt to be unbiased. His introduction claimed that George W. Bush was bombing Afghanistan not to destroy the Taliban, but rather to put in place a government that would favor American energy companies by approving the construction of a natural gas pipeline through the country.[13] Rall later spits more venom at Bush in his book *Generalissimo el Busho*.

Another atypical book focused on the artist's feelings is Art Spiegelman's *In the Shadow of No Towers*. Much larger than a standard graphic novel, the book has thick cardboard pages, similar to books for young children. Spiegelman revives classic comic strip characters from the age of yellow journalism to tell a story of confusion, terror, and emotional chaos. The connection to yellow journalism is significant, as that era's circulation wars were used to whip up "war fever." Spiegelman points out that the contemporary media climate is much the same, only with Fox News and its ilk taking the place formerly played by sensationalist newspapers.[14] (He also includes some early 1900s cartoon strips, to show how he adapts them to the world of 2004.)

Some of the new comics' characters were not as subtle. Among the comics that came out following the attacks were *SPECWAR, Kill Box, Pete the P.O.'d Postal Worker: War Journal,* and the most blatant of the lot, *Civilian Justice*. Each exploits adolescent fantasies of hunting down and killing those responsible for the atrocities. In *SPECWAR*, the characters are members of the Navy SEALs and other forces trained in specialized warfare.[15] In the first issue, written before 9/11 but published afterward, the team deals with a Middle Eastern terrorist plan to detonate an atomic bomb in New York Harbor. The plot is thwarted; the bad guys, killed. The violence is explicit and enacts the desires of the supposed audience: to avenge New York and redeem the United States.[16] The series was written by Frank Lauria, who had twenty years' experience as a SEAL. One of his reasons for creating the *SPECWAR* series was that he felt the exploits of "fellow operators" were more compelling than any fiction.[17] The third issue, finished only three days before the 9/11 attacks, discusses a terrorist attempt to obtain a briefcase nuclear bomb from a former Soviet commander. The SPECWAR group saves the day by killing all the terrorists involved.[18]

In later issues the group operates in various countries such as Somalia, where they conduct operations against scientists working on biological weapons.[19] One important story line described corrupt senior American military officers who have never seen combat, yet believe that operations in the field can be carried out in textbook fashion.[20] There is fighting against drug lords[21] and, finally, a not-very-veiled story concerning the invasion of a Middle Eastern country. The leader of the country goes into hiding but vows vengeance with weapons of mass destruction. This justifies using U.S. military power, as Americans "don't negotiate with people who are unreasonable, but meet force with force." Lauria uses his comic to call for an accounting from government, which seems to lack conviction for hunting down those responsible for 9/11. His call for action is quite explicit—"We need to be relentless in our hunt."—and he asks readers to contact their congressional officials and demand to know what is being done to wipe out terrorism.[22] However, by the time of publication, the need for retribution had worn off with some readers, and the series ended soon after the invasion of Iraq.

Civilian Justice, the second comic published following the attacks, deals with the hunt for Osama bin Laden, and it gives a nod to the patriotically dressed superheroes of World War II. Clint Martinson, the main character, loses his girlfriend in the World Trade Center attack and acts out the classic trajectory of comic book and movie heroes of the World War II era. A loner and ne'er-do-well with a troubled past (his cop father has frequently bailed him out of trouble), he finds his purpose only after 9/11 reveals the grave nature of the threat. As the superhero Civilian Justice, he rises up to avenge those closest to him and the country that he loves. On the cover, he waves an American flag, but inside he runs the flagpole through a demonic Osama bin Laden. There is no subtlety here: it is what the audience expected from the previews that appeared online and in comic book catalogs. While the writer Graig Weich noted that the terrorist attacks had also defamed Islam, the comic has a different tone. The opening lines trumpet, "A new symbol of hope . . . a hero to help us vent our rage and frustration against terrorism of any kind. For he does not attack, he defends. . . . Be warned, as Justice is coming."[23] The comic tied in to online promotions, such as a resin statue of the character and a small live-action version of the comic.[24]

Other comic books dealt with events at home. *Pete the P.O.'d Postal Worker* sought to blame Osama bin Laden for the spate of anthrax attacks made through the United States mail. It combined the stereotype of the disgruntled, homicidal postal worker of the 1990s with the superhero who punishes villains in a horrendous fashion. In one issue, Pete delivers a letter from a small child to bin Laden, asking him why he attacked the United States, killing his uncle. This comic incorporates many of the rumors about bin Laden then circulating on the Internet. Bin Laden is supposed to use a pet goat for sexual satisfaction; another rumor accuses him of cross-dressing. Also discussed is the Islamic belief that seventy virgins await terrorist "martyrs" in Paradise. It also suggests that some cable news channels either tacitly or actively support the Islamic cause. One of the more bizarre aspects of the story is that it shows bin Laden being killed by wild pigs, defiling the Islamic faith.[25]

This comic book, like the others mentioned, was not well received by young readers. The allusions and jokes were directed at an older audience, adolescents and adults, who would get the humor. How effective these comics were as propaganda is uncertain. The above three examples were published by smaller companies with limited print runs (usually no more than ten thousand copies, compared to popular titles from Marvel or DC with runs up to a hundred thousand). Some readers, no doubt, identified with the vengeance scenarios, wherein the hero vanquishes the villain (often violently). Pete the postal worker is definitely a subversive and contradictory character. On the one hand, he perfectly fits the caricature of a deranged postal worker in the 1990s: heavily armed, vindictive, and violent. On the other hand, he is so loyal to the U.S. Postal Service that he is willing to travel to Afghanistan to deliver a letter to a known terrorist. He is not a mercenary who fights for pay. Instead, in his deranged way, he fights for his organization's principles and, by extension, the ideals of the United States.

The last comic that dealt with the Middle East as a theme for military conflict was *Kill Box,* produced by Antarctic Press. The comic book centers on an American Abrams tank in the Iraqi desert, presumably there to stop terrorist activities (the Iraq War had not yet begun). The comic assumes rather bellicose values: "If America does not go to war, war will go to America."[26] This was somewhat prophetic of the Bush administration's eventual rationale for war, which was partly justified on the grounds of removing a regime that supported terrorist activities.[27] The main character is haunted by the ghost of his father, who was killed in the Gulf War (much as it is claimed George W. Bush was haunted by his father's failure to oust Saddam). Thus he needs to live up to his father's example, as well as prove his patriotic commitment to the country. Largely because the author lost interest, the series stopped being produced around the start of Operation Iraqi Freedom, despite selling well, especially in military post exchanges.[28]

Comics about 9/11 that feature women are surprisingly similar to those of the World War II era. Two of the notable entries are *Shi: Through the Ashes* and *United.* The former features Shi, an Asian American character who is a cross between a kabuki actress and a martial arts champion.[29] Like the classic war superheroes, the colors of her costume come from the American flag, but she is still depicted to appeal to what the largely male readership expected to see in comic book females: skimpy outfits that accentuate exaggerated feminine features, such as large breasts. *United* featured Lady Death, Bad Kitty, and Chastity, all of whom can take care of themselves in fights. Yet, unlike male characters, who take on terrorists directly, these female characters mostly fulfill the stereotype of nurturing women. They usually work in a rescue capacity, such as helping people trapped in collapsed buildings or those who need medical assistance.[30]

Many mainstream comic book companies went with a simpler, less fanatical form of patriotism. For instance, Marvel introduced the *The Call* in the fall of 2002. It relied on earlier 9/11 themes, featuring police (six issues), firefighters (six issues), and paramedics (four issues) in New York City, elevating them to superhero status. While the first issues were realistic, *The Call* evolved in a mythic direction, as the heroes eventually become superpowered beings. However, the desire to relate the heroes to the greater conflict against terrorism was effective.[31]

Captain America and His Iconic Roots

The 9/11 terrorist attacks revived a more traditional type of patriotism in the United States. Captain America had been out of fashion, but in the new postironic environment his undiluted patriotism, and its implicit moral superiority, made him relevant once again. When Marvel Comics reintroduced him in 2001, Captain America returned to his roots fighting the enemies of the United States.[32] In the story arc beginning with *Captain America* #1, *What Price Liberty,* Cap deals with the aftermath of 9/11, later taking on a Middle Eastern terrorist cell operating on American soil.[33] The relaunched series directly addresses such moral issues as racism and stereotyping, unlike the 1940s series, but Captain America's primary role as a symbol of America's resilience is unchanged.

Marvel was already preparing to revive *Captain America,* and John Ney Reiber and John Cassaday, the writer and artist of the new line, respectively, were already at work on new issues before the attacks. After 9/11, however, they wrote five new issues—a prequel of sorts to what they had already prepared—to deal with the new terrorist threat to freedom, democracy, and the American way of life.[34] As before, Captain America does not directly take on the world's armies but instead pursues terrorists, the twenty-first-century equivalent of spies and guerrilla fighters: combatants who use underhanded tactics, take innocent lives without qualms, and then stealthily blend into the background. In the first issue of the new series, Captain America fights off skinheads threatening the life of an Arab American merchant in New York, noting that there has to be a distinction between those who merely look different and those who wish to harm the United States.[35]

In the winter of 2002, in an issue dealing with his origins, Captain America appears in the *Ultimates* comic book in a more military-looking uniform. The traditional red, white, and blue are still there, but the mask covering his face is leather; he wears a standard American military helmet adorned with a large "A," military-style suspenders, and a utility belt resembling a regulation military web belt; and he adopts a variation of military boots instead of his usual pirate-style footwear. These changes often lead readers to assume that Captain America has a direct connection to the military units with whom he sometimes works.[36]

This was not the only possible source of confusion. By 2001 the venerable Captain had gone through many permutations since the introduction of the character sixty years earlier. The original Steve Rogers, a weakling during the Depression, was scientifically changed into the supersoldier who helped win World War II if only on the home front. After that war ended and the Cold War took over, the original Captain America disappeared (frozen, as it turned out), with several new candidates playing the part of America's most virtuous patriotic superhero. Versions of Captain America, recruited from other comic books, were woven into the story line. William Naslund, whose nom de guerre was the Patriot, a costumed figure dressed in Revolutionary War garb, became Captain America II. U.S. Agent, John Walker, fills in as Captain America V (in the guise of a heavily armored riot cop) in a three-part 2001 story, as well as a retro Captain America in the *New Invader* series. In both incarnations, Walker is more violent than the original Captain America, who was considerably less gratuitous when it came to the physical punishment of his opponents. U.S. Agent's helmet, which covered his face and hid his eyes, stands in contrast with Captain America's usual mask, through which one can at least read his eyes—giving him much more humanity.[37]

The *Invader/New Invader* series helps illuminate the difference between various superheroes' styles of patriotism. This omnibus series included clean-cut Captain America, the scruffier U.S. Agent, Miss Liberty in her red costume with white and blue shield, and Union Jack, a British lord whose costume features a large British flag across the chest. There are even nods to the original Flaming Ghost, Sub-Mariner/Prince Namor, and Spitfire. Several comic book publishers ran hypothetical story lines. Marvel produced the *What If?* series in which Captain America helps fight the Civil War, the Fantastic Four appear as Russian superheroes wearing Soviet regalia, and so on. DC Comics created *Elseworld,* which invented *Superman: Red Son.*

Captain America works for the Supreme Headquarters International Espionage Law-Enforcement Division (SHIELD).[38] A nebulous government agency that is part CIA, part Special Forces, and part National Security Agency (NSA), *SHIELD* is an espionage/spy series led by Nick Fury, now into his forties.[39] SHIELD often fights against HYDRA and A.I.M. two multinational terrorist organizations.[40]

In *Civilian Justice* (2001), the eponymous character operates not as a weapon under the direct control of the American government, but as an instrument of the will of the people, whose voices are not always heard or heeded, especially in times of war. The Shield's red, white, and blue uniform, like those of Captain America and other patriotic superheroes, shows this dedication to the people—in contrast, for example, to the Punisher's black uniform emblazoned with a skull, suggesting a lone avenger. Graig Weich incorporates an Osama bin Laden look-alike on the cover of *Civilian Justice* #1, as Simon and Kirby had done earlier with Hitler.[41] In an interview, Weich emphasized the character's change from fighting enemies of the United States on behalf of politicians to fighting for the common citizens of the world, who all hoped for peace and understanding.[42]

Traditional Roles in War Comics, Revisited or Corrected

Most of these series used only men in patriotic roles. There have been some notable exceptions, however. Miss Liberty from the *Invaders* series was the first, as well as Wonder Woman—although, despite her typical patriot's uniform, she is not technically American. Actually, she represents her native Paradise Island and its political unit of Themyscira and, by extension, the United Nations.[43] In recent years, superheroes' motivations have been explored more directly, either through hypothetical "what if" stories or by transposing their characteristics into new contexts. An example of the latter is Kyle Baker's *The Truth: Red, White and Black* (2003), which equates the fictional eugenics experiments that created Captain America with the real Tuskegee experiments on African Americans. The main genetically enhanced character, Isaiah Thomas, adopts Captain America's traditional regalia (the patriotic uniform and distinctive round shield) before going forth to battle the Nazis. The result is his detention for fifteen years in an American military prison. While the premise was controversial and interesting, sales slumped because of the comic book's unusual "hip-hop" style artwork.[44]

The storyteller uses the costume design, as well as the character's actions, to show his thoughts and politics. In recent years a notable dichotomy has developed. While the characters still represent the higher ideals of the United States, as individuals they are antitheses to what is admired by American society. They are less interested in rational analysis and negotiation. While many comic book creators tried to avoid taking openly political stances, they almost universally opposed the invasion of Iraq. These feelings affected their stories. This may also have been a backlash against the Comic Book Code, then in its death throes. It was probably also a delayed reaction to the Reagan years, the formative period for many current comic book creators, when a more aggressive and militaristic mode prevailed.

Although Saddam Hussein was surely an evil dictator, that did not, automatically, justify the Iraq War. Like the nation, comic books grappled with the moral issues that the war raised. Philosophically there was a trade-off between what was right versus what was needed. The historian Ronald Takaki has discussed how the concept of the "rational" is used to categorize the actions and beliefs of Western people, while nonwhites and non-Europeans are instead depicted as "emotional."[45] This is an ipso facto justification of Western actions because even though non-Western villains may be cunning, they are still ruled by their emotions. For example, bin Laden was supposedly inflamed by attacks on Islam and by American cultural domination, and he attacked symbols of the United States in the hope that Americans would cower in fear. This interpretation, combined with pictures of the relatively small numbers of Arabs and Muslims who celebrated the attack in the streets, supposedly proved their uncontrolled, emotional nature. Applying Takaki's thesis, the United States can dismiss its terrorist enemies as "emotional" animals, who wish to die in the name of Allah. This made it much easier for people in the West to ignore their own emotional responses and minimize any rational motivation the terrorists might have. After all, one cannot "reason" with those people.

These one-sided views were not shared by everyone. In the period from 9/11 to the start of the invasion of Iraq, the war comic came back into vogue, but many did not put the traditional emphasis on defeating the enemy, focusing instead on the futility of war and on the human condition more generally. The writer most responsible for reimagining war comics was Garth Ennis, who generally based his scripts on real events (as mentioned in chapter 5). Ennis worked with several collaborators for series of one-shot stories, under the general title *War Story*. These hit shelves in the late fall of 2001, when comparisons of the attacks on the World Trade Center and Pentagon to Pearl Harbor were at their height. Yet many news outlets debated whether to release items that might further inflame passions or cause stress.[46]

All eight stories returned to World War II subjects. Despite this, they did not make obvious comparisons to the present. One of the first stories was about the "Screaming Eagles," a mythical company of the vaunted 101st Airborne Division (which itself is known as the "Screaming Eagles" and was the parent unit of the company on which the HBO television miniseries *Band of Brothers* was based).[47] Like in the miniseries, Ennis looked at the violence that the unit endures. A replacement lieutenant, trying to impress senior staff, orders a scouting party of D-Day veterans to reconnoiter a nearby German castle, which might be used as a command center for the American general. His sergeant sees the mission as needless and wasteful, while the soldiers take a break from their mission. They loot a liquor cellar, eat food originally intended for the German staff, and vandalize abandoned German staff cars. They also take liberties with local German women, in strict violation of the official "no fraternization" policy. While reprimanded, they maintain the esprit de corps of the elite 101st Airborne.[48] In practice, their primary allegiance is to the men with whom they fight, rather than to the supposedly higher values of honor and country. This theme of comradeship is emphasized by many accounts of how soldiers actually behave in combat, whether in World War II or in Afghanistan.

Ennis went even further with the next two stories in the series. *Johann's Tiger* concerns the crew of a German King Tiger tank at the end stages of World War II. Like the *Haunted Tank* series, also from DC, it explores the relationships of the crew members, but the story takes far darker turns. The commander, Johann, haunted by his actions during the massacre of Russian civilians and POWs on the eastern front, wants to die. At the story's close, still alive, he must deal with his guilt. In fact, his main goal is to find American lines and surrender to an enemy that would treat them better than the Russians would: he and his crew might easily die in Russian hands. Despite this desperate situation, the crew continues to do their duty, even knowing Germany has lost the war. The story also describes the brutal reprisals conducted by the German Feldpolizei (Fepos) who, by the last days of the war, were mostly fanatical SS members. The Fepos operated much like the Russian NKVD "holding units," either spurring troops forward to fight or shooting deserters before a rout might ensue. By the story's end, all the crew members except for Johann are dead. He is captured by the "Amis" (Americans), but he continues to carry the guilt for his actions in Russia.[49] Such feelings were not confined to the Germans. Many military personnel are guilt-ridden about comrades they could not protect and even for causing the deaths of enemy soldiers—sometimes for the rest of their lives. These feelings can trigger post-traumatic stress disorder (PTSD), even when the actions were unavoidable at the time.[50]

D-Day Dodgers, one of the most damning issues of *War Stories,* described the actions of the Antrim Rifles, a fictional Irish unit of the British Army. The government of the Republic of Ireland was neutral in World War II, although Northern Ireland, where Ennis is from, being part of the United Kingdom, contributed troops to the British cause. (Volunteers from the republic served as well.)[51] The story, set during the Italian campaign, juxtaposes a newly arrived lieutenant with a cynical captain who has seen too many of his men die in combat. The issue's title refers to Lady Astor, a member of the British House of Lords, who famously remarked that the soldiers in Italy were dodging the wider war. While many considered Italy a "sideshow" compared to the landings in France, for the Allied troops who fought and died there the accusation was a horrible insult. As the story ends, the men—having fought and died in a bitter battle—are shown singing a song popular among the troops that, describes their travails as a "holiday."[52]

An important part of the dialogue concerns the aerial bombing of people who may or may not be combatants. The distinction meant nothing to bin Laden, who considered anyone in America part of the *Dar al-Harb* and thus an enemy of Islam.[53] The story shows the conflict between those on the ground who must fight and those far removed from the fighting who cannot understand the reasons for their actions. Captain Harris, the commanding officer, is disheartened by the constant bloodshed and derogatory comments made by politicians back home. He relates how the war even brought his family to blows: a cousin of his asked another cousin in the Royal Air Force (RAF), later killed in a bombing raid, how "they" could bomb innocent German civilians. "That's what they think of us Ross," Harris says, "behind all of the flag-waving when this war they're so fond goes beyond the cartoon version. If we do it well we're butchers. If we mess it up we're cowards."[54] Given the arguments about the retaliation for 9/11 in Afghanistan, this mirrored the larger world of contemporary politics. It also shows how comics can subtly influence readers' political opinions simply by showing what soldiers actually have to endure and contemplate.

Ennis tried to see the war from multiple angles and lesser-known perspectives. One issue, *War Stories: Condors,* is set in the Spanish Civil War not long after the bombing of Guernica. A somewhat contrived setup allows a disparate group of characters to address the issues. Four men, stuck in a bomb crater, discuss their lives up to that point. A Luftwaffe pilot sees the military as a route to adventure and escape from the poverty of Germany. A British Socialist heeds the call to fight against the Fascists. An Irishman wants the British to leave Ireland and sees Fascism as his best bet. Finally, a Spaniard is angry with all of them for using his country as a dumping ground for violence. A postscript, describing their lives after the events of the story, shows how the Spanish Civil War affected their idealism. The German dies in Russia, the Irishman blows himself up in the mid-1950s, the Spaniard runs a café catering to German tourists, and the British Socialist is beaten to death by hooligans in Thatcher-era Britain.[55] The Spanish Civil War was not a new story line for European comic books. *Black Order Brigade,* written by Enki Bilal (a Serb), tells the story of Spanish Communist veterans who reunite to fight injustice in 1970s Spain.[56]

Ennis also depicted the horrors of the war in the Arctic Circle, with two stories about Allied convoy runs taking war materials to the Russian port of Murmansk. One story, *CAM Ships,* discusses the pilots who flew escort duty on these convoy runs. Because of the severe conditions and extreme distances, the planes could not fly from airbases or regular aircraft carriers but instead took off from merchant ships fitted with catapult aircraft launchers. The pilots defend the convoys—mostly against Luftwaffe bombers based in Norway or occupied Russia—then fly on to Soviet airstrips. The story's protagonist has inadvertently shot at a superior officer during the Battle of Britain, a mistake that gets him reassigned to flight duty with the convoys. This posting is not glamorous and has none of the perks of flying over Britain, but the protection these fighters give to the convoys heading for Russia is essential to their success. The theme here is that everyone has a role to play in the war and that each is vital to the overall war effort.[57]

Finally, Ennis' signature style was to recreate famous characters and put them into new, more humanistic, settings. As *War Stories* started, Ennis also updated *Enemy Ace*, originally created by Bob Kanigher and Joe Kubert. The new two-issue miniseries *Enemy Ace: War in Heaven* returned Baron von Hammer—still the master of the dogfight he was in World War I—to the Luftwaffe, despite his hatred of Nazism, Hitler, and Goering in particular.[58] The story describes how the Germans initially swat the swarms of Soviet pilots from the skies. However, in the middle of the story, von Hammer is shot down and crashes near Leningrad. His own side picks him up, but his escort is killed. Only after his faithful wolf companion saves him from Russian partisans does he make it back to his own lines. On the way, he sees horrible things on the Russian front, including cannibalism.[59] Such events were rarely depicted in comic books, except during the underground comix era and then only for a much smaller readership. These comics appeared shortly after the events of 9/11, and while not directly connected to the attacks on the World Trade Center, the stories reflect the heightened anxieties of that time.

Ennis was not above poking fun at the war comic genre. While writing the *War Stories,* he was also working on an antithetical project. *Adventures in the Rifle Brigade* completely repurposes the standard commando squad of World War II literature, film, and comics. The stories follow the adventures of a small group of British soldiers—the typically heterogeneous bunch of stereotypes, with some modern twists. These include their commander, Captain Darcy, with his gentlemanly ideas of combat; Lieutenant Milk, a homosexual in love with the captain; Piper, a Scotsman who uses his bagpipes as a form of weaponry or torture; Sergeant Crumb, a hulking behemoth with incredible strength and the mind of a child; and two Americans—Hank the Yank, a wizard with explosives, and Corporal Geezer, a ruffian from the lower East Side, known for his skill with a blade.[60]

The series takes many of the jokes and myths of the war and spins them in odd and humorous ways. There are also references to more recent pop culture—such as an American boxer who looks and talks like Rocky Balboa. Another story compares Hitler's missing testicle to the Holy Grail. The enemies in *Rifle Brigade,* especially the main female character, the sadistic yet beautiful Gerta Gasch, harken back to 1970s exploitation movies such as *Elsa the She-Wolf of the SS.*[61] By the end of the series, Ennis, who dedicated it to the writers of 1950s British war comics, takes virtually every major war theme and warps it into something perverse.

After his work on the Yugoslavian and Palestinian conflicts, Joe Sacco was another comic book creator who returned to the World War II themes in the aftermath of 9/11. Another historical work, *Notes from a Defeatist,* was more personal and self-reflective, although he tells his personal recollections in a journalistic tone. One vignette, titled "When Good Bombs Happen to Bad People," describes the extensive, and even excessive, destruction of German cities caused by the Allied bombing campaign personified by Air Chief Marshal Arthur "Bomber" Harris of the RAF.[62] Another story, "More Women, More Children, More Quickly," tells his mother's recollections of the bombings she endured on the island of Malta during World War II.[63] The section "How I Loved the War" is about his obsessive watching of television news during the Gulf War.[64] In the final vignette, Sacco takes a step back to examine the historical development of the British Empire and the Industrial Revolution.[65]

Antiwar Comic Books Just Before the Iraq Invasion

In March 2003, just before the United States launched its first missile attacks against Iraq, Marvel sent a new comic title to press. Titled *411,* its premise was to debunk stereotypes and embrace the nonviolent traditions of Mahatma Gandhi and Martin Luther King Jr. As propaganda, the comic is interesting for doing something that earlier war comics had not: showing all characters, including enemies of the United States, as essentially equal members of humanity. The writers of *411* wanted to show that people feel the same way in all cultures and are usually willing to make sacrifices to achieve peaceful coexistence.[66] The series focused on the hard decision to *not use* violence, regardless of the cause or provocation. The vignettes from the book contain radically different depictions of Israelis, Irish Catholics, and the mujahideen of Afghanistan—and how three different individuals from these "tribes" oppose the cycle of violence that is destroying their families and communities.

One story describes an Afghan member of the mujahideen, whose commitment to fighting has caused him to miss much of his own childhood, as well as his son's. In the end, the soldier gives up the "honor" of fighting and instead volunteers to become a deminer, a man who—at great personal risk—goes into the fields to remove the mines that much of Afghanistan's landscape.[67] These comic books mean to show how problems can be worked out using nonviolence and how standing for an ideal can be as brave as facing a gun.

Another *411* story tells the true story of Jeannette Rankin, the first woman elected to the House of Representatives and a committed pacifist. She was also the only member of Congress to vote against American entry into both world wars and the single member who voted against entering World War II. It tells the story of her decision to stick to her principles despite the chance that she might lose her seat and even invite attacks on her life. The story, while only twelve pages, is a rare example of how the comics can present alternative forms of conflict resolution to their readers.⁶⁸ It was a bold experiment at a time when the war drums were already beating for the invasion of Iraq. It is interesting that it was published by Marvel, the same company that produced *Captain America,* the most patriotic of all propaganda comics.

Written and illustrated by Ryan Inzana, a relative newcomer to the comic book industry, the graphic novel *Johnny Jihad* used recent events and fears of a Muslim attack on the United States as the basis for its story. In the fall of 2001, a young American named John Walker Lindh was captured along with several dozen Taliban warriors in Afghanistan. His story became fodder for the American news media when they learned that he had previously converted to Islam and relocated to Afghanistan to join the mujahideen. (The events also brought to light various radical Islamic groups that seemed to have operations in the United States.) Unlike most of the people who the U.S. government has classified as "enemy combatants" and held indefinitely, Lindh is an American citizen, and he was tried in federal court and given a prison sentence of twenty years. Many Americans saw this decision as an insult to those who died in the 9/11 attacks (although later on, when emotions had cooled, prisoners with similar offenses were given far lighter sentences). In Inzana's introduction, he cites many of his news sources, including the story of a Muslim leader who had immigrated to the United States seeking political asylum yet nevertheless called for the country's destruction.⁶⁹ He also writes about how some people with evil purposes manipulate the idealism of young Muslims.

The attacks on September 11, 2001, were immediately compared to Pearl Harbor—and with good reason. The two attacks were on American soil, elicited strong responses of patriotism and retribution, and focused the American population on a specific enemy. Like Hitler, Hirohito, and Mussolini during World War II, bin Laden became a readily identifiable villain and the representative face of terrorism due to his media exposure on Al Jazeera and the Internet. Despite considerable anti-Muslim and anti-Arab sentiments in the wake of the attacks, the public as a whole did not necessarily lump together *all* Muslims and Arabs as terrorists (just as distinctions had usually been made to differentiate Germans and Nazis). The Japanese had not fared as well and were generally painted with the same racist brush portraying them as madmen bent on world domination. Political cynicism, however, soon replaced the unity of 9/11, as many people grew increasingly skeptical about the putative reasons for invading Iraq.

7

Comics and the Soul of Combat (2003–10)

The Beast has many heads, and on its heads are written names:
Lockheed, Bell, Monsanto, Dow, Grumman, Colt and many more.
And they are very, very hungry. So the Great Beast must be fed:
and every generation, our country goes to war to do just that. A war for
war's sake, usually. And one that could have been avoided.

—GARTH ENNIS, *Born #4*

In 2003 the United States embarked on the Iraq War, or "Operation Iraqi Freedom," the American military's name for the invasion. Its stated objectives were to remove Saddam Hussein, end his protection for terrorists, and destroy or confiscate his WMDs. As the occupation progressed, critics called it one of opportunity rather than necessity, citing the apparent lack of significant terrorist support by Saddam's government, the destruction of virtually all WMDs many years previously, and the indefinite timeline for withdrawal. Comic books reflected these tensions, and the war was the subject of various contemporary comics. Some aimed at realism, depicting the combat life for American troops in Iraq. Others drew parallels between the war and World War II, a classic historical theme in comic books, just as 9/11 was compared to Pearl Harbor. By contrast, some comics were openly critical of the war, depicting its harsh reality without the putative moral veneer. Contemporary comic books offered a wide range of perspectives on the invasion of Iraq, reflecting the cultural tensions and political opposition surrounding the war, itself.

Karl Zinsmeister's *Combat Zone* gives a generally positive portrayal of the Iraq War. Zinsmeister, a historian and field reporter, based the comic on his real-life account of combat, *Boots on the Ground*.[1] *Combat Zone* intended to bridge the gap between his histories and the popular graphic novel format. It was originally slated for release as a five-issue miniseries from Marvel. After repeated delays, with rumors of both censorship and lack of interest, the book came out as a one-volume trade paperback instead. Its formulaic story line relies heavily on depictions of American forces as heroes and liberators, drawing on comic clichés familiar to readers and moviegoers. The U.S. Army team is ethnically and racially diverse, bound by honor, and working to liberate an oppressed people. The use of these themes immediately evokes World War II–era comics and movies, as does the role of religious faith in combat; when an Iraqi soldier is killed, an American soldier responds, "God rest his soul anyway." The Iraqi militiamen, in contrast, are portrayed as dishonorable and brutal—hiding among civilians and even using them as human shields. The comic closes with a display of American honor, as a soldier rolls onto a grenade and sacrifices himself for the team. *Combat Zone* depicts the Iraqi invasion as an honorable quest, with an implicit message of American moral superiority. While boldly designed, its sales fell short of expectations.

As the Iraq War continued, photographs of American torture of Iraqi prisoners at Abu Ghraib Prison became public. When news media ran the images, critics openly doubted the morality of the American forces, something previously assumed even by many critics of the war. While some officials considered the treatment of prisoners in contravention of the Geneva Conventions' guidelines, others defended it on the legally dubious basis that Saddam and his forces had done far worse to American prisoners and his political opponents. Certain comic books were highly critical on this issue. Kyle Baker's *Special Forces*, for instance, portrays the actions of the American military as morally suspect, even dishonorable. The comic addresses such issues as prison torture, questionable recruitment procedures, and the policy of stop-loss—preventing soldiers from leaving the military once their enlistment period has technically ended. *Special Forces* introduces three main characters: a felonious woman, an autistic youth, and a military recruiter. In the story, terrorists use a wide range of media outlets—online chat rooms, webcasts, websites, Al Jazeera (at least indirectly)—to push their political agenda, as does al-Qaeda. At the end of the first issue, Baker examines the real-life story of an autistic boy recruited to fight for the U.S. Army. When ABC News made the story public, the Army annulled the enlistment.

Even Baker's cover art alone for the *Special Forces* series criticized aspects of the American military. For example, the cover of one issue shows a female soldier pointing a gun barrel through the exploded head of Mickey Mouse. Another shows the Abu Ghraib "pyramid of prisoners" photo, to which a nonchalant female soldier reacts, "What?"—suggesting the images are insignificant or unimportant. As with many comic book writers, Baker's comics express his displeasure with the Bush administration and the war in Iraq.[2] This is not surprising, as he has a history of criticizing conservative tactics, especially regarding race. His *Truth: Red, White, and Black* contains an alternative story line about an African American Captain America.[3] As noted in chapter 6, Baker tied this story to the atrocious Tuskegee experiments.

Writer and artist Joe Sacco offered a highly realistic, journalistic approach to combat in Iraq. Unlike Zinsmeister, who also worked as a reporter but wrote idealistic comic books, Sacco aims at true "comic journalism."

For the Iraq War, the British *Guardian* newspaper contracted Sacco to report on what he witnessed while embedded with U.S. forces, which led to "Complacency Kills," an eight-page comic about the lives of ground troops.[4] (He also spent time with the U.S. Marines near Haditha, joining them on patrols.) In it Sacco shows the soldiers as real people who sometimes doubt their mission and the role of the United States in Iraq, nor are they always gung-ho for battle. Sacco also shows how encounters with Iraqi citizens often changes attitudes about the war. Where other authors might lean toward satire— Ted Rall's *To Afghanistan and Back*, for example, discussed in chapter 6— Sacco remains realistic, detailed, and relatively objective. Sacco focuses on the experiences of ordinary soldiers in Iraq, mostly avoiding overt political or social commentary. He shows Marines questioning the rules of engagement and the broader purpose of their mission, and he does not shy away from depicting soldiers seriously injured in combat. Rather than developing a tightly constructed narrative like those of *Combat Zone* or *Special Forces*, Sacco's vignettes show the varying perspectives of a wide range of soldiers in combat. His decision to draw the comic in black and white only heightened its gritty psychological realism.

Sacco's follow-up to "Complacency Kills" was a work about Iraqi prisoners, "Trauma on Loan." Also published in the *Guardian* and based on the story of two Iraqi nationals imprisoned and tortured by American military personnel, it painted a far darker picture about the conduct of the war.[5] Was the United States ready and willing to do what was necessary to win—especially in a war where the enemy was unwilling to play by traditional rules of combat (such as wearing uniforms or attacking only military targets)? The "Trauma on Loan" piece was significant because it highlighted the use of torture and the detention of potential enemies of the new Iraqi government.

"Trauma on Loan" also paralleled a fictional comic book that came out at the same time, *Pride of Baghdad*, written by acclaimed writer Brian K. Vaughn. Both reflected the uncertainties of a post-Saddam Iraq. For Sacco the crux of the issue was that the American military could be as cruel as Saddam's Ba'ath Party. In Vaughn's comic, the emphasis is on something quite different: an animal's view about the postwar world. The abuse of the lions in the Baghdad Zoo, featured by various news media outlets early in the war, has become one of the symbols of the war. *Pride of Baghdad* begins with the inadvertent American bombing of the zoo, and the lions' escape and slaughter several days later. The lions were familiar on the Iraqi news, as Saddam and his sons Uday and Qusay sometimes kept them as pets. (In "Trauma on Loan," Sacco discusses how Uday would use them to terrorize his political opponents, psychologically as well as physically.) Reports like these helped to justify removing Saddam and his family from power, but it was the animals' "discussion" of current events that most appealed to readers.[6]

Tom Waltz's graphic novel *Finding Peace* also depicts combat in a realistic way, but the book's artwork makes it different from most others.[7] The drawing is rougher, done in sepia tones, giving it the appearance of scenes sketched on the battlefield. It does not discuss the morality of the war but looks unnervingly into the souls of combatants. In his foreword, professor of military history William Forstchen suggests that the comic has a "feel" many might recognize from PTSD, based on his studies of soldiers and combat. The stories are sparsely worded, relying primarily on the illustrations and the limited use of color to convey mood. The stories, which at first appear to be singular vignettes, are actually components of a larger narrative, told in a nonlinear sequence. By the end of the book, the reader understands how everything fits together in the "big picture."

David Axe, who served as an embedded reporter in Iraq, described his first-hand experience of the fighting in another graphic novel, *War Fix*. It depicts the emotional reactions of the soldiers to what they have witnessed and how his own reactions as a combat reporter affect his personal life back in the United States.[8] The title came from an encounter between Axe and a Scottish reporter diagnosed by an American military psychiatrist as a "war junkie." The doctor explained that the reporter literally "got high" from the extra adrenaline the body produces during combat. This is a widespread concept. In *Al Qaeda's Great Escape* journalist Philip Smucker explains the precise physiological mechanisms, and how their effects continue to draw reporters back into dangerous firefights.[9]

No Enemy but Peace is a one-shot comic based on real events, in the tradition of *Combat Zone*. The small publishing house Machine Gun Bob Productions wanted to tell the story of actual soldiers in combat, solely from the perspective of the soldiers and avoiding the conflict's political and moral issues. *No Enemy but Peace* describes a real Marine sergeant, Marco Martinez, involved in the fighting in Al-Tarmiya, Iraq, during 2003. Drawn in black and white, the story resembles an old newsreel more than it does the glossy approach of *Combat Zone*. This comic book has the distinction of being by a former Marine, Richard C. Meyer. As writer and assistant artist Meyer explains in the inside front cover, it is a condensed version of a graphic novel to appear later, the first of a series of comics about Marine exploits, starting with the Chosin Reservoir battle during the Korean War.[10] The theme is of ordinary men doing extraordinary things. This is clear from the comic's first line, when a soldier says (to himself), "You are not a superhero. Schwarzenegger would never play you in a movie."[11]

The World War II Comic, Revisited

As already noted, for some comic book creators during the Iraq War, it was more attractive to return to familiar battlefields. However, these new World War II stories reflect contemporary coverage of Iraq—with its regular reports of combat losses, shifting boundaries for legitimate combat targets, and the involvement of civilians—by incorporating (retroactively) greater realism. One example is *Team Zero*, written by Chuck Dixon, who has worked in the comic book field since the 1970s. The six-issue miniseries employs the tested format of a squad-sized unit on a seemingly impossible mission. The plot concerns their attack on the German missile facility of Peenemünde in the final weeks of the war. The team members are chosen for their specialized abilities, but their behavior belies more sinister psychological demons. They exhibit their true colors as the mission goes horribly wrong (missed parachute landing, killed extraction team, wrecked glider). As they contain the Germans, a new threat to the American troops becomes evident: Soviet troops. (The premise here is that the Russians are willing to use force to obtain the Germans' rocketry secrets.)[12]

Unlike Hollywood's World War II movies—in which every member of a heterogeneous team is noble, fights honestly, and shares the same universal values—*Team Zero*'s characters are decidedly unheroic. Their various atrocities include racism, rape, the shooting of innocents, and the attempted murder of team members. The entire squad, save one, fails to survive the end of the war. The miniseries questions whether such sacrifices are necessary.

Team Zero was only the first of several war-themed comics that came out after the Iraq War's initial phase. Others took traditional World War II characters, such as Sgt. Rock, and made them grapple with new sets of problems. The issue of abuse during wartime, seldom mentioned in older comic books or films, was explored more substantially in recent comics. Some existing characters, who had never conducted themselves in a savage or brutal manner, were reenvisioned in this manner. The contemporary abuses reported by the news media led many to question the actions of American military personnel, a concern that carried over to war-themed comic books.

In this changed environment, comic book legend Joe Kubert resurrected Sgt. Rock, the famous 1960s character, in two different miniseries. In *Sgt. Rock: Between Hell and a Hard Place*, Kubert worked with writer Brian Azzarello to portray the grizzled veterans of the fictitious Easy Company fighting in the Hürtgen Forest in the fall of 1944. Some German prisoners are killed during a firefight. Since the Germans have their hands tied and a few members of Easy Company are missing, suspicion falls on the Americans for killing their adversaries.

Nevertheless, the new Sgt. Rock series pulled some punches. For instance, American soldiers' cold-blooded killing of unarmed prisoners, as documented in Stephen Ambrose's *Citizen Soldiers* (among other books), is very disturbing to most readers.[13] It breaches most Americans' idealistic beliefs about the blamelessness of their troops, compared to the brutality of our enemies. After all, the "good guys" do not kill needlessly. Therefore, Sgt. Rock presents a more acceptable version of events when it is revealed that a Nazi officer has killed his own men after they surrendered, exonerating the supporting members of Easy Company who had been originally implicated as the killers.

Several rungs down on the ladder of moral concerns, this series utilizes far more swearing than earlier incarnations. The new Sgt. Rock came out under the Vertigo imprint, DC's adult line, allowing Azzarello to use coarser language to achieve a more "realistic" feel. When asked about the story's language, Kubert replied that, while stronger than he was used to, it was appropriate for such grim subject matter.[14] Azzarello is a mainstay of Vertigo Comics, but some critics from its parent company, family-friendly DC, consider his style too gritty for Sgt. Rock. They wondered if Rock should swear or act in a way that contradicts his "good guy" persona, especially as the sergeant has long been a major DC character.

Rescuing Jews from Eastern Europe, specifically Latvia, was the premise of the second miniseries, *Sgt. Rock: The Prophecy.* In it Kubert explored the idea of using Easy Company to rescue a young Jewish man (seen by some as a sort of messiah or prophet). Its "what if" placement of American troops on the eastern front was quite novel. As in other *Sgt. Rock* story lines, the core of the squad—Rock, Ice Cream Soldier, Bulldozer, Wildman, and Little Sure Shot—survives the fighting, while the company's more peripheral members meet untimely ends. This permits the graphic and grisly depiction of the loss of team members. Nevertheless, this device resembles television shows that introduce new characters only to quickly kill them. This robs the deaths of most of their potential emotional impact.[15]

Sgt. Rock was revisited with yet another approach in *Sgt. Rock: The Lost Battalion*, written and drawn by Billy Tucci, a former soldier.[16] He based it on his own research into several military actions in France after the Allied invasions of 1944. The six-issue miniseries used the familiar squad of Sgt. Rock, but with a considerable twist. Tucci first briefly describes Rock's time with the First Infantry Division on D-Day.[17] As the story evolves, Easy Company replaces struggling units; later it is attached to the Thirty-Sixth Infantry Division, which helps encircle Axis forces in southern France during October of 1944. Nevertheless, the "T-patchers" (for the *T* on their shoulder patches, representing Texas) eventually get into trouble, until rescued by members of the 100th Battalion of the 442nd Regimental Combat Team (exclusively comprising Asian Americans soldiers, mostly of Japanese descent).

The story is innovative, with Tucci assigning Rock to a real unit. (Rock being an everyman, his unit had never been identified before.) Tucci works in several references to World War II–era popular culture, including an Ernie Pyle–style reporter for *Stars and Stripes.* In one section, he shows an American soldier playing a harmonica while the surrounding Germans sing "Lili Marlene," a scenario made famous by Bill Mauldin; in fact, Tucci uses Mauldin's work as the inspiration for many details of *Sgt. Rock: Lost Battalion*."[18] He also works into the story several drawings of real soldiers, such as Audie Murphy and James Kotuba (an actual medic in the 442nd).[19] Finally, the narrative and artwork are quite realistic as far as weapons and units are concerned, creating a degree of accuracy unusual in comics.

The reinvention of Marvel's Sgt. Nicholas Fury, created by Stan Lee and Jack Kirby in the early 1960s, shows a bit more daring than Sgt. Rock's rebirth. Both characters are World War II combatants, and Fury's Howling Commandos are a counterpart to Rock's Easy Company, but it included an African American from the beginning of the series. The unit is more of an "ideal" team, with several members from immigrant groups—Italians, Jews, and Irish—often not very well educated. In theory, this showed progress in unit cohesion and cooperation, epitomizing the United Nations themes of World War II. Readers could relate to the idea of the United States with different ethnic, racial, and social groups, but the reality was often much different, with military units far more segregated.

With Fury's origins in mind, Garth Ennis once again steered the character into uncharted waters. The themes that Ennis addressed in the new version were unlike anything imagined in the 1960s original. Instead, Fury reflects on how politicians and the general population in 2003 thought about the use of American power in the Iraqi desert. The six-issue miniseries *Fury: Peacemaker* starts with the U.S. Army fighting in North Africa, its first serious challenge in the Western Hemisphere during World War II. Once the fighting begins, the leadership's promises—that tanks, aircraft, and weapons will win the day for the Americans and the troops will come home soon—fall apart. Within the first few pages, Fury points a gun at his immediate superior's head, barking that unless the lieutenant shows some leadership, Fury will kill him. In the next panel, Fury remarks that the lieutenant is dead.[20] In fact, fratricide of officers was not nearly as prevalent in World War II as it became later, but it establishes a cynical and skeptical tone from the get-go. Fury is the antithesis of a superhero here: he even consorts with "trashy women." Rather, he embodies Rudyard Kipling's idea of the "rough man," ready to do violence for the greater good or at least what is seen as the greater good.[21] The arguments between Fury and his lieutenant in the African desert of World War II could easily be mistaken for predictions made about the Iraqi campaign in 2003: the war would be quick, the resistance weak and quickly subdued, and the result a victory for the world.

Ennis uses his subversive hero to personalize the issues of violence and questionable action. Nevertheless, his characters, which are often more like antiheroes, will do heroic things, but only for personal reasons. Rather than seeking to convert the reader to their viewpoint, they are tortured instead by their own inner demons. As noted previously, compared to earlier characters Fury and the Punisher give a far more sinister look into a soldier's psychology. Ennis demonstrates this method in *Punisher: Born* (Marvel) and *Enemy Ace: War in Heaven* and the *Unknown Soldier* (both long-running DC series). In *Born,* the adrenaline rush of combat, much like the rush of a drug user, becomes the focus of Frank Castle's life. His third tour of duty in Vietnam takes him to the Cambodian border, where he seems to be the only one trying to hold back the Communists. Castle is willing to do anything, including fratricide, to silence anyone he believes to be wrong or opposed to his personal war. He lures a general who dislikes him (and threatens to send him home) to a zone where snipers operate. While Castle does not pull the trigger himself, he is definitely responsible for the general's death: he actually covers the sign warning about snipers.[22]

Later in the series, he toys with the idea of fragging the camp's commanding officer, who is trying to avoid combat during the few weeks before the entire unit is shipped to the rear. Castle sees this as weak. Instead of merely riding it out until they can go home, he believes that they should take the war to the Vietcong. Punish the enemy enough, he feels, and they will lose their will to live and to fight. While his methods are subversive and he operates outside of "proper" U.S. military methods, he does have moral beliefs about what is right for American society. To Castle, the purpose of war is to punish the bad, and killing is necessary as long as the war is won and the enemy punished. He believes in the American ideal, but thinks that the country's leadership and institutions have become corrupt.[23]

Castle's moral attitudes, while demonstrated in the context of World War II, resemble those of many people regarding Iraq. Politicians stated that the war's purpose was to rid Iraq of an increasingly dangerous tyrant who possessed weapons of mass destruction. However, after the occupation it became obvious that Saddam's Iraq was no longer much of a danger. This led many Americans to doubt the connection or relevance of interventions anywhere. Ennis focused on the fact that American government officials got away with lying, while American servicemen died in foreign wars. His depicted the abuses in combat to show that war is much more violent and chaotic than the sanitized form presented on television. Castle tends to "solve" all moral problems with deadly force. When a Marine in his unit rapes a female VC, Castle shoots the woman.[24] She is an enemy, and he cannot let her escape, so he releases her from pain in the only way he knows: with a bullet. Later on, Castle drowns the rapist.[25] In his mind at least, these are necessary acts. In effect, he conducts his own field court-martial of the soldier, in which he acts as judge, jury, and executioner.

While others use heroin to escape from the war, Castle is addicted to combat, which also increases the terror he feels from his inner demons. This reexamination of the imagery of violence and the necessity of war has drawn many readers to Ennis' work. At the end of the series, Castle makes a deal with an evil entity—either the Devil or the malevolence within himself—so he can continue to kill and punish the morally unfit.[26] The comparison between doing what was right and doing what was *seen* as right leads to an interesting turn of events. It helps explain the argument that "we would have won the Vietnam War if only the politicians had let the military fight it, rather than trying to fight it in Washington, D.C." Regardless of how war is started, as Ennis notes in this chapter's epigraph, the "beasts" (corporations) that the government serves ultimately benefit. When Ennis' comics were published, the major news media stories concerned the no-bid contracts that the U.S. government gave to such companies as Halliburton. The opening comments are somewhat prophetic; wars—whether in Vietnam or Iraq—are not really about democracy or freedom, but the profit of favored American companies that benefit from wartime exigencies and no-bid contracts.[27]

As he grew up during "the Troubles" in Northern Ireland, Ennis saw his share of violence, and its moral ambiguity was not lost on him. Even his non-war comics have a political bent. His 2002 work *The Pro*, with Amanda Conner as artist, took the superhero genre to task. The premise is a prostitute with superpowers, who nonetheless retains her "street smarts." After an incident in which her team is publicly shamed, the Pro asks its members to seriously consider their roles in society. The regular superheroes mention the need for morality and due process of law. The hooker invokes the need for realpolitik and vengeance (the last a time-honored tradition in war and patriotic comics). Her speech to the team says it all:

> You can't fight the real bastards and expect to get away scot-free. You can't make real changes unless you're prepared to piss off and hurt a lot of people. You goofs, whatever it is you think you're doing, you are of no use to this world at all. You are a lousy example to people, you are not the kind of heroes we need, and you have nothing to do with the reality they have to live in. Because this is a harsh fucking place, and it is fucked to give people the idea that someone is coming to the rescue.[28]

She asks the superhero team where they were when the planes slammed into the World Trade Center. None has a good answer. She then schools them about idealism:

> We don't need you. What we need are guys with balls to drop bombs on schools and hospitals because that's where these assholes like to hide. Or people who've got it in them to sneak up behind the motherfuckers and cut every throat in sight.

Or just some poor slob who'll run into a falling building knowing he's going to
die, but willing to throw it all away anyway. We need people who don't know shit
about hope.[29]

The Pro ultimately dies saving New York from a nuclear bomb smuggled in
by Islamic terrorists. The story captures the sense of helplessness that fuels
revenge fantasies, embodied by superheroes with no compunction about using
violence to secure peace and stability.

Ennis reinforces the fact that many innocent lives are always lost during
such interventions; people who do not anticipate this are naive. Since at least
the Gulf War, too many people have expected warfare to be clean. They think
modern "smart weapons" can target and kill only the guilty, while sparing
everyone else. This fantasy encourages them to seek immediate vengeance, but
they become squeamish when they see the results. This parallels the reports of
abuse by the American military against Iraqi citizens. The military countered
that soldiers are trained to be killers and not to maintain civil order like police.
When the military is used instead, violent incidents are inevitable. The Pro's
point is that if one wants war, people must be willing to do whatever it takes to
win (a common view in the post-Vietnam military).

Most comic book creators were against American intervention in Iraq and
distrusted the government's case for the invasion. Many thought President
George W. Bush was motivated by revenge against Saddam's assassination
plot against his father, former president George H. W. Bush. They also generally believed that helping American oil companies by taking direct control of Iraq's oil was an unstated reason for the invasion. The United States'
international mandate in Afghanistan to fight the Taliban and al-Qaeda terrorists was not enough to justify the Iraq invasion. Many saw the involvement in Afghanistan as morally justifiable, as the Taliban government had
given sanctuary to al-Qaeda operatives before and after the 9/11 attacks.
The government of Iraq, while a tyrannical nuisance, was not nearly as dangerous. Ennis followed up with *Born,* which built on a storyline that closed
out his run as a writer for the Punisher series. Titled "Valley Forge, Valley
Forge," it tells the story of a group of generals who want to use their military contacts to further their postmilitary business careers. These generals, who have never experienced combat, hire terrorists to destabilize areas
around the world. This makes their supposed expertise more valuable to
private security firms like Blackwater. In the end, the violence they espouse
comes back to haunt them.[30]

Another Ennis miniseries dealing with the immediate aftermath of 9/11
was *303,* in which he reimagines the events after the American bombing of
Afghanistan, involving the Soviet military in the action. The story centers on

a Spetsnaz (special forces) colonel coping with the realities of the post-Soviet world. While training with a Spetsnaz team in the Hindu Kush mountains of Afghanistan, he receives orders from Moscow to find a crashed American plane and secure whatever information is located in the wreck. SAS forces harass his team until an American special operations helicopter strafes and kills the British unit. Every member of the Soviet team dies, except him. Arriving alone, before the Americans arrive, he discovers a cache of secret documents aboard the plane. These explain a plot to fabricate a war in Afghanistan to precipitate U.S. intervention. The real motive for the war is building a pipeline linking the Russian oilfields to the Pakistani coast, so American interests can profit. At this point, he takes up a British Lee Enfield .303-caliber rifle—hence the title—which he uses to enforce his own moral code, assassinating the people responsible. In an interview concerning the miniseries, Ennis noted that the writing reflects his fears that events had overtaken people, making war inevitable.[31]

Antarctic Press, the current leader in historically themed comic books, has also released several comics that use historical events as evidence to justify war or at least vilify the enemy (directly or by association). A good example is Ted Nomura's series *Dictators of the Twentieth Century*. The first four issues deal with the life of Adolf Hitler.[32] Nomura's style is heavily influenced by the expressionistic style of Japanese manga comic books. Nomura researched his topic well, and Hitler's life is well documented.[33] Nomura's description of Hitler gives a human feel to the historical figure, and some readers found the portrayal of Hitler as a tormented person with good qualities as morally equivocal. He followed up the series with a similar treatment of Saddam.[34] As with the Hitler series, Nomura spends much of the first issue explaining the conditions that led to the dictator's rise. There are only two Saddam issues, and there is not as much artwork as in the Hitler series, especially in the second part, *Saddam Hussein—The Fall*.[35] The *Dictators* series was not reflexively prowar, but Nomura was implicitly making the case that Saddam was as dangerous as Hitler and that there is sometimes a need to remove truly evil people.[36]

Another Antarctic series was the two-part *Pearl Harbor*, which, like other titles from the publisher, is well researched (it even provides a bibliography). The book has a similar feel to the movie *Tora, Tora, Tora*; it presents both sides of the story without *taking* sides.[37] Nevertheless, the subject matter implies a comparison to 9/11. Even though Pearl Harbor was a clear defeat, a World War II story remained more satisfying in moral terms. The Nazis and Imperial Japan were clearly defined enemies, and the seriousness of their threat to the world was obvious. This was less true of Saddam and even bin Laden (if few would disagree that the latter was dedicated to hurting the United States).

Patriotic Themes and the Death of Captain America

Superhero figures serve as iconic political symbols, although usually in a broadly defined manner. Superman's dedication to "truth, justice, and the American way," for example, is not a very controversial platform. At the same time, these figures of fantasy sometimes act out "what if" scenarios that explore competing and sometimes unpopular ideas. For instance, the *Elseworld* series has taken famous DC characters and placed them into alternate realities. In *Superman: Red Son*, the scenario has Kal-El (who grows to become Superman) landing in the Ukraine in 1938, rather than the American Midwest. This version of Superman has a red cape and a gray uniform, with a large hammer and sickle replacing the original stylized S.[38]

The use of patriotic themes in comics does not mean automatically supporting the government in real life. Many in the news media expressed concerns about parts of the Patriot Act, as well as the crackdown on anti-war protests, and comic books reflected these concerns.[39] In his comic book *Liberality for All*, writer Mike Mackey has a character modeled on conservative pundit and radio talk-show host Sean Hannity comment on how a liberal American government has sold out the ideals of the United States. The series' premise was that if Al Gore had won the 2000 election, bin Laden would have been regarded as a "misguided person"—with legitimate reasons to say and do what he did—rather than as a terrorist. In the comic, by 2021 the United States has become part of a United Nations–controlled world government, and Afghan ambassador to the United Nations bin Laden attempts to defeat the United States with a nuclear weapon.

One of the letters to the creators in the first issue complains that comics have become too liberal. Another letter writer is very upset about the changes to Superman's costume in *Red Son*, which he believes shows how the "liberal media" have corrupted even American icons.[40] While the letter has nothing to do with *Liberality for All*, the comic provided a friendly platform for someone on the political right. Many comic book writers use their artwork as an outlet for their politics, fears, and even hopes. The politics that have permeated comic books show the vocal divisions in American society concerning the wars in Iraq and Afghanistan and the merits of American intervention. At minimum, this can lead people to think about current events; at most, it might cause them to reevaluate their convictions. Sales statistics show that historically themed comics and "visual histories" sell well, so there should be more issues of this type.[41]

Perhaps one of the most ambitious new comic books was the 2007 Marvel series *Civil War*. About battles between superheroes (it had nothing to do with the American Civil War), this "maxi-series" included several different comic book titles, and its characters looked at current news issues and politics (like the original Captain America series). The original story line, which involves almost every Marvel character, was the brainchild of Mark Millar and Steve McNiven. As the series evolved, however, almost all the writers and artists within the Marvel franchise also became involved.[42] The premise of the story line is, simply, that power corrupts.

In the opening story arc, a group of lesser superheroes, known as the New Warriors, attempt to apprehend some supervillains for the purpose of better television ratings. Nitro, one of the villains, causes a powerful explosion in Stamford, Connecticut, that kills over six hundred people, including many students from a nearby school.[43] This sets in motion the main story, about the Superhero Registration Act and its effects on the superhero community (through their registration and potential control or confinement by the government). Congress debates the role of superheroes as if they require regulation, like guns or driver's licenses. The act is pushed through following the Stamford incident, and any unregistered superheroes are considered in violation and subject to detention in the "negative zone."[44] This is a specially created prison in another dimension, with portals located in Rikers Island in New York City, in Los Angeles, and eventually in all fifty states.

The superheroes are split over the regulation. Supporters include Iron Man, Hank Pym, and Reed Richards of the Fantastic Four. Opponents, led by Captain America, believe that the government is acting in a totalitarian manner that recalls the governments he fought in World War II. As the fighting over registration increases, the heroes find themselves in an awkward situation. People attack superheroes in public. Some switch allegiances. The story line transparently refers to current events, as the Registration Act mirrors the Patriot Act, which passed with almost no opposition and virtually no debate, although it gave law enforcement unprecedented powers to spy on all citizens.

The *Civil War* story line mirrors the real arguments over the "Global War on Terror," about whether the price of security requires sacrificing one's civil rights, such as freedom of speech. While not matching the divisiveness of Vietnam, the policies of the American government after 9/11 created strong views on both sides, which comic books such as *Civil War* reflect. Readers often align their own stances with different opposing heroes. Does Captain America have to become an outlaw to defend the ideals his uniform represents? Does Iron Man, under the guise of controlling terrorism, need to restrict the freedoms that Americans regard as their birthright? When Captain America dies, does it also represent the death of "American values"? In the post-Communist world of the early twenty-first century, it became difficult to reconcile American unilateralism with the concept of an international community.

The story directly addresses moral issues that have been rare in comic books, especially in such a central way. Superheroes question themselves about why, and for what, they fight. Why should they use their powers to help others if they can be punished for it? Some, like Spider-Man, wonder if the public "outing" of their real identities might lead to threats against their families and friends. Most important, some ask what ultimately motivates them—helping society or their own glory? Cap pointedly asks himself this after part of New York City is reduced to rubble by a fight between pro- and antiregistration forces.[45] Others question the motives of supervillains now fighting on the side of law and order. As the war continues, Iron Man and Captain America both seek out assistance and information from such criminals as Wilson Fisk, aka Kingpin, who manipulates events to his own liking. Even characters like the Watcher, Dr. Strange, and the Punisher have a say, though they avoid taking sides.

The debate associated with the Superhero Registration Act relates to the wholesale imprisonment of other groups in American history. In fact, in one part of the series, two story lines are drawn in parallel, with the superhero fight running next to a discussion of Japanese Americans' internment during World War II. Only following a nasty battle between the two groups in downtown Manhattan, leading to the destruction of several blocks like 9/11 had, does Captain America realize that the toll of such fighting over the Superhero Registration Act is not worth the cost. He turns himself in to the authorities, only to be assassinated by Crossbones on his way to trial.

Results of the civil war within the Marvel universe include Tony Stark's rise to command SHIELD; the Fifty State Initiative, in which each state gets its own superhero team; and, most pointedly, the assassination of Captain America. That event leads to a deeper exploration of Cap's story line, in which presidential elections are manipulated by groups controlled by the infamous Red Skull, creating unrest and chaos. In reality, Captain America's death was reported in many news sources as if he were a major real-life hero. The *New York Times*, for instance, ran the story under the headline "Captain America Is Dead; National Hero since 1941."[46] Cap's cocreator, Joe Simon, commented, "It's a hell of a time for him to go, we really need him now."[47]

Because the story arc of the *Civil War* series is so wide and continues over many different comic book titles, it is often difficult to follow. Like a soldier in the foxhole, readers can only see a limited view of the battle. Making it more complicated, readers also see what the characters *might* do in alternate realities, such as what the Punisher or Captain America would do if placed in the same situation. Marvel gathered all the stories into trade paperbacks that followed a particular character or theme, making it easier to grasp the overlapping story lines. With the entire story told in trades, readers could obtain a "strategic overview," instead of trying to make sense of events as they were serialized. In the comics, as with war, a good overview makes a big difference.

The Marvel staff went two steps beyond the norm with its follow-up to the death of Captain America. The first step was a five-part series titled the *Death of Captain America*, in which each issue deals with one of the five stages of grief: denial, anger, bargaining, depression, and finally acceptance. Various characters involved on both sides of the civil war speak about Captain America's commitment to the ideals for which he fought. While many of his allies want revenge on Iron Man for his part in Cap's death, it ultimately shows that the United States will go forward, based on Captain America's principles. The death of an American icon, even a fictional one, elicited responses from the real world, showing that Americans could still be united behind their country.

After *Captain America* #25, in which the original Cap is killed, the series shifted to the question of who would be his replacement. One suggestion was Frank Castle, aka the Punisher. Many comic book readers did not like this possibility, for several reasons.[48] The first was that while the Punisher indisputably gets things done, he remains what he has always been: an antihero. Captain America had been a conversion hero. The second problem was that the Punisher is too much like the modern-day United States: possessing awesome firepower but lacking in finesse. His attitude toward war is like America's: go in hard and fast and destroy everything in the way. The Punisher remained a fantasy choice for some and a nightmare for others. The eventual replacement was, in a roundabout way, the most logical: Bucky, Cap's partner from the 1940s. While Bucky had supposedly been killed diverting a German V-1 rocket from hitting London late in the war, in the new arc it is discovered that he had been retrieved by the Soviets from the North Sea and turned into an assassin.[49] Only after the end of the Cold War, and Captain America's recognition of his old sidekick, was Bucky restored to his former life. In some ways, the story resembles that of American Army sergeant Charles Jenkins, who defected to North Korea in 1965 and was a propaganda tool for the Sung regime until 2007, when he was able to return to the United States.[50] After his experiences, the grown-up Bucky is both more and less idealistic: more committed than ever to American ideals but more cynical about how the world really works.

The new direction of the main series does not mean the immediate end of Captain America, as he remained part of other unfolding story lines.[51] One of these is that of *Captain America: Chosen*, a six-part series that linked the story of a Marine in Afghanistan to the death of Captain America, albeit through extrasensory means. The emphasis of the story is how—simply by carrying on in the face of adversity—all soldiers are heroes. While trying to save the men in his squad, the Marine, Cpl. James Newman, also has to face his own fears.[52] At the same time, Newman somehow sees and converses with Captain

America, who apparently helps him do extraordinary things. As the miniseries culminates, the reader comes to learn that Captain America was dying at the same time and was using his remaining strength to telepathically pick possible replacements. Candidates are Americans with the can-do attitude to overcome adversity and do what is needed for the greater good.[53]

Many military memoirs and histories have made the same point. They describe soldiers who overcame their own doubts to do their jobs, often without realizing how amazing—and dangerous—those jobs actually were. Those decorated for valor often say that they are not heroes (or by extension, superheroes) but were simply doing their jobs and helping their friends. This attitude permeates *Captain America: Chosen*, and it carries over to comics created specifically for the military audience though the Army–Air Force Exchange System (AAFES).

Comics for the Troops

The six comics produced by Marvel Comics for AAFES are direct descendants of earlier comic books meant for the troops. The series, started in 2005, incorporates superheroes into military scenarios. These comics feature the New Avengers, with cameos from the Fantastic Four, Spider-Man, and Captain America. The new Marvel line was well received, with the AAFES website noting that the first issue, titled *The New Avengers: Pot of Gold*, had an initial run of three hundred thousand. The comic addresses the base/post exchange program, as well as the military's entire Morale, Welfare, and Recreation (MWR) system. In the story line, a mechanically augmented terrorist—presumably of crypto-Islamic origin, given the use of such phrases as "Great Satanic Empire" and "Fist of God"—is manipulated by the criminal mastermind Kingpin. He aims to steal the $250 million that the MWR generates each year but is unsuccessful, naturally. At the conclusion, Kingpin and the terrorist face imprisonment for their illegal acts.[54]

One of the most successful comics produced was *The New Avengers: Letters Home*.[55] In the story, the terrorist group HYDRA, originally a foil to Captain America, takes over a satellite housing a communications transmitter. The satellite is important for morale; therefore, Captain America has to round up other superheroes to maintain military communications during Christmas. With the help of the Silver Surfer, the Ghost Rider, and the Punisher, Captain America delivers holiday messages from their families to the soldiers in the field (superheroes with their own families are exempt from this duty). This comic returned to comics' first purpose for the military: morale. Produced for troops fighting in Iraq and Afghanistan, it was sold only at post and base exchanges.[56]

According to the AAFES history page, *Pot of Gold* had a run of one million copies and was received well enough that the comics in the series have come out twice a year since then.[57] However, the comics produced for AAFES sometimes make egregious mistakes. Many soldiers noticed the reversed chevrons on the uniform of a U.S. Army soldier in the 2007 issue of the *New Avengers*.[58] Civilian readers might not catch this sort of minor error. In real life, such a mistake would result in punishment for the soldier who sewed his stripes on upside down. Marvel should have checked such details before sales to the military.

Comic book imagery has affected the military in other ways. It turns up, for instance, in Evan Wright's book *Generation Kill*, a unit history that chronicles the Iraq invasion in 2003. He notes that one of the captains in the Marine reconnaissance unit was sarcastically called Captain America, because he seemed to panic or overreact in every situation, exactly the opposite of the comic book character.[59] Another soldier was nicknamed "Manimal," based on both the comic book and the 1970s television show.[60] The book also contained photos taken by the author showing Marines relaxing by reading comic books—not very surprising given that many were still in their teens. Various special operations teams have even incorporated the Punisher skull emblem into their unofficial insignia. One SEAL unit in Iraq designed patches with the skull emblem in the center, with the slogan "God will judge our enemies, we'll arrange the meeting." This was consistent with the character's original role—as a weapon to punish the guilty for their crimes against society, a mission that remains the same whether they are mafiosi or fedayeen.[61] This theme of the military reading war comics could be developed more in the future.

Conflict and Comics in Recent Years

As shown throughout this book, modern events and social conditions have always permeated the comics. This shift toward a more adult readership has only reinforced this tendency in recent years. At times, the related artistic media of comics and cartoons are almost used as a form of journalism. As with the news media, the question arises: do comics that "report" these events convey them accurately, or do they help "create" them instead? Clearly, World War II comics rarely strayed from the official view of the war. Beginning with the Korean War, a few comics tried to show war's darker side, an approach that became even more common during Vietnam. This trend began to reverse with the Gulf War, and many recent war comics about the military situation in Iraq and Afghanistan have tried to tell these tales in traditional terms of heroism and valor. Sometimes they succeed, but sometimes they appear more like propaganda. As with real reporters embedded with military units during the Iraq War, their objectivity is often questionable.

What happens when the comics describe war reporters who, in turn, are describing a war? This is the premise of the graphic novel *Shooting War*, released in 2007. Inspired by the combat reporting done in the Iraq War, its story focuses on how some combat journalists propagandize or even misrepresent facts to put the conflict in the best possible light. The main character, Jimmy Burns, becomes an overnight Internet sensation when he witnesses and reports on a terrorist bombing in his New York City neighborhood. The "Global News Network," a news channel that slants the news to promote the government's agenda, then hires him. Unfortunately, reporting on the terrorists—even unfavorably—gains exposure for their cause, even as it gives the news media better ratings. To give the graphic novel a more authentic feel, the former CBS News anchorman Dan Rather appears as a character in the book.[62]

Some creators now express their war experiences in graphic novel form to help the healing process, for themselves and for veterans or serving combatants. Their war comics take on the role of therapeutic autobiographies. Two excellent examples, based on two different wars, describe their authors' psychological scars. *Alan's War* tells the history of Alan Cope, an American soldier who served in the European theater in World War II. Cope's memoir is not a combat story but the reflections of an average soldier who spent most of his time behind the fight. It is a story about camaraderie and his experience during the late stages of the war and the occupation of postwar Europe.[63] While his unit was sometimes involved in active patrolling, combat plays only a small role in the story. Another graphic novel of this type is *Waltz with Bashir*. Ari Folman writes of his suppressed memories of the Christian Phalangist massacre of Palestinians at the Sabra and Shatilla refugee camps while he and Israeli army comrades just stood by (a topic already treated in Joe Sacco's graphic novel *Palestine*).

Children in Recent War Comics

As previously noted, the use of child soldiers has long been a contentious issue. It is always reprehensible if the enemy uses children; when the United States relies on child commandos, even indirectly, they are freedom fighters. Some recent comic books have reexamined this issue. One graphic novel that obliquely told of the suffering of children was *Children of the Grave* from IDW Comics. It describes a three-man American reconnaissance team sent into a fictional—but clearly Islamic—country to kill a turban-wearing leader. This fanatical leader is dangerous because he has no compunction about killing anyone who opposes his version of Islam. The story incorporates much of the imagery that has come from Afghanistan since the end of the Taliban regime. The turbaned leader bent on revenge resembles both bin Laden and Mullah Omar, the Taliban leader of Afghanistan before the American invasion. In fighting similar to that between Afghan tribal clans, he masterminds the murder of innocent children of an opposing tribal group. Finally, the graphic novel shows the videotaped beheadings of civilians as propaganda for the Islamic cause. It also depicts the Islamic leader's viewpoint: he sees American compassion as a weakness and believes that the stronger side should destroy the weaker one. [64] In the conclusion, the ghosts of the murdered children—serving now as spirit guides to American forces—help strike down their killers. Despite this supernatural element, using propaganda to influence children, as well as using children as combatants or even shields, is unfortunately very real.

A second comic book that has returned to the subject of child soldiers is the ongoing reimaging of DC's *Unknown Soldier* under Vertigo, its more mature imprint. It is also a political statement about Africa, as the new Unknown Soldier is a former doctor (with homicidal tendencies) named Moses Lwanga, who goes back to help his ancestral homeland of Rwanda. He is haunted by ghostly images and eventually is lured into a civil war.[65] This psychic split somehow allows Moses to become a superior soldier, yet without a clear initial concept of right or wrong. Later in the story, it turns out that Moses had been subjected to psychological conditioning by the CIA to make him into the perfect assassin, with no compunctions about killing. As the story develops, his conditioning unravels, and more information about his past is revealed. The writer, Joseph Dysart, gives a history of actual events in Rwanda, Uganda, and Burundi (most of the story takes place in the three countries) and explains how they tie into the fictional story.[66] The story deals with child soldiers, rape, and the CIA's machinations in the local political scene. The *Unknown Soldier* changes from conversion hero to a subversive one, as he fights all sorts of entities who undermine his own convictions. He even changes his physical appearance by cutting his own face.

In addition, newer comics have increasingly incorporated popular culture and references to the war to inform the readers. DC has reimagined its popular *Haunted Tank* series to better reflect modern American society. One such current DC title is *Army at Love*. Writer Rick Veitch and artist Gary Erskine created a comic about a motivational and morale unit (MoMo) in a fictionalized Afghanistan. They have a very satirical take on this situation. The unit recruits special-needs people into the military, using catchy pop tunes and mythology to motivate people to join. In a society already addicted to caffeine, adrenaline, and even sex, the unit gives drugs to the soldiers to raise their endorphin levels to make them more eager warriors. As the story progresses, Veitch writes himself into the story line: he is tortured in Camp X-Ray at Guantanamo Bay, Cuba. He has been taken there because, in the first part of the series, he revealed too much of what the government was really doing. At first, these seem to be only his paranoid delusions, but they turn out to be real. Apparently Veitch has discovered part of some larger secret plan, which he has accidently exposed. The message is that too much information, even in a comic book, can be dangerous.[67]

Chuck Dixon's *Storming Paradise* is another notable new comic book miniseries from DC that uses an alternate history to tell its story. The question is, how historically accurate is it? Where does the story line go? In the fall of 2008, DC Comics embarked on three more war comic books. The company reworked *Sgt. Rock* into a six-part miniseries drawn by Billy Tucci, best known for Shi, the Japanese female assassin. It revived *The Haunted Tank* and set it during the Iraq invasion of 2003, with an interesting twist. In the Kanigher and Kubert 1960s original, only a direct relative could see the ghost of the Confederate general Stuart. In the 2008 series, the tank commander is an African American, Jamal Stuart—who turns out to be descended from General Stuart.[68]

The final title introduced in the fall of 2008 was a miniseries written by Chuck Dixon and illustrated by Butch Guice. Titled *Storming Paradise*, the story line posits that the first atomic bomb test had failed, and the American military had to invade the southern Japanese island of Kyushu.[69] If this and a subsequent invasion planned for Honshu (the main island) had been carried out, conservative estimates of American casualties might have numbered close to half a million. In this alternate history, Gen. George Patton, who actually died in the fall of 1945 after a car accident, is instead killed by Japanese troops in early 1946.[70] Dixon is also responsible for many of the issues of *The 'Nam,* specifically the issues that deal with the pain of downed pilots and the second major story line involving the Punisher.[71] As usual, many readers—from both ends of the political spectrum—wrote in with their opinions about these alterations to such well-known characters that represented cherished American ideals. When a formula is altered to meet new conditions, people react in different ways.

8 Conclusion: Concepts of War through Comic Books

War comics have always appealed to readers as tales of trial by fire, combat, and privation. Recent (and current) war comics have also emphasized the realistic, the political, and the artistic. Overall, however, the comics published in the past seventy years have displayed three general themes or attributes, realism, politics, and aesthetics:

- *Realism.* Recent war comics navigate the fog of war. Confusion on the battlefield, the immediacy of violence and retribution, and the chaos of action have become more pronounced, especially in work of Garth Ennis. (This is not to say that such creators as Harvey Kurtzman and Joe Kubert, both military veterans, have shied away from the realities of war.) With the shift in readership toward adults, the texts have taken on a more mature tone, as well as the more graphic depictions of war's danger and destruction.
- *Politics.* In many of the works penned by Garth Ennis, political motivation has been crucial. While this is not entirely new, political motivations and machinations have been intrinsic to his story lines. Ennis' *303* starts in Afghanistan in the fall of 2001 and ends with the assassination of the American president—the result of political and economic deals by major American leaders. The text is an illustration and extension of Carl von Clausewitz's maxim "War is politics by other means." In several ways, the war comic has taken on a polemical role, akin to the political cartoon but with greater depth and complexity.
- *Aesthetics.* For comics that seek to eschew bias, the majority have adopted a documentary style. Many have been presented in black and white for its stark impact, which is reminiscent of the news footage that permeated black-and-white television and documentaries during the 1950s and 1960s.

As a genre, war comics can give historians much insight into how wars were perceived by the American public. They can show how enemies were vilified, heroes were created, and ideals (justice, democracy, diligence, or prosperity) were espoused and often propagandized. This is because the creators' perspective often reflected the views of their readers, if only because they had to fulfill their expectations enough to ensure future sales. Thus, these comics have often been far more antiwar (sometimes subversively) than many realize, which can give historians insight into dissenting contemporary points of view as well.

Many war comic books were closely geared to the government's desires, even in the absence of direct government pressure. This visual medium, originally aimed at children, also offered a simple and effective way to rally older people around patriotic conceits. The heroes, whether playing Lary May's conversion or subversion roles, helped introduce readers to the government's rationales for fighting and the promotion and preservation of "American ideals."

At the same time, this survey of war comics reveals that there was substantial production of antiwar comics throughout each of America's major military incursions after World War II. The tone of many of these antiwar comics was decidedly moralistic, and the early ones did not survive beyond a few issues. The major antiwar comics such as *Frontline Comics* and *Two-Fisted Tales* in the 1950s and *Blazing Combat* from 1965 to 1966 did not directly question America's involvement in Korea or Vietnam, but they influenced readers by taking issue with the way combat had previously been depicted. These stories often tried to show the absolute brutality and moral ambiguity of combat, as well as attitudes toward the enemy, especially in depictions of torture conducted by or for the United States. In this way, war comic books could subtly undermine the arguments for a war by demonstrating the specific behaviors that the war engendered. Recognizing this ambiguity or ambivalence, major distributers and conservative forces, such as the American Legion, argued that comics undermined American ideals.

By the late 1960s, social unrest in the United States, partially fueled by doubts over Vietnam, encouraged the emergence of "underground comix," which openly challenged the propaganda that their creators felt major media outlets were facilitating. Even some major comics publishers shifted attention toward larger social issues to stay relevant. Admittedly, many still maintained an unrealistic or even antirealistic perspective—and continued to present a fantasy version of combat.

By the 1980s, when the news media were embracing the objectives of the Reagan administration, comics resumed their role actively supporting the military. Comic book creators tried to engage readers in traditional military discourse through the discussion of antiterrorism in *G.I. Joe*, a realistic reappraisal of the events of Vietnam in *The 'Nam*, or even pacifism in *Real War Stories*. In general, however, the comics enlisted patriotic heroes to rally middle America during times of crisis or uncertainty.

One of the most significant limitations of these comics was that many creators lacked military and combat experience. This blind spot limited the comics' depiction of the true nature (and terror) of combat. There remained in their stories a glorified presentation of combat that lent legitimacy to their pro-war stories and, often, did not question American policies or the government. The stories of some creators, such as Sam Glanzman, adopted a right-wing, pro-America stance; other creators, like Joe Kubert, concentrated on the small unit, with relatively infrequent causalities. Slowly, however, the American public caught up to their heroes and gradually reembraced the military once again as the decade wore on. *G.I. Joe*, Ronald Reagan, and Pete "Maverick" Mitchell combined to win audiences and restore virtue in the institutions that had once let John Rambo and America down.

By the 1990s, the end of the Cold War and the resulting "peace dividend" forced some comic book creators to look for new enemies. Some characters from the World War II era were carried into newer events; other characters finally admitted their connection to various conflicts around the globe, such as Vietnam and real-world, CIA-sponsored activities. Flag-draped characters such as Uncle Sam no longer sought to defend America from outside dangers, but looked at America itself instead. How could the United States lead the world when it was rotting from within? Comic book creators also reimagined familiar characters with symptoms of PTSD or battle-induced psychosis. One trailblazer in this field was not a military veteran or even American. The Northern Irishman Garth Ennis has maintained a greater distance, and sense of moral ambiguity, than most American comic book creators. From his point of view, combat and war rarely produce clear winners.

The attacks of September 11, 2001, brought many comparisons to Pearl Harbor and consequently revived some World War II attitudes in war comics. This renewed patriotism nevertheless displayed some significant changes. Post-9/11 comics emulated World War II comic books in that they sought justice for the guilty but did not blindly attack anyone for being "different." Their goal was to protect the innocent but also to avoid mistreatment like the internment of Japanese Americans during World War II. Of course, some stories also entertained xenophobic revenge fantasies, but these were normally the output of limited-production comic book companies.

The start of the Iraq War also produced a series of war comics. However, many of these (especially the series *411*) did not applaud heroics or rally readers around the flag and troops. Instead, they opposed the war as unjust and called for peace and dialogue. Prowar comics became the exception to the rule. While 9/11 had been a rallying point for American ideals, the Iraq War fostered distrust of American political leadership. Comic books also aimed at "first version history" by reporting events in the field as soon as possible. Joe Sacco's work was so timely that it had a journalistic feel.

War genre comics still contain the basic elements of any combat story: the coalescence of a multiethnic, yet cohesive, fighting unit; the manufacture or demonization of an enemy; the demarcation of the high moral ground occupied by the United States; and a sense of realism about combat (however heightened or stylized). While "reality" is often far different from what is presented, its promise remains perennially attractive, drawing readers into the stories and keeping them there.

Appendix

The Comics Code

Code of the Comics Magazine Association of America, Inc.
(adopted October 26, 1954)

Preamble

The comic-book medium, having come of age on the American cultural scene, must measure up to its responsibilities.

Constantly improving techniques and higher standards go hand in hand with these responsibilities.

To make a positive contribution to contemporary life, the industry must seek new areas for developing sound, wholesome entertainment. The people responsible for writing, drawing, printing, publishing, and selling comic books have done a commendable job in the past, and have been striving toward this goal.

Their record of progress and continuing improvement compares favorably with other media in the communications industry. An outstanding example is the development of comic books as a unique and effective tool for instruction and education. Comic books have also made their contribution in the field of letters and criticism of contemporary life.

In keeping with the American tradition, the members of this industry will and must continue to work together in the future.

In the same tradition, members of the industry must see to it that gains made in this medium are not lost and that violations of standards of good taste, which might tend toward corruption of the comic book as an instructive and wholesome form of entertainment, will be eliminated.

Therefore, the Comics Magazine Association of America, Inc. has adopted this code, and placed strong powers of enforcement in the hands of an independent code authority.

Further, members of the association have endorsed the purpose and spirit of this code as a vital instrument to the growth of the industry.

To this end, they have pledged themselves to conscientiously adhere to its principles and to abide by all decisions based on the code made by the administrator.

They are confident that this positive and forthright statement will provide an effective bulwark for the protection and enhancement of the American reading public, and that it will become a landmark in the history of self-regulation for the entire communications industry.

Code for Editorial Matter

General standards—Part A

1. Crimes shall never be presented in such a way as to create sympathy for the criminal, to promote distrust of the forces of law and justice, or to inspire others with a desire to imitate criminals.
2. No comics shall explicitly present the unique details and methods of a crime.
3. Policemen, judges, Government officials and respected institutions shall never be presented in such a way as to create disrespect for established authority.
4. If crime is depicted it shall be as a sordid and unpleasant activity.
5. Criminals shall not be presented so as to be rendered glamorous or to occupy a position which creates a desire for emulation.
6. In every instance good shall triumph over evil and the criminal punished for his misdeeds.
7. Scenes of excessive violence shall be prohibited. Scenes of brutal torture, excessive and unnecessary knife and gunplay, physical agony, gory and gruesome crime shall be eliminated.
8. No unique or unusual methods of concealing weapons shall be shown.
9. Instances of law-enforcement officers dying as a result of a criminal's activities should be discouraged.
10. The crime of kidnapping shall never be portrayed in any detail, nor shall any profit accrue to the abductor or kidnaper. The criminal or the kidnaper must be punished in every case.
11. The letters of the word "crime" on a comics-magazine cover shall never be appreciably greater in dimension than the other words contained in the title. The word "crime" shall never appear alone on a cover.
12. Restraint in the use of the word "crime" in titles or subtitles shall be exercised.

General standards—Part B

1. No comic magazine shall use the word horror or terror in its title.
2. All scenes of horror, excessive bloodshed, gory or gruesome crimes, depravity, lust, sadism, masochism shall not be permitted.
3. All lurid, unsavory, gruesome illustrations shall be eliminated.
4. Inclusion of stories dealing with evil shall be used or shall be published only where the intent is to illustrate a moral issue and in no case shall evil be presented alluringly, nor so as to injure the sensibilities of the reader.

5. Scenes dealing with, or instruments associated with walking dead, torture, vampires and vampirism, ghouls, cannibalism, and werewolfism are prohibited.

General standards—Part C
All elements or techniques not specifically mentioned herein, but which are contrary to the spirit and intent of the code, and are considered violations of good taste or decency, shall be prohibited.

Dialogue
  1. Profanity, obscenity, smut, vulgarity, or words or symbols which have acquired undesirable meanings are forbidden.
  2. Special precautions to avoid references to physical afflictions or deformities shall be taken.
  3. Although slang and colloquialisms are acceptable, excessive use should be discouraged and, wherever possible, good grammar shall be employed.

Religion
  1. Ridicule or attack on any religious or racial group is never permissible.

Costume
  1. Nudity in any form is prohibited, as is indecent or undue exposure.
  2. Suggestive and salacious illustration or suggestive posture is unacceptable.
  3. All characters shall be depicted in dress reasonably acceptable to society.
  4. Females shall be drawn realistically without exaggeration of any physical qualities.

NOTE. It should be recognized that all prohibitions dealing with costume, dialog, or artwork applies as specifically to the cover of a comic magazine as they do to the contents.

Marriage and sex
  1. Divorce shall not be treated humorously nor represented as desirable.
  2. Illicit sex relations are neither to be hinted at nor portrayed. Violent love scenes as well as sexual abnormalities are unacceptable.
  3. Respect for parents, the moral code, and for honorable behavior shall be fostered. A sympathetic understanding of the problems of love is not a license for morbid distortion.
  4. The treatment of live-romance stories shall emphasize the value of the home and the sanctity of marriage.

5. Passion or romantic interest shall never be treated in such a way as to stimulate the lower and baser emotions.

6. Seduction and rape shall never be shown or suggested.

7. Sex perversion or any inference to same is strictly forbidden.

Code for Advertising Matter

These regulations are applicable to all magazines published by members of the Comics Magazine Association of America, Inc. Good taste shall be the guiding principle in the acceptance of advertising.

1. Liquor and tobacco advertising is not acceptable.

2. Advertisement of sex or sex instruction books are unacceptable.

3. The sale of picture postcards, "pinups," "art studies," or any other reproduction of nude or seminude figures is prohibited.

4. Advertising for the sale of knives or realistic gun facsimiles is prohibited.

5. Advertising for the sale of fireworks is prohibited.

6. Advertising dealing with the sale of gambling equipment or printed matter dealing with gambling shall not be accepted.

7. Nudity with meretricious purpose and salacious postures shall not be permitted in the advertising of any product; clothed figures shall never be presented in such a way as to be offensive or contrary to good taste or morals.

8. To the best of his ability, each publisher shall ascertain that all statements made in advertisements conform to fact and avoid misrepresentation.

9. Advertisement of medical, health, or toiletry products of questionable nature are to be rejected. Advertisements for medical, health, or toiletry products endorsed by the American Medical Association, or the American Dental Association, shall be deemed acceptable if they conform with all other conditions of the Advertising Code.

Source: Senate Committee on the Judiciary, *Comic Books and Juvenile Delinquency*, Interim Report (Washington, DC: Government Printing Office, 1955).

Notes

Preface

1. *Sgt. Rock* (New York: DC Comics, 1959–) and *Haunted Tank* (New York: DC Comics, 1961–).
2. New York Comic Book Museum website, www.nyccomicbookmuseum.org/concierge/concierge.htm, accessed April 12, 2006.
3. *Frontline Combat* (New York: Warren, 1951–54), *Blazing Combat* (New York: Warren, 1965–66), *Two-Fisted Tales* (New York: EC Comics, 1950–55).
4. Bradford Wright, *Comic Book Nation: The Transformation of Youth Culture in America* (Baltimore: Johns Hopkins University Press, 2001), 18.
5. *The Shield* (New York: Archie Comics, 1940–45, 1965–), *Captain America* (New York: Marvel Comics, 1941–), *Uncle Sam* (New York: DC Comics, 1940–44, 1973–), *Wonder Woman* (New York: DC Comics, 1941–), and *SuperPatriot* (Berkeley, CA: Image Comics, 1992–).
6. *Alpha Flight* (New York: Marvel Comics/Marvel UK, 1979–), *The Vindicator* (New York: Marvel Comics/Marvel UK, 1980–), *Captain Britain* (New York: Marvel Comics/Marvel UK, 1976–), *Union Jack* (New York: Marvel Comics/Marvel UK, 1991–), *Captain Canuck* (Winnipeg, Manitoba: Comely Comix, 1975–), and *Jack Staff* (Berkeley, CA: Image Comics, 2000–).
7. *Captain America* (New York: Marvel Comics, 1940–48, 1964–), *Sgt. Rock* (New York: DC Comics, 1958–88), *Iron Man* (New York: Marvel Comics, 1963–).
8. Lary May, ed., *Recasting America: Culture and Politics in the Age of the Cold War* (Chicago: University of Chicago Press, 1988), and Lewis A. Erenberg and Susan E. Hirsch, eds., *The War in American Culture* (Chicago: University of Chicago Press, 1996).
9. William W. Savage Jr., *Commies, Cowboys, and Jungle Queens: Comic Books and America, 1945–1954* (Hanover, NH: Wesleyan University Press, 1998); Roger Sabin, *Comics, Comix & Graphic Novels: A History of Comic Art* (London: Phaidon, 1997); Wright, *Comic Book Nation*; and James Steranko, *The History of Comics*, 2 vols. (Reading, PA: Supergraphics, 1970, 1972).
10. John W. Dower, *War without Mercy: Race and Power in the Pacific War* (New York: Pantheon, 1986).

Chapter 1. Entertaining and Informing the Masses

1. The cartoon appeared in Ben Franklin's newspaper *The Pennsylvania Gazette* on May 9, 1754. It accompanied an editorial by Franklin about "the present disunited state of the Brtish Colonies" and pictures a snake divided into pieces to represent the separate colonial governments. See Chris Lamb, *Drawn to Extremes* (New York: Columbia University Press, 2004), 43.
2. Stephen Hess and Sandy Northrop, *Drawn and Quartered: The History of American Political Cartoons* (Montgomery, AL: Elliot & Clark, 1996), 8.
3. Harold Schechter, *Savage Pastimes: A Cultural History of Violent Entertainment* (New York: St. Martin's, 2005), 18–19, and Sabin, *Comics, Comix and Graphic Novels*, 11–14.

4. Thomas Nast, "The Day We Celebrate," in *Drawn and Quartered,* ed. Hess and Northrup, 57.

5. Robert C. Harvey, *Children of the Yellow Kid: The Evolution of the American Comic Strip* (Seattle: University of Washington Press, 1998), 36.

6. Sabin, *Comics, Comix and Graphic Novels,* 20.

7. David Perlmutter, *Visions of War: Picturing Warfare from the Stone Age to the Cyber Age* (New York: St. Martin's 1999), 8–9.

8. Will Eisner, *Graphic Storytelling and the Visual Narrative* (Tamarac, FL: Poorhouse, 1996), 21.

9. Nicky Wright, *The Classic Era of American Comics* (Lincolnwood, IL: Contemporary Books, 2000), 11–12.

10. Flagg first painted his famous Uncle Sam portrait for the July 4, 1916, issue of *Leslie's* magazine. After the United States entered World War I, the government contacted Flagg, requesting him to adapt his famous figure into a war poster.

11. Maurice Rickards, *Posters of World War I* (New York: Walker, 1968), 50.

12. Ronald Shaffer, *America in the Great War: The Rise of the War Welfare State* (New York: Oxford University Press, 1996), 9.

13. Harvey, *Children of the Yellow Kid,* 33.

14. Ibid., 26.

15. Albert W. Bryce, *Halt Friends!* (New York: publisher unknown, 1924), 4.

16. "Big foot humor" is like that of clowns: the exaggeration of characteristics, movements, or the like for a humorous effect.

17. The common image of machine gunners was that they played dirty and were often killed on the spot if captured because of the incredible damage they inflicted. See Alban B. Butler, *Happy Days* (New York: Coward-McCann, 1929), 86.

18. Ibid., 16.

19. Wright, *Classic Era of American Comics,* 14.

20. Mike Benton, *The Comic Book in America* (Dallas: Taylor, 1993), 15.

21. The most notable of these suits involved the similarity between DC Comics' Superman and Fawcett Comics' Captain Marvel. The courts eventually ruled in favor of DC, sidelining Captain Marvel until DC later licensed, and then acquired, the rights to all of Fawcett's characters. See Wright, *Comic Book Nation,* 18–19.

22. Carl Burgos, *Marvel Mystery Comics #9* (New York: Marvel Comics, July 1940).

23. Wright, *Classic Era of American Comics,* 64–65.

24. Stella Ress, "Bridging the Generation Gap: Little Orphan Annie in the Great Depression," *Journal of Popular Culture* 43, #4 (Summer 2010): 11–12.

25. Wright, *Comic Book Nation,* 11.

26. Ibid., 11–12.

27. William Young, "The Serious Funnies: Adventure Comics during the Depression, 1929–1938," in *Things in the Driver's Seat: Readings in Popular Culture,* ed. Harry Russell Huebe (Chicago: Rand McNally, 1972), 86–87.

28. Robert Harvey, *Meanwhile: A Biography of Milton Caniff, Creator of Terry and the Pirates and Steve Canyon* (Seattle: Fantagraphics Books, 2007), 200.

29. Dower, *War without Mercy,* 33–35.

30. Joe Simon (w) and Jack Kirby (a), *Captain America,* vol. 1 (New York: Marvel Comics, 1991, reprints of 1941 comics), 33, 94–96.

31. Young, "Serious Funnies," 90.

32. Harvey, *Children of the Yellow Kid,* 95.

33. Simcha Weinstein, *Up, Up, and Oy Vey! How Jewish History, Culture and Values Shaped the Comic Book Superhero* (Baltimore: Leviathan, 2006), 16–17.

34. Frederic Spotts, *Hitler and the Power of Aesthetics* (New York: Overlook, 2003), 107.

35. Jerry Siegel (w) and Joe Shuster (a), "How Superman Would End the War," *Look,* February 27, 1940, 8–10.

36. Stan Lee (w) and Jack Binder (a), "The Destroyer," in *All Winners,* vol. 1 (New York: Marvel Comics, 1941, reprinted 2005), 98.

37. Ronin Ro, *Tales to Astonish: Jack Kirby, Stan Lee, and the American Comic Book Revolution* (New York: Bloomsbury, 2005), 29.

38. Todd DePastino, *Bill Mauldin: A Life up Front* (New York: Norton, 2008), 125–26.

39. Both the title and the character are the Spirit (aka Denny Colt).

40. Will Eisner (w) and Chuck Cuidera (a), *Blackhawk Archives,* vol. 1 (New York: DC Archive Editions, 2001), 12.

41. Rogers, Rangers were scouts in the Revolutionary War who utilized Indian tactics. They inspired the Ranger battalions of the U.S. Army in World War II.

42. Allen, *True Comics,* #15–25.

43. *Remember Pearl Harbor: Battle of the Pacific* (New York: Street & Smith, February 23, 1942), 2–6.

44. Dower, *War without Mercy,* 33–35.

45. May, *Recasting America,* 82–83.

Chapter 2. Fighting for Freedom (1939–45)

1. Carl Burgos and Bill Everett, "Marvel Comics Presents the Human Torch and Sub-Mariner Fighting Side by Side," in *Marvel Mystery Comics* #17 (New York: Marvel Comics, March 1941), reprinted in *The Golden Age of Marvel Comics,* vol. 1, ed. Stan Lee (New York: Marvel Comics, 1997), 45–48.

2. Jules Feiffer, *The Great Comic Book Heroes* (Seattle: Fantagraphics Books, 2003), 24–26, and Wright, *Comic Book Nation,* 11.

3. Joe Kubert, *Yossel: April 18, 1943* (New York: iBooks, 2003), 2.

4. Steven J. Ross, "Hollywood, Jews, and America," *Reviews in American History* 30, #4 (December 2002): 626.

5. Arie Kaplan, *From Krakow to Krypton: Jews in Comic Books* (Philadelphia: Jewish Publication Society, 2008), 58.

6. *PM* was an afternoon newspaper published in New York City by Ralph Ingersoll from 1940 to 1948 with the financial backing of Chicago millionaire Marshall Field III.

7. "SNAFU" is the U.S. military acronym for Situation Normal: All Fucked Up.

8. "Don't Help the Enemy," in *How Boys and Girls Can Help Win the War* (New York: Marvel Comics, Parents Magazine Institute, and True Comics, 1942), 24. The prices for the same ordnance vary a great deal in similar comic book advertisements. They are almost certainly all fictional; after all, would the War Department have allowed comic books to publish such sensitive information?

9. This was shown by several advertisements in the back of *Captain America* comic books, in particular #9 (December 1941), reprinted in Joe Simon and Jack Kirby, *Captain America,* vol. 2 (New York: Marvel Comics, 1994), 31.

10. Cheryl Hoganson, *Fighting for American Manhood: How Gender Politics Provoked the Spanish–American and Philippine–American Wars* (New Haven, CT: Yale University Press, 2000), 67.

11. Young, "Serious Funnies," 89.

12. The Four Freedoms were first outlined in President Franklin Roosevelt's 1941 State of the Union address, delivered to Congress on January 6, 1941.

13. *Das Schwarze Korps,* German Propaganda Archive, April 25, 1940, 8, http://www.calvin.edu/academic/cas/gpa/superman.htm (accessed February 2, 2011).

14. Blackhawk first appeared in *Military Comics* #1 (New York: Quality Comics, August 1941). Reprinted in DC Archives edition: *The Blackhawk Archives* vol. 1 (New York: DC Comics, 2001).

15. Thomas Powell, "The War Writers Board and Comic Books," *Historian: A Journal of History* 59, #4 (Summer 1997): 795, 798.

16. Allan Winkler, *The Politics of Propaganda* (New Haven, CT: Yale University Press, 1978), 45.

17. Various advertisements from comic books of the day.

18. "Don't Help the Enemy," 58–59.

19. *True Aviation Stories* #7, Parents Magazine Institute (Spring 1944), 12–13.

20. John Franklin, author interview, October 1999.

21. Fred Van Lente (w) and Ryan Dunlavey (a), *Comic Book Comics #2: Our Artists at War!* New York: Evil Twin Comics (July, 2008), 9.

22. Paul Castiglia, ed., *The Shield: America's First Patriotic Comic Book Hero* (Mamaroneck, NY: Archie Comics, 2002), 67–75.

23. Ibid., 55.

24. See Turner Catledge, "Our Policy Stated in Soviet-Nazi War," *New York Times,* June 24, 1941.

25. Edwin Black, *War against the Weak: Eugenics and America's Campaign to Create a Master Race* (New York: Four Walls, Eight Windows, 2003), 7.

26. Many Jewish German scientists such as Einstein were forced into exile before World War II. After the war, along with some non-Jewish German scientists, they found themselves on different sides of the Iron Curtain. By the 1960s, Marvel had rewritten Captain America's origin story, renaming Reinstein as Erskine, probably to play down any possible Nazi associations with German names. This confused some readers who had followed the story lines from inception.

27. Simon and Kirby, *Captain America,* vol. 1 (New York: Marvel Comics 1994).

28. *U.S.A. Comics* was a Marvel umbrella title, published from the summer of 1941 to the fall of 1945, which introduced Captain America (before he got his own stand-alone comic) and brought together tales of various minor superheroes.

29. The "Dead End Kids" was a fictional band of teenage boys from an underprivileged neighborhood in New York City. They first appeared on Broadway in the 1935 play *Dead End,* then in a Hollywood film of the same name produced by Samuel Goldwyn

in 1937. Under various other monikers, most famously as "The Bowery Boys," they appeared together in dozens of short films until 1958.

30. Joe Simon (w) and Jack Kirby (a), *Young Allies* #1 (New York: Marvel Comics, June 1941), 11.

31. Gary Groth, "Interview with Jack Kirby," in *The Comics Journal: Jack Kirby* (Seattle: Fantagraphics Books, 2002), 20–21.

32. *Young Allies* #3 (New York: Marvel Comics, March 1942), 4.

33. Lary May, "Making the American Consensus: The Narrative of Conversion and Subversion in World War II Films," in *War in American Culture*, ed. Erenberg and Hirsch, 72.

34. Ibid.

35. *Young Allies* #5 (New York: Marvel Comics, September 1942).

36. May, "Making the American Consensus," 76–77.

37. *Military Comics* (May 1941), 2–11, reprinted in Will Eisner (w) and Chuck Cuidera (a), *Blackhawk Archives*, vol. 1 (New York: DC Archive Editions, 2001).

38. Ibid., 6.

39. May, "Making the American Consensus," 82.

40. The Shield and Captain America are utterly upright characters. They always uphold traditional American democracy, fighting for home, family, and morality. They only fight those who would destroy American values.

41. Maurice Scott, "Shock Gibson," *Speed Comics* (New York: Harvey Comics, 1939–48), reprinted in *War Heroes Classics* #1 (Larchmont, NY: Lorne-Harvey, 1991), 10–17.

42. May, "Making the American Consensus," 83–85.

43. Joe Simon (w) and Jack Kirby (a), "Major Liberty," in *USA Comics* #2 (New York: Marvel Comics, November 1941), 19.

44. Stan Lee, ed., *Golden Age of Marvel Comics*, vol. 2 (New York: Marvel Comics, 1999), 23–34.

45. Wright, *Comic Book Nation*, 43, and Michael Uslan, ed., *America at War: The Best DC War Comics* (New York: DC Comics, 1978), 44.

46. Uslan, *America at War*, 47–58.

47. Trina Robbins, *The Great Women Cartoonists* (New York: Watson-Guptill, 2001), 58–60.

48. Sabin, *Comics, Comix, and Graphic Novels*, 86–88.

49. No exact ages are ever given, but they appear to be about ten to fourteen years old, or the approximate age of Boy Scouts—and, for that matter, of the Hitler Youth.

50. Joe Simon (w) and Jack Kirby (a), *Boy Commandos* #1 (New York: DC Comics, Winter 1942–43), 4.

51. Paul Fussell, *The Boys' Crusade: The American Infantry in Northwestern Europe, 1944–1945* (New York: Modern Chronicles Library, 2003), 6.

52. Lewis Erenberg, "Swing Goes to War: Glenn Miller and the Popular Music of World War II," in *War in American Culture*, ed. Erenberg and Hirsch, 158.

53. John Keegan, *The Second World War* (New York: Penguin, 1989), 404.

54. "Girl Commandos," in *War Heroes Classics* (Larchmont, NY: Lorne-Harvey, 1991), 21–27.

55. May, "Making the American Consensus," 87, 89.

56. Garrett McGurn, *Yank: The Army Weekly–Reporting the Greatest Generation* (Golden, CO: Fulcrum, 2004), 67.

57. Ibid., 116, and Benton, *Comic Book in America,* 127.

58. DePastino, *Bill Mauldin,* 69.

59. Frank Brandt, ed., *Cartoons for Fighters* (Washington, DC: Infantry Journal, 1945), 35–36.

60. U.S. Information Service, *A Pocket Guide to China* (Washington, DC: Department of the Army, 1943), 65–75.

61. Joe Simon and Jim Simon, *The Comic Book Makers* (New York: Vanguard Publishing, 2003), 58.

62. Ibid., 66–67.

63. Ro, *Tales to Astonish,* 34.

64. "There Are No Master Races," in *True Comics* #39 (New York: Parents Magazine, September–October 1944), 41.

65. Ibid., 27.

66. Amy Kiste Nyberg, *Seal of Approval: The History of the Comics Code* (Jackson: University Press of Mississippi, 1998), 7.

67. *Real Heroes* #1 (New York: Parents Comics Institute, 1941), 1.

68. DePastino, *Bill Mauldin,* 2–3.

69. Ibid., 137.

70. Albert Delacorte, ed., *USA Is Ready* (New York: Dell, 1941), 59–60.

71. Bill Mauldin, *The Willie and Joe Years,* vol. 1 (Seattle: Fantagraphics Books, 2008), 113.

72. Joe Simon (w) and Jack Kirby (a), *Captain America* #6 (September 1941), reprinted in *Captain America: The Classic Years, vol. 2,* #1–3 (New York: Marvel Comics; 2000.)

73. Dower, *War without Mercy,* 98.

74. Joe Simon (w) and Jack Kirby (a), *Captain America* #5 (August 1941), reprinted in *Captain America: The Classic Years, vol. 2,* #5–10 (New York: Marvel Comics, 1998).

Chapter 3. The Cold War Erupts, and Comics—Mostly—Toe the Line (1945–62)

1. This Cap, originally named William Burnside, was a PhD candidate in American history. In the course of his research, he read the notes about the Super-Soldier Serum and became so enamored of the project that he legally changed his name to Steve Rogers (the name of the original Captain America; there have been five in total). He later taught history at Lee High School while serving as Captain America. http://marvel.com/universe/Captain_America_(William_Burnside) (accessed March 7, 2011).

2. John Romita Sr., "Back from the Dead," in *Young Men Comics,* vol. 2, #24 (New York: Marvel Comics, December 1953), reprinted in *The Golden Age of Marvel Comics,* vol. 1, ed. Stan Lee (New York: Marvel Comics, 1997), 145.

3. Jerry Weist and Jim Steranko, *100 Greatest Comic Books: An Appreciation of the Comics and Their Stories* (Atlanta: Whitman, 2004), 55.

4. Savage, *Commies, Cowboys and Jungle Queens,* 102–3.

5. *Atom-Age Combat* #3 (New York: St. John Publications, January 1953), 21.

6. *Atom-Age Combat* #4 (New York: St. John Publications, January 1953).

7. Belief in this Communist conspiracy was widespread in American society and government at the time. Its most fanatical promoters included Rep. Richard Nixon, Rep. J. Parnell Thomas, Sen. Estes Kefauver, and—most famously—Sen. Joe McCarthy. There were many other self-aggrandizing anti-Communists, including Roy Cohn, and myriad variations of the putative conspiracy. Nevertheless, there were also a number of genuine Communist agents, some

quite high-level, brought to trial during this period. These included former State Department official Alger Hiss and the atomic spy Julius Rosenberg (eventually executed along his wife, Ethel, a more dubious case). Still others, such as the nuclear physicist Klaus Fuchs, fled to the Soviet Union in fear of imminent exposure. It was Fuchs, a British national, not Rosenberg, who made the most significant disclosures of American atomic secrets to the Soviets.

8. *Is This Tomorrow: America under Communism!* (St. Paul, MN: Catechetical Guild Educational Society, 1947).

9. Ibid., 3.

10. Ibid., back cover. "The Ten Commandments of Democracy" were originally drawn up by Edith Lehman, the wife of the former governor of New York.

11. Alfred Usndel, ed., *The World around Us: Spies* (New York: Gilbertson World Wide, August 1961).

12. The documentary film *The Atomic Cafe*, directed by Jayne Loader, Kevin Rafferty, and Pierce Rafferty (1982), explored the subject as treated in the movies and television of the period.

13. *Treasure Chest of Fun and Fact* was a Catholic-oriented comic book published by George A. Pflaum of Dayton, Ohio, from 1946 to 1972 and provided to parochial school students.

14. Few secular comic books invoked Christianity or religion in general, except to distinguish the United States from "godless communism." See Norah Smaridge, "Red Victim: The Story of Bishop Walsh," *Treasure Chest*, vol. 9, #15 (November 1963), 23–28.

15. *Atomic War* #1 (New York: Ace Comics, 1952), 3.

16. Examples include *Red Dawn*, directed by John Milius (1984), *Damnation Alley*, directed by Jack Smight (1977), and *The Day After*, directed Nicholas Meyer (television, 1983).

17. *Atomic War* #1, 6.

18. "Operation Vengeance," in *Atomic War* #2, 13.

19. "Snorkel of the Wolfpack," in *Atomic War* #3, 21–22.

20. *General Douglas MacArthur* (New York: Fox Feature Syndicate, 1951).

21. *Heroic Comics* #16 (New York: Famous Funnies, January 1943).

22. *Heroic Comics* #77 (New York: Famous Funnies, November 1952), 2–4.

23. Alfonso Greene, "G.I. Jap—American Hero!," in *Heroic Comics* #34 (New York: Famous Funnies, January 1946), 15–16.

24. *Heroic Comics* #77 (New York: Famous Funnies, November 1952), 6–7.

25. Department of the Navy, *Li'l Abner Joins the Navy* (Washington, DC: U.S. Department of the Navy, 1950).

26. Stokes Walesby (w) and Theodore Roscoe (a), *Navy: History and Tradition* #1–4 (Washington, DC: Stokes Walesby, 1959.)

27. Castiglia, *The Shield*, 2.

28. Joe Simon and Jack Kirby, *Fighting American*, vol. 1 (New York: Marvel Comics, 1989).

29. Wright, *Classic Era of American Comics*, 154–55.

30. Some had spent the war away from war zones, but many comic book creators—such as Jack Kirby, John Severin, Wally Wood, and Harvey Kurtzman—had extensive combat experience. The last three were dominant in EC comics, and the comic book field overall, for years. Many of the creators of *Frontline Combat* or *Two-Fisted Tales* mentioned that their World War II experiences had inspired some of EC's horror comics as well. See John Week "Letters to Frontline Combat Comics," in *Frontline Combat* #7 (West Plains, MO: Gemstone, 1996) 22–23.

31. "Corpse on the Imjin," in *Two-Fisted Tales* #25 (New York: EC Comics, February 1952), reprinted in *Two-Fisted Tales: The EC Archives,* vol. 2 (West Plains, MO: Gemstone, 2007).
32. Ibid., 67.
33. Harvey Kurtzman, "Rubble," in *Two-Fisted Tales* #24 (November–December 1951), 29–33.
34. See "Buzz Bomb," in *Two Fisted Tales,* #25.
35. U.S. Marines were using older maps with the Japanese name, so Marines and soldiers who fought there called it Chosin (or sometimes "Frozen Chosin"). Kurtzman used Changjin, the correct Korean name.
36. Kurtzman, Harvey, and Wallace Wood. Two-Fisted Tales. Timonium, Md.: Gemstone, 2007.
37. Russ Heath, "Basic Training," in *Combat Casey* #23 (Atlas Comics, 1955), 18–22.
38. Savage, *Commies, Cowboys and Jungle Queens,* 53, 55.
39. Frederic Wertham, *Seduction of the Innocent* (Port Washington, NY: Kennikat 1954), 293, 246.
40. Ibid., 284, 292.
41. Nyberg, *Seal of Approval,* 56.
42. Savage, *Commies, Cowboys and Jungle Queens,* 52; and Philip Wylie, *Generation of Vipers* (Champaign, IL: Dalkey Archive, 1955), 208.
43. The Comics Code of 1954 lasted for nearly two decades in its original form. After two revisions, in 1973 and 1991, the industry has generally ignored it. Enforcement is now a matter of self-regulation, and a few titles still abide by its restrictions. See appendix A.
44. As a result of this destruction, many comics from the golden age (formerly defined as 1938–55 and encapsulating World War II and the Korean War) are now highly valued among collectors with some mint condition fetching anywhere from ten thousand dollars to more than one million on the market. When these comics sold at auction in the early 1990s, it fueled a speculative market of comics as an investment, which drove prices up and drove off collectors in the 1990s. The speculation ended in the early 2000s, when many investors realized that the market for comics from recent years would not pay such dividends. See Sabin, *Comics, Comix, and Graphic Novels,* 67–68, and Weist and Steranko, *100 Greatest Comic Books,* 18–19.
45. Wright, *Comic Book Nation,* 179.
46. Nyberg, *Seal of Approval,* 33–35.
47. Brian Lanker and Nicole Newnham, *They Drew Fire: Combat Artists of World War II.* New York: TV Books 2000), 87.
48. *Foxhole* was picked up later by Charlton Comics, then rereleased by Super Comics in 1963, where the issues ran from #10 to #18. http://www.atomicavenue.com/foxhole (accessed January 22, 2009).
49. Joe Simon(w) and Jack Kirby (a), "League of the Handsome Devils," in *Fighting American* #2 (New York: Prize, June 1954), 2.
50. Joe Simon (w) and Jack Kirby (a), "Stranger from Paradise," in *Fighting American* #3 (New York: Prize, (September 1954), 22–23.
51. Ibid., viii.
52. Although set in World War II, *Combat's* first twenty-seven issues were created in the 1960s. The remaining comics in the series were recycled from the title's earlier run.
53. AtomicAvenue.com, http://www.atomicavenue.com/atomic/TitleDetail.aspx?TitleID=14229 (accessed February 13, 2002).

54. Sam Glanzman, "Monte Cassino," in *Combat* #9 (New York: Dell Comics, 1962), 1.

55. Robert Kanigher (w) and Joe Kubert (a), *Our Army at War* #81 (New York: DC Comics, April 1959), 8–11.

56. Mark Chiarello, foreword to *DC Archives Editions: Sgt. Rock Archives,* vol. 3 (New York; DC Comics, 2005), 6.

57. Interview with Joe Kubert, May 2001, Slush Factory, slushfactory.com/features/articles/052502-kubert.php.

58. Kubert's artwork from this time became part of a "what if?" story line that evolved into the DC Comics graphic novel *Yossel.* Kubert notes in its foreword that had his parents not immigrated to the United States in the late 1920s, he might very well have been fighting in the Warsaw Ghetto in April 1943.

59. Compiled from Bob Kanigher et al., *DC Showcase Presents: Haunted Tank,* vols. 1 and 2. (New York: DC Comics, 2007, 2008).

60. Wright, *Comic Book Nation,* 194.

61. Ibid., 199.

62. *Toonpedia,* s.v. "Charlton Comics," http://www.toonopedia.com/charlton.htm (accessed March 17, 2009).

63. These topics along with others from *PS: The Preventive Maintenance Monthly* can now be accessed and searched for at https://www.logsa.army.mil/psmag/pshome.cfm (accessed April 24, 2011).

64. U.S. Army, *Five Years Later . . . Where Will You Be?* (Washington, DC: Government Printing Office, 1962), 8.

65. *Guadalcanal Diary,* directed by Louis Seiler (1943), *Battleground,* directed by William Wellman (1949), and *A Walk in the Sun,* directed by Lewis Milestone (1945).

66. Bob Kanigher (w) and Joe Kubert (a), *Sgt. Rock* #95 (New York: DC Comics, July 1960), 4.

67. Bob Kanigher (w) and Joe Kubert (a), *Sgt. Rock* #113 (New York: DC Comics, December 1961), 1.

68. Bob Kanigher (w) and Joe Kubert (a), *Sgt. Rock* #85 (New York: DC Comics, August 1959), 2.

69. Bob Kanigher (w) and Joe Kubert (a), *Sgt. Rock* #127 (New York: DC Comics, February 1963), 1.

70. Kanigher and Kubert *Sgt. Rock* #113, 1.

71. Fredrik Strömberg. *Black Images in Comics: A Visual History* (Seattle: Fantagraphics Books, 2003), 161.

72. Given that war comics usually depict idealized and exaggerated ideas of manhood and virility, there have yet to be any openly gay characters. Even recently, the subject has been treated indirectly at best. When characters exhibited less than stereotypical ideas of manhood, it was often attributed to being "British." The closest thing to a gay character was Lt. Milk in the three issue mini-series *Adventures in the Rifle Brigade* (New York: DC Comics/Vertigo 2001). Garth Ennis, the writer of that series (Carlos Ezquerra was the artist), parodied the portrayal of effeminate characters and employed stereotypical situations to get the commander to physically touch Milk, but it never went further than that. The character's name recalls Harvey Milk, the San Francisco supervisor and first openly gay man elected to public office in California, who was assassinated in 1977.

73. Richard Slotkin, *Gunfighter Nation: The Myth of the Frontier in Twentieth-Century America* (Norman: University of Oklahoma Press, 1998), 322–23.

74. Marvel's *The Fantastic Four, Spider-Man,* and the *Hulk* often looked at wider social issues, including race. Eisner chose the Hulk's original gray skin color to avoid suggesting any particular race, but as this caused technical printing problems he changed it to green. *X-Men* addressed the struggles of being different more cleverly, by substituting mutants for minorities.

75. Stan Lee, Larry Leiber, and Don Heck, "Iron Man Is Born," in *Tales of Suspense* #39 (New York: Marvel, March 1963).

Chapter 4. War Comics in a Time of Upheaval (1962–91)

1. *G.I. Joe: A Real American Hero* (New York: Marvel Comics, 1982–1994).

2. Joe Gill (w) and Enio Legisamo (a), "Terror in a Vietcong Tunnel," in *Army War Heroes* #20. Derby, CT Charlton Comics, July 1967), 28–32.

3. Ibid., 26.

4. Throughout its publishing history, from the beginning of the comic book era, Dell produced some 351 titles. Of these, only 21 had war themes. Many of these ran only a year or two, *Wings* and *Combat* being notable exceptions. Most 1960s war comic titles were adaptations of television shows or films, including *The Rat Patrol, Hogan's Heroes, McHale's Navy,* and *Zulu.* http://www.atomicavenue.com/publishers/dell (accessed February 26, 2009).

5. Otto Binder (w) and Carl Pfeufer (a), "Rebel Rat-Hole," in *Tod Holton: Super Green Beret* #1 (New York: DC Comics/Lightning Comics, April 1967), 13–17.

6. Otto Binder (w) and Carl Pfeufer (a), "White Magic in the Black Forest," in *Tod Holton: Super Green Beret* #1 (New York: DC Comics/Lightning Comics), 23–31.

7. Otto Binder (w) and Carl Pfeufer (a), "The Lion God of Mokuru," in *Tod Holton: Super Green Beret* #2 (New York: DC Comics/Lightning Comics, June 1967), 1–10.

8. Otto Binder (w) and Carl Pfeufer (a), "Dawn of American Freedom," in *Tod Holton: Super Green Beret* #2 (New York: DC Comics/Lightning Comics, June 1967), 27–30, 35–41.

9. Bill Schelly, *Joe Kubert: Man of Rock* (Seattle: Fantagraphics Books, 2008), 168.

10. Ibid., 174.

11. Robin Moore (w) and Joe Kubert (a), *Tales of the Green Berets* #1 (New York: DC Comics, January 1967). Reprinted in *The Tales of the Green Beret,* vol. 1 (El Cajon, CA: Blackthorne Publishing, 1986).

12. Bob Haney (w) and Joe Kubert (a), "Invasion Game," in *Star Spangled War Stories* #155 (New York: DC Comics, March 1971). Reprinted in Joe Kubert et al., *DC Showcase Presents: The Unknown Soldier,* vol. 1 (New York: DC Comics, 2006), 57–69.

13. Glanzman often illustrated the stories in the later issues. Shotgun Harker was originally created by Bill Montes (a) and Charles Nicholas (w), and first appeared in *Fightin' Marines* #78 (Derby, CT: Charlton Comics, January 1968), 2–4.

14. Michael Catron, "A Conversation with James Warren," in *Blazing Combat Collection* (Seattle: Fantagraphics Books, 2009), 191.

15. Ibid., 189–90.

16. Archie Goodwin (a) and Joe Orlando (w), "Viet Cong," in *Blazing Combat* #1 (Philadelphia: Warren Publishing, October 1965). Reprinted in Archie Goodwin (a) and Joe Orlando (w), *Blazing Combat* (Seattle: Fantagraphics Books, 2009), 4.

17. Archie Goodwin (a) and Joe Orlando (w), "Landscape!," in *Blazing Combat* #2 (Philadelphia: Warren Publishing, January 1966). Reprinted in Goodwin and Orlando, *Blazing Combat*, 46–53.

18. Julian Bond (w) and T. G. Lewis (a), *Vietnam: An Antiwar Comic Book* (1967). See "The Sixties Project," http://www3.iath.virginia.edu/sixties/HTML_docs/Exhibits /Bond/Bond_comic_page_02.html (accessed February 21, 2011).

19. Ibid.

20. Calley was court-martialed, convicted, and originally sentenced to ten years in prison for his role in the My Lai Massacre. Calley served only three and a half years, however, under house arrest.

21. Tom Veitch (w), Greg Irons (a), et al., "The Legion of Charlies," in *The Legion of Charlies* (San Francisco: Last Gasp, January 1971). Reprinted in Tom Veitch and Greg Irons, *The Mammoth Book of the Best War Comics* (New York: Carroll & Graf, 2007), 253–56.

22. Greg Irons, "Raw War Comics," in *Hydrogen Bomb and Biochemical Warfare Funnies* (San Francisco: Rip Off, May 26, 1971), 37–41.

23. Fred Schrier, "The Last Laugh," in *Hydrogen Bomb and Biochemical Warfare Funnies*, 44–46.

24. Robert Kanigher (w) and Russ Heath (a), "No Loot for the Hellcats," in *Our Fighting Forces, Featuring Lt. Hunter's Hellcats* (New York: DC Comics, 1968) 5–7.

25. *The Dirty Dozen,* directed by Robert Aldrich (1967).

26. *Kelly's Heroes,* directed by Brian G. Hutton (1970).

27. Gary Friedrich (w) and Dick Ayers (a), *Combat Kelly and the Deadly Dozen* (New York: Marvel Comics, 1972–73), 4–8.

28. Sgt. Alvin C. York was one of the most decorated American soldiers of World War I, despite initially being a pacifist because of his religious beliefs as a member of the Church of Christ in Christian Union. In his most famous exploit, he led an attack on a German machine-gun emplacement, killing 28 German soldiers and capturing 132 others. This feat won him a Medal of Honor. Gary Cooper immortalized him in the film *Sergeant York,* directed by Howard Hawks (1941).

29. Archie Goodwin (w) and Al McWilliams (a), *Savage Combat Tales, Featuring Sgt. Stryker's Death Squad* #1 (New York: Atlas Comics, 1975), 5–8.

30. Bob Kanigher, David Micheline (w), and Ed Davis (a), *Men of War #1–2* (New York: DC Comics, 1977–80).

31. Bob Kanigher (w) and Russ Heath (a), "Let Me Live . . . Let Me Die," in *G.I. Combat* #141 (New York: DC Comics, May 1970). Reprinted in *DC Showcase Presents: Haunted Tank,* vol. 2 (New York: DC Comics, 2008).

32. Bob Kanigher, David Micheline (w), and Ed Davis (a), *Men of War* #1 (New York: DC Comics, August 1977), and *Men of War* #2 (New York: DC Comics, September 1977), 22.

33. Roger McKenzie (w) and Dick Ayers (a), *Men of War* #6 (New York: DC Comics: May 1978).

34. Roger McKenzie (w) and Dick Ayers (a), *Men of War* #11 (New York: DC Comics, December 1978), 9–11.

35. See Slotkin, *Gunfighter Nation,* and Warren Susman, *Culture as History: The Transformation of American Society in the Twentieth Century* (New York: Pantheon, 1984). The idea is more amusingly distilled by Oscar Wilde's self-serving epigram "Life imitates Art far more than Art imitates Life" in his essay *The Decay of Lying* (1889).

36. Doug Murray and Michael Golden. "5th of the 1st," in *Savage Tales #1*. (New York: Marvel Comics, 1984.)

37. Andrew Dagilis, "Uncle Sugar vs. Uncle Charlie: An Interview with *The 'Nam*'s Creator, Doug Murray," *Comics Journal* #136 (Seattle: Fantagraphics Publishing, July 1990), 62–84.

38. The Punisher appears in *The 'Nam* #52–53, #67–69, and finally in *Punisher Invades the 'Nam*.

39. David Anthony Kraft, "Interview with Wayne Vansant," in *David Anthony Kraft's Comics Interview* #53 (New York: Fictioneer Press, 1987), 20–31.

40. Brian Jacks, "Interview: Doug Murray," Slush Factory, May 25, 2002, http://slushfactory.com/features/articles/052502-murray.php (accessed August, 20, 2008).

41. Cap went to Vietnam to rescue a single person from a prison, not to fight alongside American forces. See Stan Lee (w) and Gene Colan (a), *Captain America* #125 (New York: Marvel Comics, May 1970).

42. Doug Murray (w) and Wayne Vansant (a), "Back in the Real . . . ," in *The 'Nam* #41 (New York: Marvel Comics, February 1990), 29.

43. *Vietnam Journal* (Series: 1987–90, 2002), Apple Comics, http://www.atomicavenue.com/atomic/TitleDetail.aspx?TitleID=8803 (accessed January 26, 2010).

44. Durand said that the Army gave him drugs to improve his night vision. Unfortunately, when mixed with alcohol, these caused psychotic episodes. See Don Lomax and Bob Durand, *High Shining Brass* #3 (Bethel, CT: Apple Comics, 1991), 26.

45. Central Intelligence Agency, *The Freedom Fighters Manual* (New York: Grove, 1983), http://www.ballistichelmet.org/school/free.html (accessed March 8, 2011).

46. Antonio Langdon, *Grenada: Rescued from Rape and Slavery* (New York: Victims of International Communist Emissaries Press, 1983), 2.

47. Ibid., 16.

48. Long-range reconnaissance patrols (LRRPs, pronounced "lurps") were small four- to six-man teams sent on particularly risky missions deep into hostile territory during the Vietnam War.

49. Larry Hama (w), Steve Leialoha (a), *G.I. Joe: A Real American Hero* #26 (New York, Marvel Comics, August 1984), 26.

50. Larry Hama (w) and Herb Trimpe (a), *G.I. Joe Special Missions* #1 (New York, Marvel Comics, October 1986), 16.

51. Larry Hama (w), Rod Whigham (a), and Andy Mushynsky (a), *G.I. Joe: A Real American Hero* #39 (New York, Marvel Comics, September 1985), 19.

52. Monroe Arnold (w) and Rich Buckler (a), *Reagan's Raiders* #3 (New York: Solson Comics, 1987), 3.

53. Mark Barr (w) and Frank Springer (a), *Captain America* #241 (New York: Marvel Comics, June 1980).

54. *Death Wish*, directed by Michael Winner (1975).

55. Barr and Springer, *Captain America* #241, 19.

56. Ibid., 15.

57. Ibid., 23.

58. Ibid., 27.

59. Ibid., 30.

60. *Top Gun,* directed by Tony Scott (1986).

61. Alan Moore (w) and Bill Sienkiewicz. *Brought to Light: A Graphic Docudrama* (Forestville, CA: Eclipse Books, 1989).

62. Central Committee for Conscientious Objectors. *Real War Stories* (Forestville, CA: Eclipse Comics, 1987, 1991).

Chapter 5. The Resurgence of Superheroes after the Fall of Communism (1991–2001)

1. Francis Fukuyama, *The End of History and the Last Man* (New York: Simon & Schuster, 1992).

2. Jerry Lembcke's *The Spitting Image: Myth, Memory, and the Legacy of Vietnam* (New York: New York University Press, 1998) and Bob Greene's *Homecoming: When the Soldiers Returned from Vietnam* (New York: Putnam, 1989) offered conflicting views of whether or not returning servicemen were actually spat upon. Regardless, feelings were strong about the war in Vietnam and the responsibility of those who fought there. The potency of such events depends upon whether they are believed, not their veracity—even more so in the already mythic world of comic books.

3. Charles Marshall (w) and Ernie Stiner (a), "Overkill," in *Desert Storm: Send Hussein to Hell* (Wheeling, WV: Innovation Publishing, April 1991), 8.

4. *Rocky and His Friends* and *The Bullwinkle Show,* animated television series, Jay Ward Productions, 1959–64.

5. George Broderick Jr. (w) and Don Martinec (a), "The Adventures of Iraqi and Abdulwinkle," in *Desert Storm: Send Hussein to Hell* (Wheeling, WV: Innovation Publishing, April 1991), 9.

6. Comic Book Database, http://www.cbdb.com (accessed December 16, 2010).

7. Dagilis, "Uncle Sugar vs. Uncle Charlie."

8. "Letters to the Editor," *The 'Nam* #84 (New York: Marvel Comics, September 1993), 32.

9. Murray and Vansant, "Back in the Real . . . ," 30.

10. Siegel and Shuster, "How Superman," 9–10.

11. Chuck Dixon (w) and Kevin Kobasiac (a). "Creep," in *The 'Nam* #66 (New York: Marvel Comics: March 1992).

12. The Vietcong had no legal right to collect "taxes" in South Vietnam, but that is how they described what was, essentially, a protection racket.

13. Don Lomax, "Editor's Note," in *The 'Nam* #84 (New York: Marvel Comics, September 1993), 32.

14. Tom Tuohy, introduction to *Punisher Invades the 'Nam : Final Mission,* by Don Lomax (w) and Alberto Saichann (a) (New York: Marvel Comics, February 1994), 3.

15. This was a reference to the Japanese doctors of Unit 731, who experimented on Allied POWs during World War II, similarly to Dr. Josef Mengele's experiments on Nazi concentration camp inmates.

16. Don Lomax (w) and Alberto Saichann (a), *Punisher Invades the 'Nam: Final Mission* (New York: Marvel Comics, February 1994).

17. *First Blood,* directed by Ted Kerchief (1982); *Rambo: First Blood Part II,* directed by George P. Cosmatos (1985); and *Rambo* III, directed by Peter MacDonald (1988). Stallone later reprised the role in *Rambo* (2008), which he directed.

18. Ed Herron (w) and Jack Kirby (a), *Captain America* #1 (New York: Marvel Comics, March 1941), 20.

19. Alex Schomburg, *All Winners* #7 (New York: Marvel Comics, January 1943), 244.

20. Ed Brubaker (w) and Steve Epting (a), "The Death of Captain America," in *Captain America* #25 (New York: Marvel Comics: March 2007), 30.

21. Simon Furman (w) and Art Nichols (a), "What if the Punisher Became Captain America?," in *What If?*, vol. 2, #51 (New York: Marvel Comics, July 1993).

22. Ironically, John Walker was also the name of a Navy cryptologist who was part of a major Soviet spy ring that was broken in the late 1980s. Walker, his son, and brother-in-law were arrested for selling secrets to the Soviet Union for surprisingly small amounts of money.

23. Greg Wright (w) and Tod Smith (a). *The Punisher: No Escape.* (New York: Marvel Comics, 1990), 28.

24. Furman and Nichols, "What If the Punisher Became Captain America?," 32–33.

25. Ibid., 48.

26. Mike Baron (w) and Bill Reinhold (a), *Punisher: Empty Quarter* (New York: Marvel Comics, 1994), 22–23.

27. In the twentieth century, the United States occupied Nicaragua five times, Haiti and Cuba four times each, and at different times it has annexed or "leased" land in Panama and Cuba to enforce American policies in the region. See Max Boot's *The Savage Wars of Peace* (New York: Basic Books, 2002).

28. D. G. Chichester (w) and Klaus Janson (a), *Punisher–Captain America: Blood and Glory* (New York: Marvel Comics, 1991), 16–17.

29. Stephen E. Ambrose : The US Army from the Normandy Beaches to the Bulge to the Surrender of Germany (New York: Simon & Schuster, 1997). Ambrose, *Citizen Soldiers*; Paul Fussell, *Wartime: Understanding and Behavior in the Second World War* (New York: Oxford University Press, 1989); Peter Schrijvers, *Crash to Ruin: American Combat Soldiers in Europe During World War II* (New York: New York University Press, 1998) and *The GI War against Japan: American Soldiers in Asia and the Pacific during World War II* (New York: New York University Press, 2002).

30. Chichester and Janson, *Punisher–Captain America*, 17.

31. Ibid., 26.

32. Ibid., 43.

33. Ibid., 44. Cap carries a shield, which he can use as a weapon in extremis.

34. Ibid., 18.

35. Ibid., 31.

36. Mike Conroy, *500 Comic Book Villains* (Hauppauge, NY: Barron's Educational Series, 2004), 227.

37. "Comic with First Superman Story Sells for $1.5m," *The Independent* (London), March 30, 2010, http://www.independent.co.uk/news/world/americas/comic-with-first-superman-story-sells-for-15m-1930852.html (accessed March 30, 2010).

38. Jerry Siegel and Joe Shuster had to sue DC Comics to recover any profits from their Superman character, and it took more than thirty years in the courts before they saw any profits. Marvel owns Captain America, so Joe Simon and Jack Kirby did not see any profits either. Now creators of new comic book characters hold the intellectual property rights.

39. David Rawson, Pat McGreal (w), and Greg LaRocque (a), *Fighting American* (New York: DC Comics, 1994).

40. Ibid., #1 (February 1994), 3.

41. Ibid., #2 (March 1994), 28

42. Ibid., #1–6 (February–July 1994).

43. James Robinson and Paul Smith, *Elseworlds: The Golden Age* (New York: DC Comics, 1997) 20, 24, This is a trade paperback reprint that republished the four comics that were originally published separately in 1993.

44. Ibid., 60. The gimmick of placing Hitler's brain into another living entity was also used in the *SuperPatriot* miniseries.

45. Howard Chaykin's American Flagg was a dysfunctional character trying to set America right. Alex Ross reimagined Uncle Sam for DC Comics and also Captain America for Marvel Comics.

46. Steve Darnall (w) and Alex Ross (a), *U.S.* (New York: DC Comics/Vertigo, 1997).

47. Greil Marcus, "The Man on the Street," in *Give Our Regards to the Atomsmashers!,* edited by Steve Howe (New York: Pantheon Books, 2004): 190–1.

48. Darnall and Ross, *U.S.,* 96.

49. Walt Kelly, poster of Pogo for Earth Day, 1970. http://www.igopogo.com/we_have_met.htm

50. *Agent Liberty* first appeared in *Superman,* vol. 2, #60 (New York: DC Comics, October 1991).

51. Dan Jurgens et al., *Agent Liberty* #1 (New York: DC Comics, 1992), 14.

52. Erik Larsen, author e-mail interview, October 18, 2005.

53. Erik Larsen (w), Keith Giffen (w), and Dave Johnson (a), *SuperPatriot* (Berkeley, CA: Image Comics, July 1993).

54. Larsen, author interview.

55. Don Lomax, *Vietnam Journal* (Bethel, CT: Apple Comics, November 1987–April 1991).

56. Matt Brady, *Garth Ennis on Battlefields: Night Witches,* Newsarama.com, http://www .newsrama.com/comics/080818-Ennis-Battlefields.html (accessed August 18, 2008).

57. Alex Alonso, "Editor's Note," in Garth Ennis (w) and Killian Plunkett (a), *The Unknown Soldier* (New York: DC Comics, 1997), 6.

58. Ennis and Plunkett, *Unknown Soldier,* 12.

59. This was the original (albeit, reimagined) Unknown Soldier looking for a third one to succeed the second one, who had died—in short, a replacement for his replacement. See ibid., 94–100.

60. Ibid., 102–3.

61. Garth Ennis (w) and Jim Lee (a), "Nosh and Barry and Eddie and Joe," in *Weird War Stories Annual* (New York: DC Comics, 2000), 1–10.

62. Wayne Vansant, *Semper Fi* (New York: Marvel Comics, 1988–89).

63. Ibid.

64. Wayne Vansant, *Days of Darkness* (Bethel, CT: Apple Comics, 1995).

65. Rod Ledwell, *WW2.* Norwood, MA: New England Comics, 2000–1, 2003–6).

66. This sort of speculation caused many investors to see the comics not as entertainment but as a future payout. In turn, it caused many to quit collecting comics, due to the variant covers that permeated the industry. By early 2000, the market had dropped off when investors realized that their comics were not worth what they had originally thought. See Weist and Steranko, *100 Greatest Comic Books.*

67. Most revived titles were reprints of the complete runs of older comics. There were some limited exceptions: Apple Comics reprinted *Blazing Combat* and *Vietnam Journal* with the addition of a few newly created stories.

68. Aubrey Singer (w) and Dave Matthews (a), *Strange Combat Tales* #4 (New York: Epic Comics, January 1994).

69. Joe Lansdale (w) and Sam Glanzman (a), "The Elopement," in *Weird War Tales* # 2 (New York: DC Comics, 1997), 21–32.

70. Gordon Rennie (w) Randy DuBurke (a), "Tunnel Rats," in *Weird War Tales* #1 (New York: DC Comics, June 1997).

71. David Lloyd, "Looking Good, Feeling Great," in *Weird War Tales* #2 (New York: DC Comics, July 1997) 1–10.

72. Joe Kubert, *Fax from Sarajevo* (Milwaukie, OR: Dark Horse Comics, 1998).

73. Art Spiegelman, *Maus: A Survivor's Tale,* 2 vols. (New York: Pantheon Books, 1986, 1991).

74. Joe Sacco, *Palestine* (Seattle: Fantagraphics Books, 1994), *Safe Area Goražde: The War in Eastern Bosnia 1992–1995* (Seattle: Fantagraphics Books, 2000), and *The Fixer* (Montreal: Drawn and Quarterly, 2003).

75. Sacco, *Safe Area Goražde,* 19–23.

76. Joe Kubert, *Medal of Honor Special Edition* #1 (Milwaukie, OR: Dark Horse Comics, April 1994).

77. Will Eisner, *Last Day in Vietnam,* (Milwaukie, OR: Dark Horse, 2000), 3–5.

78. Jim Ottaviani et al., *Fallout: J. Robert Oppenheimer, Leo Szilard, and the Political Science of the Atomic Bomb* (Ann Arbor, MI: G.T. Labs, 2001).

79. Keiji Nakazawa, *I Saw It: The Atomic Bombing of Hiroshima—A Survivor's True Story* (San Francisco: Educomics, 1982).

80. Jim Ottaviani, interview on the G.T. Labs website, http://www.gtlabs.com/interview .html (accessed June 4, 2008).

Chapter 6. The Role of Comics after 9/11 (2001–3)

1. Stan Lee (w) and Steve Ditko (a), *Spider-Man* (New York: Marvel Comics, 1964–). See Wright, *Comic Book Nation,* 238.

2. The film *Spider-Man,* shot before 9/11 but released afterward, demonstrated this dilemma. As originally written, Spider-Man catches some villains in a gigantic web he spins between the twin towers. This scene had to be reshot, for obvious reasons, and it was partly replaced with a scene set at New York City's Roosevelt Island Tramway. Significantly, the standard superhero scenario is nearly reversed: instead of the solitary Spider-Man coming to the rescue by himself, a group of average New Yorkers help him thwart the Green Goblin's attempt to drop a tramcar full of children (and Peter Parker's girlfriend, Mary Jane) into the East River. *Spider-Man,* directed by Sam Raimi (2002).

3. Joe Quesada, ed., *Amazing Spider-man* #36 (New York: Marvel Comics, 2001), 2–15.

4. John Ney Rieber (w) and John Cassaday (a), "The New Deal," in *Captain America* #1 (New York: Marvel Comics, 2002), 31.

5. Geoff Johns, David Goyer, Humberto Ramos, and Sandra Hope, "A Burning Hate," in *9/11,* vol. 2 (New York: Marvel Comics, 2001), 189–94.

6. John Ney Rieber (w) and John Cassaday (a), "Fight Terror," in *Captain America* #2 (New York: Marvel Comics, 2002).

7. Will Eisner, "Reality," in *9–11: Emergency Relief,* ed. Jeff Mason (Gainesville FL: Alternative Comics, 2001), 45.

8. Frank Miller, "The Power of Faith," in *9–11: Artists Respond*, vol. 1 (Milwaukie, OR: Dark Horse, 2001), 64–65.

9. John McRae and P. Craig Russell, "In Flanders Field," in *9–11*, vol. 1, 5–6.

10. Sam Glanzman, "There Were Tears in Her Eyes," in *9–11: Artists Respond*, vol. 2 (Milwaukie, OR: Dark Horse, 2001), 189–93.

11. Ibid., 192.

12. Ted Rall, "The Day My Train Stood Still," in *9–11: Emergency Relief*, ed. Jeff Mason (Gainesville, FL: Alternative Comics, 2001), 80–83.

13. Ted Rall, *To Afghanistan and Back* (New York: NBM, 2002).

14. Art Spiegelman, *In the Shadow of No Towers* (New York: Pantheon, 2004), 11.

15. Frank Lauria, ed., *SPECWAR: Special Warfare* #1–7 (San Diego, CA: Peter Four Productions, 2002). "SEALs" is the acronym for the SEa, Air, and Land special forces of the U.S. Navy, which highlights the arenas where SEALs can operate. http://www .specwarnet.net/americas/SEALs.htm (accessed February 25, 2011).

16. Lauria, *SPECWAR* #1, 2, 32.

17. Lauria, *SPECWAR* # 2, 1.

18. Lauria, *SPECWAR* #3, 32.

19. Lauria, *SPECWAR* #4, 1.

20. Richard Marcinko wrote two nonfiction books about his SEAL experiences. He reported on a commander who never went on missions, yet had no compunction about ordering others into seemingly unnecessary and often fatal situations. It is possible that the same commander was referenced here. See Lauria, *SPECWAR* #5.

21. Lauria, *SPECWAR* #6, 2–6.

22. Lauria, *SPECWAR* #5, 1.

23. Graig Weich, *Civilian Justice* #1 (New York: Beyond Comics, 2002). http://www .civilianjustice.com (accessed February 10, 2010).

24. Ibid., 34.

25. Marcus Meleton and Pete Garcia, *Pete the P.O'd Postal Worker: War Journal* (Costa Mesa, CA: Sharkbait, 2002), 1, 3. Pigs are considered unclean in Islamic culture. Thus, to die by being trampled and eaten by pigs would be an especially disturbing event for Muslims.

26. Brian Denham, *Kill Box* #1 (San Antonio, TX: Antarctic, December, 2002), 1.

27. Ibid., 10–11.

28. Rod Espinoza, author and Antarctic Press publisher, author e-mail interview, February 10, 2005.

29. *Shi* means death in Japanese; her real name is Ana Ishikawa. It is also, of course, a pun on the English word "she." The character first appeared in William Tucci's *Razor Annual* #1 (Bayport, NY: Crusade Comics, 1993).

30. Brian Augustyn (w) and Ron Adrian (a), *United* #1 (Scottsdale, AZ: Chaos Comics, May 2002), cover, 18, 20.

31. Chuck Austen (w) and Patrick Olliffe (a), *The Call* #1–4 (New York: Marvel Comics, June–September 2003). The prequel comics were Chuck Austen (w) and David Finch (a) *The Call of Duty: Brotherhood* (New York: Marvel Comics, July–December 2002, January 2003); Bruce Jones (w) and Tom Mandrake (a), *The Call of Duty: The Precinct* (New York: Marvel Comics, August–December, 2002, January 2003); and Chuck Austen (w) and Danijel Zededj (a), *The Call of Duty: The Wagon* (New York: Marvel Comics, October 2002–January 2003).

32. *Captain America* had been in "suspended animation," and not for the first time. The original series was cancelled in the early 1950s, although he was brought back from 1963 to 1965. After another brief hiatus, he returned in 1968 and continues to the present. During this forty-three-year run, Cap has fought mostly criminal elements and the like. Vol. 1 comprises 1968–95; vol. 2 ran from 1995 to 1997; vol. 3 from 1997 to 2002; vol. 4 from 2002 to 2004; and vol. 5 from 2004 to 2009. Marvel "rebooted" the original story line from the first volume in 2009 (#600).

33. Cassaday and Rieber, *Captain America* #1.

34. *Wizard: The Comics Magazine* #133 (October 2002), 39.

35. Cassaday and Rieber, *Captain America* #1, 28–33.

36. Mark Millar, Bryan Hitch, and Andrew Currie, *The Ultimates* #1 (New York: Marvel Comics, 2002), 17.

37. Jerry Ordway and Karl Kesel, *U.S. Agent* #1–3, mini-series (New York: Marvel Comics, 2001).

38. Not to be confused with *The Shield*. The role of the Shield is as intriguing, as the character is directly controlled by a real government agency, specifically the FBI. Director J. Edgar Hoover is the only one who knows the Shield's identity, calling on him when needed to fight for the government. The Shield was created in an era when belief in science and trust in the government was widespread. While popular in his day, the character was only reissued in a vintage collection of back issues. Given that *The Shield* was published by Archie Comics, with their wholesome image of yesteryear, the nostalgia is understandable.

39. Marvel comics had introduced Nick Fury, the main character, in 1963 in *Sgt. Fury and his Howling Commandos,* a World War II series. Stan Lee (w) and Jack Kirby (a), *Sgt. Fury and His Howling Commandos* #1.

40. SHIELD originated in Stan Lee (w) and Jack Kirby (a), *Strange Tales* #135 (New York: Marvel Comics, May 1965).

41. Weich, *Civilian Justice* #1 (New York: Beyond Comics, September 2002).

42. Graig Weich, author interview, March 19, 2006.

43. Alex Ross and Paul Dini, *Wonder Woman: Spirit of Humanity* (New York: DC Comics, 2001), 8.

44. The characters are drawn in more stylized form and give off a different "feel." This may have been indicative of the artist's desire to mix art and politics. See Kyle Baker (w) and Robert Morales (a), *Truth: Red, White, and Black* #1–6 (New York: Marvel Comics, 2003).

45. Ronald Takaki, *A Different Mirror: A Multicultural History of America* (New York: Back Bay Books, 1993), 41.

46. HBO contemplated not running *Band of Brothers* as scheduled in the fall of 2001, as some thought that the date was too soon after the attacks. The worry was that it might distress some viewers, who would not wish to watch something so graphic. It played as scheduled and got very high ratings.

47. *Band of Brothers,* produced by Steven Spielberg and Tom Hanks (2001).

48. Garth Ennis (w) and Dave Gibbons (a), *War Story: Screaming Eagles* (New York: DC Comics/Vertigo, February 2002).

49. Garth Ennis (w), Chris Weston (a), *War Story: Johann's Tiger,* vol. 1 (New York: DC Comics/Vertigo, November 2001).

50. Ibid., 32.

51. Garth Ennis (w) and David Lloyd (a), *War Story,* vol. 2 (New York: DC Comics/Vertigo, March 2006, 3.

52. Garth Ennis (w) and John Higgins (a), *War Story: D-Day Dodgers,* (New York: DC Comics/Vertigo, Dec., 2001).

53. *Dar al-Harb,* or "house of war," refers to countries where Muslim law is not in force. Countries that have nonaggression or peace treaties with Muslims are known as *Dar al-Ahd* or *Dar al-Sulh.* Central Intelligence Agency, *The World Factbook,* s.v. "Religions," https://www.cia.gov/library/publications/the-world-factbook/geos /us.html (accessed February 24, 2011).

54. Ennis and Higgins, *War Story: D-Day Dodgers,* 35.

55. Garth Ennis (w) and Carlos Ezquerra (a), *War Story: Condors* (New York: DC Comics/ Vertigo, March 2003), 32.

56. Pierre Christin (w) and Enki Bilal (a), *Black Order Brigade,* trans. Frank Wynne (Hollywood, CA: Humanoids, 1979).

57. Garth Ennis (w) and Gary Erskine (a), *War Story: Archangel* (New York: DC Comics/ Vertigo, April 2003).

58. Garth Ennis et al., *Enemy Ace: War in Heaven* (New York: DC Comics/Vertigo, July 2001), 7.

59. Ennis et al. *Enemy Ace,* 40.

60. Ennis and Ezquerra, *Adventures in the Rifle Brigade,* 9–11.

61. *Elsa the She-Wolf of the SS,* directed by Don Edmonds (1975).

62. Joe Sacco, "When Good Bombs Happen to Bad People," in *Notes from a Defeatist* (Seattle: Fantagraphics Books 2003), 119–29.

63. Sacco, "More Women, More Children, More Quickly," in ibid., 131–53.

64. Sacco, "How I Loved the War," in ibid., 153–89.

65. Sacco, "Apocrypha" in ibid., pp. 202–215.

66. Arun Gandhi, "Understanding the Culture of Violence," in *411* #1 (New York: Marvel Comics, 2003), 1–2.

67. David Rees (w) and Tony Salmons (a), "Seeds," in *411* #1 (New York: Marvel Comics, June 2003), 24–31.

68. Brian K. Vaughn (w) and Leonardo Manco (a), "The Clarion Call," in *411* #2 (New York: Marvel Comics, July 2003), 2–13.

69. A reference to Sheik Abdel Rahman, who was expelled from Egypt for his connections to the Islamic Brotherhood.

Chapter 7. Comics and the Soul of Combat (2003–10)

1. Karl Zinsmeister, *Boots on the Ground: A Month with the 82nd Airborne in the Battle for Iraq* (New York: Truman Talley Books/St. Martin's, 2003).

2. Kyle Baker, *Special Forces* #1 (Berkeley, CA: Image Comics, 2008), 32.

3. Baker and Morales, *Truth.*

4. Joe Sacco, "Complacency Kills," *Guardian Weekend,* February 26, 2005.

5. Joe Sacco, "Trauma on Loan," *Guardian Weekend,* January 21, 2006.

6. Brian K. Vaughn (w) and Niko Henrichon (a), *Pride of Baghdad* (New York: DC Comics, 2006).

7. Tom Waltz (w) and Nathan St. John (a), *Finding Peace* (New York: IDW, 2008).

8. David Axe (w) and Steven Olexa (a), *War Fix* (New York: NBM ComicsLit, 2006).

9. Philip Smucker, *Al Qaeda's Great Escape: The Military and the Media on Terror's Trail* (Washington, D.C.: Brassey's, 2004).

10. Richard C. Meyer (w), Martin Montiel Luna (a), and Richard C. Meyer (a), *No Enemy but Peace* (Laredo, TX: Machinegun Bob Productions, 2008), 1.

11. Ibid., 2.

12. Chuck Dixon (w) and Doug Mahnke (a), *Team Zero* (New York: DC Comics, 2005–6).

13. Ambrose, *Citizen Soldiers: The US Army from the Normandy Beaches to the Bulge to the Surrender of Germany*, 354.

14. Joe Kubert interview, http://www.comicsbulletin.com/interviews/3602/brian-azzarello-crafting-stories-from-mistakes/ (accessed December 15, 2013).

15. Joe Kubert, *Sgt. Rock: The Prophecy,* #1 (New York: DC Comics, 2006).

16. Tucci gained much of his fame for the comic *Shi,* a very successful issue of which was part of the massive outpouring of comic books after 9/11.

17. Billy Tucci, *Sgt Rock: The Lost Battalion* #1 (of 6). (New York: DC Comics, January 2009), 2–5.

18. Bill Mauldin and Todd DePastino, *Willie and Joe: The World War II Years,* vols 1–2. (Seattle: Fantagraphics, 2009), vol. 2, 97.

19. Tucci, *Sgt. Rock: The Lost Battalion* #1, 15, and Tucci, *Sgt. Rock the Lost Battalion* #4, (2009), 23.

20. Garth Ennis (w) and Darick Robertson (a), *Fury: Peacemaker* #1 (New York: Marvel Comics, 2006).

21. "Good people sleep peaceably in their beds at night only because rough men stand ready to do violence on their behalf," a quotation frequently attributed to George Orwell, has not been substantiated. However, in an essay about Kipling, Orwell refers to the concept, which Kipling expressed in somewhat similar words in his poem *Tommy* (1892).

22. Ennis and Robertson, *Born* #1, 31–32.

23. *The Marvel Encyclopedia: The Definitive Guide to the Characters of the Marvel Universe,* s.v. "The Punisher" (New York: DK, 2006).

24. Garth Ennis (w), Darrick Robertson (a), and Jimmy Palimiotti (a), *Born* #2 (New York: Marvel Comics, July 2003), 21–22.

25. Ibid., 24–25.

26. Garth Ennis (w), Darrick Robertson (a), and Jimmy Palimiotti (a), *Born* #4 (New York: Marvel Comics, September 2003–4), 29–31.

27. Ibid., 1.

28. Garth Ennis (w) and Amanda Conner (a), *The Pro* (New York: Image Comics, 2002), 40.

29. Ibid.

30. Garth Ennis (w) and Goran Parlov (a), "Valley Forge, Valley Forge," in *The Punisher Book* #10 (New York: Marvel Comics, May–October 2008), 137–139, 143–146.

31. Garth Ennis (w) and Jacen Barrows (a), *303* #1–6 (Rantoul, IL: Avatar, 2004), and http://www.comicbookresources.com/news/printthis.cgi?id=4044 (accessed May 12, 2008).

32. Ted Nomura, *Dictators of the Twentieth Century Series: Hitler* #1–4 (San Antonio, TX: Antarctic, 2004).

33. Japanese manga-style comics are known for exaggerated physical features, stylized violence, and kinetic movement. The style has become popular and has been emulated

around the world. See Scott McCloud, *Understanding Comics: The Invisible Art* (San Francisco: Kitchen Sink, 1993).

34. Ted Nomura, *Dictators of the Twentieth Century: Saddam Hussein–The Fall* #2 (San Antonio, TX: Antarctic, 2004).

35. Ibid.

36. Nomura, introduction, ibid.

37. *Tora, Tora, Tora,* directed by Richard Fleischer, Kinji Fukasaku, and Toshio Masuda (1970).

38. Mark Millar (w) and Dave John (a), *Superman: Red Son* (New York: Elseworld/DC Comics, 2003).

39. The USA PATRIOT Act, or "Patriot Act," is an act of Congress that was quickly developed and passed (in October 2001) as antiterrorism legislation in response to the 9/11 attacks. It broadly expanded domestic law enforcement and foreign intelligence agencies' investigative and search and surveillance powers. The act's official title is the "Uniting and Strengthening America by Providing Appropriate Tools Required to Intercept and Obstruct Terrorism Act of 2001."

40. See Mike Mackey (w) and Donny Lin (a), *Liberality for All* #2 (Lexington, KY: ACC Studios, 2005), 30.

41. Osprey Publishing produced "graphic histories" based on World War II and American Civil War battles. Statistics on monthly sales are available from *Previews Magazine,* a monthly catalog of comic books, graphic novels, and related merchandise. It also publishes the monthly sales figures for comics, graphic novels, etc. http://previewsworld.com /support/previews_docs/Bestsellers/Top100comics_2007.pdf (accessed February 1, 2011).

42. Mark Millar (w) and Steve McNiven (a), *Civil War,* miniseries (New York: Marvel Comics, 2006–7).

43. Millar and McNiven, *Civil War* #1, 7–10.

44. Millar and McNiven, *Civil War* #1, 18–20.

45. Millar and McNiven, *Civil War* #7, 17–25.

46. George Gene Gustines, "Captain America Is Dead; National Hero Since 1941," *New York Times,* March 8, 2007, http://www.nytimes.com/2007/03/08/books/08capt.html? pagewanted=all (accessed March 3, 2011).

47. "Comic Hero Captain America Dies," BBC News, March 8, 2007, http://news.bbc .co.uk/2/hi/entertainment/6431619.stm (accessed March 11, 2011).

48. Ben Morse, "Who Will Be Captain America?" *Wizard* #187 (New York: Marvel Comics, May 2007), 28–29.

49. Both Bucky and Captain America fell into the North Sea after the rocket bomb they were diverting from London blew up in mid-air. This was the same plot strand used to revive Cap in the early 1960s. (The Sub-Mariner found him in suspended animation inside a block of ice.) The same idea was used to reintroduce the original Bucky in 2004.

50. Jim Frederick, "The Long Mistake," *Time,* December 6, 2004, http://www.time.com/time /magazine/article/0,9171,880313,00.html (accessed February 1, 2011).

51. The original Steve Rogers was reintroduced in 1962, and the *Captain America* title resumed in 1968. Rogers was killed off in 2007, and the original Bucky assumed the mantle and shield of Captain America. In *Captain America: The Chosen,* the story is mostly set in modern

Afghanistan. But Captain America's death (in the United States) is different. Rather than dying immediately, he uses his heretofore unknown telepathic powers to contact the deserving soldier in Afghanistan who will take his place. These alternate and overlapping story lines are a major reason why some people do not like comic books or quit reading after they can no longer follow the complicated narratives. At the same time, these reiterations of characters and themes are typical of all mythology and are an attraction for other readers.

52. David Morrell (w) and Mitch Breitweiser (a), *Captain America: The Chosen* #1 (New York: Marvel Comics, November 2007), 2–8.

53. David Morell (w) and Mitch Breitweiser (a), *Captain America: The Chosen* #6 (New York: Marvel Comics, March, 2008), 19–22.

54. Paul Jenkins (w) and Graham Nolan (a), *The New Avengers: Pot of Gold* (New York: Marvel Comics/AAFES, 2005).

55. Stuart Moore (w) and Cliff Richards (a), *The New Avengers: Letters Home* (New York: Marvel Comics/AAFES, January 2007).

56. AAFES comics can now be purchased by civilians through websites such as eBay.

57. Army and Air Force Exchange Service, http://www.aafes.com/pa/history-page.htm (accessed February 1, 2011).

58. Stuart Moore (w) and Cliff Richards (a), *New Avengers: Fireline* (New York: Marvel Comics/AAFES, 2008).

59. Evan Wright, *Generation Kill: Devil Dogs, Captain America, and the New Face of War* (New York: Berkley Caliber, 2005), 68.

60. Ibid., 7.

61. Advertised on eBay as unofficial patches for SEAL Team 5 and SEAL Team 8. (SEAL Team 6 probably sells better after the bin Laden killing.) Also used as unofficial logos for several other units.

62. Anthony Lappe (w) and Dan Goldman (a), *Shooting War* (New York: Grand Central, 2007), 105.

63. Emmanuel Guibert and Alan Cope, *Alan's War: The Memories of G.I. Alan Cope* (New York: First Second Press, 2008).

64. Tom Waltz (w) and Casey Maloney (a), *Children of the Grave* (New York: IDW, 2006).

65. Joe Dysart (w) and Alberto Ponticelli (a), *Unknown Soldier* #1 (New York: DC Comics, 2008), 28.

66. Ibid., 32.

67. Rick Veitch (w) and Gary Erskine (a), *Army at Love: The Art of War* #1 (New York: DC Comics, 2009), 2–3.

68. Frank Marraffino (w) and Henry Flint (a), *The Haunted Tank* #1–6 (New York: Vertigo/DC Comics, 2009).

69. Plans to invade Japan actually had been made. Operation Olympic and Operation Downfall were to be the equivalents of Operation Overlord (the Normandy invasion) in Europe—amphibious assaults to invade two of the Japanese main islands and end the war.

70. Chuck Dixon (w) and Butch Guice (a), *Storming Paradise* #4 (New York: DC Comics/Wildstorm, 2008).

71. *The 'Nam,* issues 58–69.

Bibliography

Allen, William, ed. *True Comics* #8. New York: Parents Magazine Institute, January 1942.

Alonso, Alex. "Editor's Note." In *The Unknown Soldier*. New York: DC Comics, 1997.

Ambrose, Stephen. *Citizen Soldiers: The US Army from the Normandy Beaches to the Bulge to the Surrender of Germany*. New York: Simon & Schuster, 1997.

_____. *D-Day, June 6, 1944: The Climactic Battle of World War I*. New York: Simon & Schuster, 1996.

Ambrose, Stephen, and Douglas G. Brinkley. *Rise to Globalism: American Foreign Policy since 1938*. New York: Penguin, 1998.

American Historical Association. *Perspectives on Audiovisuals in the Teaching of History*. Washington, DC: American Historical Association, 1999.

Anderson, Benedict R. *Imagined Communities: Reflections on the Origin and Spread of Nationalism*. New York: Verso, 1991.

Andreas, Joel. *Addicted to War: Why the U.S. Can't Kick Militarism*. Oakland, CA: AK, 2004.

Anonymous. Ad for Pearson's soap. *Cosmopolitan*, April 1899.

Appleby, Joyce, Lynn Hunt, and Margaret Jacob. *Telling the Truth about History*. New York: Norton, 1995.

Appy, Christian. *Patriots: The Vietnam War Remembered from All Sides*. New York: Viking, 2003.

_____. *Working-Class War: American Combat Soldiers and Vietnam*. Chapel Hill: University of North Carolina Press, 1993.

Army and Air Force Exchange Service. http://www.aafes.com/pa/history-page.htm. Accessed February 1, 2011.

Arnold, Monroe, and Rich Buckler. *Reagan's Raiders* #1–3. New York: Solson Comics, 1987.

Asherman, Allan. "The Why of Blitzkrieg." In *Blitzkrieg* #1. New York: DC Comics, January–February 1976.

Atom-Age Combat #3–4. New York: St. John Publications, January 1953.

AtomicAvenue.com, s.v. "Combat." http://www.atomicavenue.com/atomic/TitleDetail .aspx?TitleID=14229. Accessed February 13, 2002.

_____, s.v. "Dell Publishing History." http://www.atomicavenue.com/publishers/dell .Accessed February 26, 2009.

_____, s.v. "Foxhole." http://www.atomicavenue.com/foxhole. Accessed January 22, 2009.

Atomic War #1. Philadelphia, PA: Ace Comics, November 1952.

Augustyn, Brian (w), and Ron Adrian (a). *United* #1. Scottsdale, AZ: Chaos! Comics, May 2002.

Austen, Chuck (w), and David Finch (a). *The Call of Duty: Brotherhood*. New York: Marvel Comics, July 2002–January 2003.

Austen, Chuck (w), and Patrick Olliffe (a). *The Call* #1–4. New York: Marvel Comics, June–September 2003.

Austen, Chuck (w), and Danijel Zededj (a). *The Call of Duty: The Wagon*. New York: Marvel Comics, October 2002–January 2003.

Axe, David (w), and Steven Olexa (a). *War Fix*. New York: NBM ComicsLit, 2006.

Azzarello, Brian (w), and Joe Kubert (a). *Sgt. Rock: Between Hell and a Hard Place*. New York: DC Comics, 2003.

Bacevich, Andrew J. *American Empire: The Realities and Consequences of U.S. Diplomacy*. Cambridge, MA: Harvard University Press, 2002.

Baker, Kyle. *Special Forces* #1–4. Berkeley CA: Image Comics, 2008.

Baker, Kyle (w), and Robert Morales (a). *Truth: Red, White and Black* #1–6. New York: Marvel Comics, 2003–4.

Barat, Peter, Beth Lewis, and Paul Barat, eds. *Persuasive Images*. Princeton, NJ: Princeton University Press, 1992.

Baron, Mike (w), and Bill Reinhold (a). *Punisher: Empty Quarter*. New York: Marvel Comics, November 1994.

Barr, Mark (w), and Frank Springer (a). *Captain America* #241. New York: Marvel Comics, June 1980.

Barson, Michael. *Red Scared: The Commie Menace in Propaganda and Popular Culture*. San Francisco: Chronicle Books, 1999.

Barthes, Roland. *Mythologies*. New York: Hill & Wang, 1972.

Bell, John. *Guardians of the North: The National Superhero in Canadian Comic Book Art*. Ottawa: National Archives of Canada, 1992.

Bennett, Greg, Charles Brownstein, and Chris Pitzer, eds. *SPX 2004: War*. New York: Comic Book Legal Defense Fund, 2004.

Benton, Mike. *The Comic Book in America*. Dallas: Taylor, 1993.

Bernays, Edward. *Propaganda*. New York: Ig, 2004.

Binder, Otto (w), and Carl Pfeufer (a). "Dawn of American Freedom." In *Tod Holton, Super Green Beret* #2. New York: DC Comics / Lightning Comics, June 1967.

_____. "The Lion God of Mokuru." In *Tod Holton, Super Green Beret* #2. New York: DC Comics / Lightning Comics, June 1967.

_____. "Rebel Rat-Hole." In *Tod Holton, Super Green Beret* #1. New York: DC Comics/ Lightning Comics, April 1967.

_____. "White Magic in the Black Forest." In *Tod Holton, Super Green Beret* #1. New York: DC Comics/Lightning Comics, April 1967.

Black, Bill, ed. *Miss Victory: Golden Anniversary Issue*. Longwood, FL: AC Comics, 1991.

Black, Edwin. *War against the Weak: Eugenics and America's Campaign to Create a Master Race*. New York: Four Walls, Eight Windows, 2003.

Bond, Julian (w), and T. G. Lewis (a). *Vietnam: An Antiwar Comic Book*. The Sixties Project, 1967. http://www3.iath.virginia.edu/sixties/HTML_docs/Exhibits/Bond/Bond _comic _page_02.html. Accessed February 21, 2011.

Boot, Max. *The Savage Wars of Peace*. New York: Basic Books, 2002.

Boyer, Paul. *By the Bomb's Early Light: American Thought and Culture at the Dawn of the Atomic Age*. Chapel Hill: University of North Carolina Press, 1994.

Brady, Matt. *Garth Ennis on Battlefields: Night Witches*. Newsarama.com. http://www .newsrama.com/comics/080818-Ennis-Battlefields.html. Accessed August 18, 2008.

Brandt, Frank, ed. *Cartoons for Fighters*. New York: The Infantry Journal, 1945.

Bremner, Charles. "Swiftian Sister of Social Satire." *The Times* (London), April 22, 1991.

Broderick, George, Jr., and Don Martinec. "The Adventures of Iraqi and Abdulwinkle." In *Desert Storm: Send Hussein to Hell*. Wheeling, WV: Innovation Publishing, April 1991.

Brubaker, Ed (w), and Steve Epting (a). "The Death of Captain America." In *Captain America* #25. New York: Marvel Comics, April 2007.

Bryce, Albert W. *Halt Friends!* New York: publisher unknown, 1924.

Burgos, Carl. *Marvel Mystery Comics* # 9. New York: Marvel Comics, July 1940.

Burgos, Carl, and Bill Everett. "Marvel Comics Presents the Human Torch and Sub-Mariner Fighting Side by Side." In *The Golden Age of Marvel Comics*, vol. 1 edited by Stan Lee. New York: Marvel Comics, 1997.

Burks, Cramer. *Spy Toys*. Sherman Oaks, CA: Windmill Group, 1999.

Butler, Alban B. *Happy Days*. New York: Coward-McCann, 1929.

Campbell, J. Scott. Wizard: *The Comics Magazine* #133. New York: Wizard Entertainment, October 2002.

Casey, Robert Francis, IV. *The Visual Depictions of the Stages of Grief within 9/11 Comics*. Mobile: University of South Alabama Press, 2003.

Cassaday, John, and John Ney Rieber. *Captain America*, vol. 4, #1–10. New York: Marvel Comics, 2001–3.

Castiglia, Paul, ed. *The Shield: America's First Patriotic Comic Book Hero*. Mamaroneck, NY: Archie Comics, 2002.

Catledge, Turner. "Our Policy Stated in Soviet-Nazi War." *New York Times*, June 24, 1941. http://query.nytimes.com/mem/archive/pdf?res=FA0B1EFC3E5B147B93C6AB 178DD85F458485F9. Accessed February 12, 2011.

Catron, Michael, ed. "A Conversation with James Warren." In *Blazing Combat Collection*. Seattle: Fantagraphics Books, 2009.

Central Intelligence Agency. *The Freedom Fighter's Manual*. New York: Grove, 1985. www .ballistichelmet.org/school/free.html. Accessed March 8, 2011.

————. *The World Factbook*. s.v. "Religions." https://www.cia.gov/library/publications /the-world-factbook/geos/us.html. Accessed February 24, 2011.

Chafe, William. *Unfinished Journey: America since World War II*. New York: Oxford University Press, 1996.

Chang, Iris. *The Rape of Nanking: The Forgotten Holocaust of World War II*. New York: Penguin, 1997.

Chaykin, Howard. *American Flagg: Hard Times*. New York: First Comics, 1986.

Chiarello, Mark. "Foreword." *DC Archives Editions: Sgt. Rock Archives*, vol. 3. New York: DC Comics, 2005.

Chichester, D. G., and Klaus Janson. *Punisher–Captain America: Blood and Glory*. New York: Marvel Comics, 1991.

Chinnock, Frank W. *Nagasaki: The Forgotten Bomb*. New York: World, 1969.

Chomsky, Noam. *Media Control: The Spectacular Achievements of Propaganda*. New York: Seven Stories, 1991.

Christin, Pierre (w), and Enki Bilal (a). *Black Order Brigade*. Trans. Frank Wynne. Hollywood, CA: Humanoids, 1979.

Churchill, Sir Winston, and Denis Kelly. *The Second World War*. London: Penguin, 1989.

Clark, Beverly Lyon. *Girls, Boys, Books, Toys: Gender in Children's Literature and Culture*. Baltimore: Johns Hopkins University Press, 2000.

Clark, Toby. *Art and Propaganda in the Twentieth Century*. New York: Abrams, 1996.

Coles, Robert. *Children of Crisis*. New York: Back Bay Books, 2003.

Coll, Steve. *Ghost Wars: The Secret History of the CIA, Afghanistan, and bin Laden, from the Soviet Invasion to September 10, 2001*. New York: Penguin, 2004.

Comely, Richard. *Captain Canuck*. Winnipeg, Manitoba: Comely, 1978.

"Comic Hero Captain America Dies." BBC News, March 8, 2007. http://news.bbc.co.uk/2/hi/entertainment/6431619.stm. Accessed March 11, 2011.

"Comic with First Superman Story Sells for $1.5m." *The Independent* (London), March 30, 2010. http://www.independent.co.uk/news/world/americas/comic-with-first -superman -story-sells-for-15m-1930852.html. Accessed March 30, 2010.

Conroy, Mike. *500 Comic Book Villains*. Hauppauge, NY: Barron's Educational Series, 2004.

———. *War Stories: A Graphic History*. New York: Harper Design, 2009.

Craig, Matthew. "Ninth Art: Special Relationship." http://www.thematthewcraig.com /twocaptains.htm. Accessed July 26, 2004.

Croci, Pascal. *Auschwitz*. New York: Abrams, 2004.

Curtis, Arthur. *37 Greatest Army Heroes*. Washington, DC: National, 1968.

Dagilis, Andrew. "Uncle Sugar vs. Uncle Charlie: An Interview with *The 'Nam*'s Creator, Doug Murray." *Comics Journal* #136. Seattle: Fantagraphics July 1990. http://www .comicbookresources.com/?page=article&id=18745. Accessed February 15, 2010.

Dann, Thomas. "The Axis Powers as Depicted in US Superhero Comics 1938–1945." Master's thesis, California State University, Dominguez Hills, 2003.

Danna, Sammy, ed. *Advertising and Popular Culture*. Bowling Green, OH: Bowling Green University Popular Press, 1992.

Darnall, Steve (w), and Alex Ross (a). *U.S.* New York: DC Comics/Vertigo, 1997.

Das Schwartze Korps. German Propaganda Archive, April 25, 1940. http://www.calvin .edu/academic/cas/gpa/superman.htm. Accessed February 2, 2011.

Dean, Michael. "9/11, Benefit Comics, and the Dog-Eat-Dog World of Good Samaritanism." *Comics Journal* #247 (October 2002).

DeFalco, Tom, ed. *Semper Fi* #1–9. New York: Marvel Comics, December 1988–August 1989.

Delacorte, Albert, ed. *USA Is Ready*. New York: Dell, 1941.

Delisle, Guy. *Pyongyang: A Journey to North Korea*. Montreal: Drawn and Quarterly, 2005.

Denham, Brian. *Kill Box* #1–3. San Antonio, TX: Antarctic, December 2002.

Denning, Michael. *The Cultural Front: The Laboring of American Culture in the Twentieth Century*. New York: Verso, 1998.

Department of the Navy. *Li'l Abner Joins the Navy*. Washington, DC: Department of the Navy, 1950.

DePastino, Todd. *Bill Mauldin: A Life Up Front*. New York: Norton, 2008.

Diana, Fred, Dave Baggley, and Ron Kasman. *American Annihilator*. Islington, Ontario: Night Realm Comics, 1995.

Dini, Paul, et al. *Captain America: Red, White, and Blue*. New York: Marvel Comics, 2002.

Dini, Paul (w), and Alex Ross (a). *Wonder Woman: Spirit of Humanity*. New York: DC Comics, 2001.

Dixon, Chuck (w), and Butch Guice (a). *Storming Paradise* #4. New York: DC/Wildstorm, 2008.

Dixon, Chuck (w), Butch Guice (a), and Rick Burchett (a). *Storming Paradise* #1–6. New York: DC/Wildstorm, 2008–9.

Dixon, Chuck (w) and Doug Mahnke (a). *Team Zero*. New York: DC Comics, 2005–6.

"Don't Help the Enemy." In *How Boys and Girls Can Help Win the War*. New York: Marvel Comics, Parents Magazine Institute, and True Comics, 1942.

Doubler, Michael. *Closing with the Enemy: How GIs Fought the War in Europe, 1944–1945*. Lawrence: University Press of Kansas, 1995.

Douglas, Susan. *Where the Girls Are: Growing Up Female with the Mass Media*. New York: Three Rivers, 1997.

Dower, John W. *War without Mercy: Race and Power in the Pacific War*. New York: Pantheon, 1986.

Dysart, Joe (w), and Alberto Ponticelli (a). *The Unknown Soldier* #1–25. New York: DC Comics, 2008-2010.

Eisner, Will. *Graphic Storytelling and the Visual Narrative*. Tamarac, FL: Poorhouse, 1996.

———. *Last Day in Vietnam*. Milwaukie, OR: Dark Horse, 2000.

———. "Reality." In *9-11: Emergency Relief*, edited by Jeff Mason. Gainesville, FL: Alternative Comics, 2001.

Eisner, Will, ed. *9-11: Artists Respond*, vol. 1. New York: DC Comics, 2002.

Eisner, Will (w), and Chuck Cuidera (a). *Blackhawk Archives*, vol. 1. New York: DC Archive Editions, 2001.

Ellis, John. *Eye Deep in Hell*. Baltimore: Johns Hopkins University Press, 1976.

———. *The Social History of the Machine Gun*. Baltimore: Johns Hopkins University Press, 1975.

Ellul, Jacques. *Propaganda: The Formation of Men's Attitudes*. New York: Vintage Books, 1973.

Engelhardt, Tom. *The End of Victory Culture: Cold War America and the Disillusioning of a Generation*. New York: Basic Books, 1995.

Ennis, Garth, ed. *War Story*, vol. 1. New York: DC Comics/Vertigo, 2004.

Ennis, Garth (w), and Jacen Barrows (a). *303* #1–6. Rantoul, IL: Avatar. http://www.comicbookresources.com/2004.news/printthis.cgi?id=4044. Accessed May 12, 2008.

Ennis, Garth (w), and Amanda Conner (a). *The Pro*. New York: Image Comics, 2002

Ennis, Garth (w), and Gary Erskine (a). *War Story: Archangel*. New York: DC Comics/Vertigo, April 2003.

Ennis, Garth (w), and Carlos Ezquerra (a). *Adventures in the Rifle Brigade*. New York: DC Comics/Vertigo, 2005.

_____. *War Story: Condors.* New York: DC Comics/Vertigo, March 2003.

Ennis, Garth (w), and Dave Gibbons (a). *War Story: Screaming Eagles.* New York: DC Comics/Vertigo, January 2002.

Ennis, Garth (w), and John Higgins (a). *War Story: D-Day Dodgers.* New York: DC Comics/Vertigo, December 2001.

Ennis, Garth (w), and Bob Kanigher (w). *Enemy Ace: War in Heaven.* New York: DC Comics, 2001.

Ennis, Garth (w), and Jim Lee (a). "Nosh and Barry and Eddie and Joe." In *Weird War Stories Annual.* New York: DC Comics, April 2000.

Ennis, Garth (w), and David Lloyd (a), eds. *War Stories* vol. 2. New York: DC Comics/Vertigo, March 2006.

Ennis, Garth (w), and Jimmy Palimiotti (a). *Punisher: Born.* New York: Marvel Comics, 2004.

Ennis, Garth (w), and Goran Parlov (a). "Valley Forge, Valley Forge." In *The Punisher* #55-60 (7th Series). New York: Marvel Comics, 2008.

Ennis, Garth (w), and Killian Plunkett (a). *The Unknown Soldier.* New York: DC Comics, 1997.

Ennis, Garth (w), Darrick Robertson (a). *Born* #2. New York: Marvel Comics, July 2003.

_____. *Born* #4. New York: Marvel Comics, September 2003–September 2004.

_____. *Fury: Peacemaker* #1–6. New York: Marvel Comics, 2008.

Ennis, Garth (w), and Chris Weston (a). *War Story: Johann's Tiger,* vol 1. New York: DC Comics/Vertigo, November 2001.

Ennis, Garth (w), Chris Weston, Christian Alamy, and Russ Heath. *Enemy Ace: War in Heaven.* New York: DC Comics/Vertigo, July 2001.

Erenberg, Lewis A., and Susan E. Hirsch, eds. *The War in American Culture: Society and Consciousness Curing World War II.* Chicago: University of Chicago Press, 1996.

Espinoza, Rod. Author e-mail interview, February 10, 2005.

Feiffer, Jules. *The Great Comic Book Heroes.* Seattle: Fantagraphics Books, 2003.

Finch, Lynette. "Psychological Propaganda: The War on Ideas during the First Half of the Twentieth Century." *Armed Forces and Society* 26, #3 (Spring 2000).

Foner, Eric. *Who Owns History? Rethinking the Past in a Changing World.* New York: Hill & Wang, 2003.

Franklin, Benjamin. "Join or Die." *Pennsylvania Gazette,* May 9, 1754. http://www.benfranklin300.org/frankliniana/result.php?id=406&sec=1. Accessed March 11, 2011.

Franklin, John. Author interview, October 1999.

Frederick, Jim. "The Long Mistake." *Time,* December 6, 2004. http://www.time.com/time/magazine/article/0,9171,880313,00.html. Accessed February 1, 2011.

Friedrich, Gary (w), and Dick Ayers (a). *Combat Kelly and the Deadly Dozen.* New York: Marvel Comics, 1972–73.

Fukuyama, Francis. *The End of History and the Last Man.* New York: Simon & Schuster, 1992.

Furman, Simon (w), and Art Nichols (a). "What If the Punisher Became Captain America?" In *What If?,* vol. 2, #51 (New York: Marvel Comics, July 1993).

Fussell, Paul. *The Boys' Crusade: The American Infantry in Northwestern Europe, 1944–1945.* New York: Modern Chronicles Library, 2003.

_____. *Wartime: Understanding and Behavior in the Second World War*. New York: Oxford University Press, 1989.

Gabriel, David Jay. *A Brief History of First Amendment Issues in Comic Books, 2001*. http://www.scribd.com/doc/97297109/A-Brief-History-of-Comic-Books-and-First-Amendment-Issues-Well-Illustrated

Gage, Christos (w), Jeremy Hawn (a), and Mark Morales (a). *Civil War: Iron Man*. New York: Marvel Comics, 2006–7.

Gaiman, Neil. *9-11: The World's Finest Comic Book Writers and Artists Tell Stories to Remember*, vol. 2. New York: DC Comics, 2002.

Gandhi, Arun. "Understanding the Culture of Violence." In *411#1* New York: Marvel Comics, 2003.

Gannon, Michael. *Operation Drumbeat: The Dramatic True Story of Germany's First U-Boat Attacks along the American Coast in World War II*. New York: Harper Perennial, 1990.

General Douglas MacArthur. New York: Fox Feature Syndicate, 1951.

G.I. Joe: A Real American Hero. New York: Marvel Comics. Series 1982–94.

Gill, Joe (w), and Enio Legisamo (a). "Terror in a Vietcong Tunnel." In *Army War Heroes* #20. Derby, CT: / Comics Charlton, July 1967.

"Girl Commandos." In *War Heroes Classics*. Larchmont, NY: Lorne-Harvey, 1991.

Glanzman, Sam. "Monte Cassino." In *Combat* #9. New York: Dell Comics, September 1963.

_____. "There Were Tears in Her Eyes." In *9/11: Artists Respond*, vol. 2. Milwaukie, OR: Dark Horse, 2001.

Goodwin, Archie (w), and Al McWilliams (a). *Savage Combat Tales, Featuring Sgt. Stryker's Death Squad* #1. New York: Atlas Comics, 1975.

Goodwin, Archie (w), and Joe Orlando (a). *Blazing Combat*. Seattle: Fantagraphics Books, 2009.

Goulart, Ron. *Comic Book Culture: An Illustrated History*. Portland, OR: Collectors, 1998.

Grant, John. *Masters of Animation*. New York: Watson-Guptill, 2003.

Gravett, Paul, and Peter Stansbury. *Holy Sh*t! The World's Weirdest Comic Books*. New York: St. Martin's, 2009.

Greene, Alfonso. "G.I. Jap-American Hero!" In *Heroic Comics* #34. New York: Famous Funnies, January 1946.

Greene, Bob. *Homecoming: When the Soldiers Returned from Vietnam*. New York: Putnam, 1989.

Grossman, Dave. *On Killing: The Psychological Cost of Learning to Kill in War and Society*. New York: Back Bay Books, 2009.

Groth, Gary. "Interview with Jack Kirby." In *The Comics Journal Library: Jack Kirby*. Seattle: Fantagraphics Books, 2002.

Groth, Gary, and Anne Elizabeth Moore, eds. *Comics Journal Special Edition: Cartoonists on Patriotism*, Winter 2003.

Guggenheim, Marc (w), Humberto Ramos (a), and Carlos Cuevas (a). *Civil War: Wolverine*. New York: Marvel Comics, 2007.

Guibert, Emmanuel, and Alan Cope. *Alan's War: The Memories of G.I. Alan Cope*. New York: First Second Press, 2008.

Gustines, George Gene. "Captain America Is Dead: National Hero Since 1941." *New York Times*, March 8, 2007. http://www.nytimes.com/2007/03/08/books/08capt .html?pagewanted=all. Accessed March 3, 2011.

Hama, Larry (w), and Steve Leialoha (a). *G.I. Joe: A Real American Hero* #26. New York: Marvel Comics, August 1984.

Hama, Larry (w), and Herb Trimpe (a). *GI Joe Special Missions* #1. New York: Marvel Comics, 1986.

Hama, Larry (w), Rod Whigham (a), and Andy Mushynsky (a). *G.I. Joe: A Real American Hero* #39. New York: Marvel Comics, September 1985.

Haney, Bob (w), and Joe Kubert (a). "Invasion Game." In *Star Spangled War Stories* #155. New York: DC Comics, March 1971.

Harvey, Robert C. *Children of the Yellow Kid: The Evolution of the American Comic Strip*. Seattle: University of Washington Press, 1998.

_____. *Meanwhile: A Biography of Milton Caniff, Creator of Terry and the Pirates and Steve Canyon*. Seattle: Fantagraphics Books, 2007.

Heath, Russ. "Basic Training." In *Combat Casey* #23. New York: Atlas Comics, August 1955.

Hein, Susan, and Mark Seldon, eds. *Censoring History*. Armonk, NY: M. E. Sharpe, 2000.

Heller, Steven. "A Cold Eye: Fighting the Image Wars." In *Print* 58, #5 (September–October 2004).

Heroic Comics #16. New York: Famous Funnies Publications, January 1943.

Heroic Comics #77. New York: Famous Funnies Publications, November 1952.

Herron, Ed, and Jack Kirby. *Captain America* #1. New York: Marvel Comics, March 1941.

Hess, Stephen, and Sandy Northrop. *Drawn and Quartered: The History of American Political Cartoons*. Montgomery, AL: Elliot & Clark, 1996.

History Channel. *Comic Book Superheroes Unmasked*. Triage Entertainment, 2003.

Hixson, Walter. *Parting the Curtain: Propaganda, Culture and the Cold War*. New York: Palgrave Macmillan, 1998.

Hoganson, Cheryl. *Fighting for American Manhood: How Gender Politics Provoked the Spanish–American and Philippine–American Wars*. New Haven, CT: Yale University Press, 2000.

Holocaust Encyclopedia, s.v. "German American Bund." United States Holocaust Memorial Museum. http://www.ushmm.org/wlc/media_ph.php?lang=en& ModuleId=10005684& MediaId=2742. Accessed February 15, 2011.

Honey, Maureen. *Creating Rosie the Riveter*. Amherst, MA: University of Massachusetts Press, 1985.

Horan, Deborah. "Army's Propaganda War Collides with Reality." *Chicago Tribune*, July 9, 2004.

Howell, Thomas. "The Writer's War Board." *Historian: A Journal of History* 59, #4 (Summer 1997).

Huchthausen, Peter. *America's Splendid Little Wars: A Short History of U.S. Military Engagements: 1975–2000*. New York: Viking, 2003.

Inge, M. Thomas. *Comics as Culture*. Jackson: University Press of Mississippi, 1990.

Irons, Greg. "Raw War Comics." In *Hydrogen Bomb and Biochemical Warfare Funnies* #1. San Francisco: Rip Off, May 26, 1971.

Is This Tomorrow: America under Communism! St. Paul, MN: Catechetical Guild Educational Society, 1947.

Izureta, Ryan. *Johnny Jihad.* New York: NBM, 2003.

Jacks, Brian. "Interview: Doug Murray." Slush Factory, May 25, 2002. http://slushfactory.com/features/articles/052502-murray.php. Accessed August, 20, 2008.

_____. "Interview: Joe Kubert." Slush Factory, October 14, 2013. http://slushfactory.com/features/articles/052502-kubert.php. Accessed April 25, 2011.

Jacobson, Aileen. "Kids Have History of Eating up Tales of Doom, Gloom." *Chicago Tribune*, January 4, 2005.

Jacobson, Allan, C. P. Smith, Chris Walker, and Dave Sharpe. *The New Invaders* #1–8. New York: Marvel Comics, 2004.

Jacobson, Sidney, and Ernie Colón. *After 9/11: America's War on Terror (2001–).* New York: Hill and Wang, 2008.

_____. *The 9/11 Report: A Graphic Adaptation.* New York: Hill & Wang, 2006.

Jansen, Klaus, D. G. Chichester, Margaret Clark, and John Wellington. *Captain America–Punisher: Blood and Glory.* New York: Marvel Comics, 1992.

Jenkins, Paul (w), Ramon Bachs (a), Steve Lieber (a), and Lee Weeks (a). *Civil War: Front Line*, vol. 1. New York: Marvel Comics, 2007.

Jenkins, Paul (w), and Graham Nolan (a). *The New Avengers: Pot of Gold.* New York: Marvel/AAFES, 2005.

Jewett, Robert, and John Shelton Lawrence. *Captain America and the Crusade against Evil: the Dilemma of Zealous Nationalism.* Grand Rapids, MI: Eerdmans, 2003.

Johns, Geoff, Dale Eaglesham, and Art Thibert. *JSA 81.* New York: DC Comics, 2006.

Johns, Geoff, David Goyer, Humberto Ramos, and Sandra Hope. "A Burning Hate." In *9/11*, vol. 2. New York: Marvel Comics, 2001.

Jones, Bruce (w), and Tom Mandrake (a). *The Call of Duty: The Precinct.* New York: Marvel Comics, August 2002–January 2003.

Jurgens, Dan. *Superman*, vol. 2, #60. New York: DC Comics, October 1991.

Jurgens, Dan (w), Dusty Abell (a), Jackson Guice (a), Steve Mitchell (a), and Brad Vancata (a). *Agent Liberty* #1. New York: DC Comics, January 1992.

Kamalipour, Yahya, ed. *War, Media, and Propaganda: A Global Perspective.* and Nancy Snow, eds. Lanham, MD: Rowman & Littlefield, 2004.

Kanfer, Stefan. *Serious Business: The Art and Commerce of Animation in America.* Cambridge, MA: Da Capo, 2000.

Kanigher, Bob (w), and Russ Heath (a). "No Loot for the Hellcats." In *Our Fighting Forces, Featuring Lt. Hunter's Hellcats.* New York: DC Comics, 1968.

Kanigher, Bob (w), and Russ Heath, Irv Novick, Jerry Grandenetti, Jack Adler, Joe Kubert, Jack Abel (a). *DC Showcase Presents: The Haunted Tank*, vols. 1–2. New York: DC Comics, 2006, 2008.

_____. *DC Showcase Presents: The War That Time Forgot*, vols. 1–2, New York: DC Comics, 2006.

Kanigher, Bob (w), and Joe Kubert (a). *DC Showcase: Haunted Tank*, vols. 1–2. New York: DC Comics, 2007–8.

_____. *Enemy Ace Archives*, vols. 1–2. New York: DC Comics, 2002, 2004.

_____. "Let Me Live . . . Let Me Die." In *DC Showcase Presents: Haunted Tank*, vol. 2. New York: DC Comics, 2008.

_____. *Our Army at War* #81. New York: DC Comics, April 1959.

_____. *Sgt. Rock* #85. New York: DC Comics, August 1959.

_____. *Sgt. Rock* #95. New York: DC Comics, July 1960.

_____. *Sgt. Rock* #113. New York: DC Comics, December 1961.

_____. *Sgt. Rock* #127. New York: DC Comics, February 1963.

Kanigher, Bob (w), David Micheline (w), and Arvell Jones and Ed Davis (a). *Men of War* #1–2. New York: DC Comics, August–September 1977.

Kaplan, Arie. *From Krakow to Krypton: Jews and Comic Books*. Philadelphia, PA: Jewish Publication Society, 2008.

Katz, Harry, ed. *Cartoon America*. New York: Abrams, 2006.

Keegan, John. *The Face of Battle*. New York: Penguin, 1988.

_____. *The Second World War*. New York: Penguin, 1989.

Keen, Sam. *Faces of the Enemy*. San Francisco: Harper & Row, 1986.

Keene, Jennifer. *The United States and the First World War*. London: Pearson Education, 2000.

Kelly, Robin. *Race Rebels*. New York: Free Press, 1996.

Kendall, David, ed. *The Mammoth Book of the Best War Comics*. New York: Carroll & Graf, 2007.

Kipling, Rudyard. "Tommy." In *Barrack-Room Ballads, 1892*. http://monologues.co.uk/Military/Tommy.htm. Accessed March 13, 2011.

_____. "White Man's Burden." In *McClure's Magazine*, February 1899.

Kirby, Jack. Interview. *The Comics Journal* 134 (February 1990).

_____. *The Losers*. New York: DC Comics, 2009.

Kraft, David Anthony. "Interview with Wayne Vansant." In *David Anthony Kraft's Comics Interview* #53. New York: Fictioneer, Press 1987.

Kubert, Joe. *Fax from Sarajevo*. Milwaukie, OR: Dark Horse Comics, 1998.

_____. *Medal of Honor Special Edition* #1. Milwaukie, OR: Dark Horse Comics, April 1994.

_____. *Sgt. Rock Archives*, vols. 1–2. New York: DC Comics, 2002.

_____. *Sgt. Rock Archives*, vol. 3. New York: DC Comics, 2005.

_____. *Sgt. Rock: The Prophecy* #1–6. New York: DC Comics, 2006.

_____. *Yossel: April 18, 1943*. Ann Arbor, MI: iBooks, 2003.

Kubert, Joe, Irv Novick, Archie Goodwin, Bob Haney, Robert Kanigher, Frank Robbins, David Michelinie (w), and Joe Kubert, Irv Novick, Jack Sparling, Gerry Talaoc, Dan Spiegle, Doug Wildey (a). *DC Showcase Presents: The Unknown Soldier*. New York: DC Comics, 2006.

Kurtzman, Harvey. "Rubble!" In *Two-Fisted Tales* #24. New York: EC Comics, November–December 1951.

Lamb, Chris. *Drawn to Extremes: The Use and Abuse of Editorial Cartoons*. New York: Columbia University Press, 2004.

Langdon, Antonio. *Grenada: Rescued from Rape and Slavery*. New York: Victims of International Communist Emissaries Press, 1983.

Lanker, Brian, and Nicole Newnham. *They Drew Fire: Combat Artists of World War II.* New York: TV Books, 2000.

Lansdale, Joe (w), and Sam Glanzman (a). "The Elopement." In *Weird War Tales* #2. New York: DC Comics, 1997.

Lappe, Anthony (w), and Dan Goldman (a). *Shooting War.* New York: Grand Central, 2007.

Larsen, Erik. Author e-mail interview, October 18, 2005.

Larsen, Erik (w), Keith Giffen (w), and Dave Johnson (a). *SuperPatriot.* Berkeley, CA: Image Comics, July 1993.

Lauria, Frank, ed. *SPECWAR: Special Warfare* #1–7. San Diego: Peter Four Productions, 2002.

Ledwell, Rod. *WW2.* Norwood, MA: New England, 2000–1, 2003–6.

Lee, Stan (w), and Jack Binder (a). "The Destroyer." In *All Winners* #1. New York: Marvel Comics, 2005.

Lee, Stan (w), and Gene Colan (a). *Captain America* #125. New York: Marvel Comics, May 1970.

Lee, Stan (w) and Steve Ditko (a). *Spider-Man.* New York: Marvel Comics, 1964–.

Lee, Stan (w), and Jack Kirby (a). *Sgt. Fury and His Howling Commandos* #1. New York: Marvel Comics, May 1963.

_____. *Strange Tales* #135. New York: Marvel Comics, August 1965.

Lee, Stan (w), Jack Kirby (a), and Dick Ayers (a). *Marvel Masterworks: Sgt. Fury.* New York: Marvel Comics, 2005.

Lee, Stan (w), Larry Leiber (a), and Don Heck (a). "Iron Man Is Born." In *Tales of Suspense* #39. New York: Marvel Comics, March 1963.

Lembcke, Jerry. *The Spitting Image: Myth, Memory, and the Legacy of Vietnam.* New York: New York University Press, 1998.

Levine, Laurence. *Highbrow/Lowbrow: The Emergence of Cultural Hierarchy in America.* Cambridge, MA: Harvard University Press, 1988.

Linderman, Gerald. *The Mirror of War.* Ann Arbor: University of Michigan Press, 1996.

Lipsitz, George. *A Rainbow at Midnight.* Champaign: University of Illinois Press, 1984.

Lloyd, David. "Looking Good, Feeling Great." In *Weird War Tales* #2. New York: DC Comics, July 1997.

Lobdell, Scott (w), Clayton Henry, and Mark Morales. *Alpha Flight: You Gotta Be Kidding Me.* New York: Marvel Comics, 2004.

Lobdell, Scott (w), and Mark Pacella (a). *Alpha Flight* #106, *The Walking Wounded.* New York: Marvel Comics, March 1992.

Loewen, James. *Lies My Teacher Told Me: Everything Your History Textbook Got Wrong.* New York: Touchstone, 1995.

"Log of the Snorkel Wolf Pack." In *Atomic War* #3. Philadelphia, PA: Ace Comics, 1953.

Lomax, Don. "Editor's Note." In *The 'Nam* #84. New York: Marvel Comics, September 1993.

_____. *Gulf War Journal.* New York: ibooks, 2004.

_____. *Tet '68.* Bethel, CT: Apple Comics, 1992.

_____. *Vietnam Journal.* Bethel, CT: Apple Comics, 1987-1990, 2002.

_____. *Vietnam Journal: Bloodbath at Khe Sanh*. Bethel, CT: Apple Comics, 2010. http://
www.atomicavenue.com/atomic/TitleDetail.aspx?TitleID=8803. Accessed January 26,
2011.

_____. "Vietnam Journal: The 5.56 Blues." In *Blazing Combat: Vietnam and Korea* #1.
Bethel, CT: Apple Comics, August 1993.

_____. *Vietnam Journal: Valley of Death* #1. Bethel, CT: Apple Comics, 1994.

Lomax, Don (w), Bob Durand (w), and Don Lomax (a). *High Shining Brass* #1–4. Bethel,
CT: Apple Comics, 1991.

Lomax, Don (w), and Alberto Saichann (a). *Punisher Invades the 'Nam: Final Mission*.
New York: Marvel Comics, February 1994.

Lutes, Jason. *Berlin: City of Stones*. Montreal: Drawn and Quarterly, 2000.

Mackey, Mike (w), and Donny Lin (a). *Liberality for All* #1–4. Lexington, KY: ACC Studios
2005.

Magnussen, Anne, and Hans-Christian Christiansen. *Comics and Culture: Analytical
and Theoretical Approaches to Comics*. Amsterdam: Museum Tusculanem, 2000.

Mann, Ron. *Comic Book Confidential* #1. Toronto, ON: Sphinx Productions, 1988.http://
www.amazon.com/Comic-Book-Confidential-Lynda-Barry/dp/B0033W23Q6/ref=sr
_1_2?ie=UTF8&qid=1384622514&sr=8-2&keywords=comic+book+confidential.

Marchand, William. *Advertising the American Dream: Making Way for Modernity, 1920–
1940*. Berkeley, CA: University of California Press, 1985.

Marcus, Greil. "The Man on the Street." In *Give Our Regards to the Atomsmashers! Writers
on Comics*, edited by Sean Howe. New York: Pantheon Books, 2004.

Marlin, Randal. *Propaganda and the Ethics of Persuasion*. Orchard Park, NY: Broadview,
2002.

Marraffino, Frank (w), and Henry Flint (a). *The Haunted Tank* #1–6. New York: Vertigo/ DC
Comics, 2009.

Marshall, Charles (w), and Ernie Stiner (a). "Overkill." In *Desert Storm: Send Hussein to
Hell*. Wheeling, WV: Innovation, April 1991.

The Marvel Encyclopedia: The Definitive Guide to the Characters of the Marvel Universe, s.v.
"The Punisher." New York: DK, 2006.

Marvel Universe Wiki., s.v. "Captain America." http://marvel.com/universe/Captain
America(William_Burnside). Accessed March 7, 2011.

Mason, Jeff, ed. *9-11: Emergency Relief*. Gainesville, FL: Alternative Comics, 2001.

Mauldin, Bill. *Bill Mauldin's Army*. San Francisco: Presidio, 1979.

_____. *Up Front*. New York: Norton, 1995.

_____. *The Willie and Joe Years*, vol. 1. Seattle: Fantagraphics Books, 2008.

May, Lary. "Making the American Consensus: The Narrative of Conversion and Subversion in World War II Films." In *War in American Culture: Society and Consciousness
during World War II*, edited by Lewis Erenberg and Susan Hirsch. Chicago: University
of Chicago Press, 1996.

_____, ed. *Recasting America: Culture and Politics in the Age of the Cold War*. Chicago:
University of Chicago Press, 1989.

McCloud, Scott. *Reinventing Comics*. New York: Harper Perennial, 2000.

_____. *Understanding Comics: The Invisible Art*. San Francisco: Kitchen Sink, 1993.

McGreal, Pat (w), Dave Rawson (w), Greg LaRocque (a), and Richard Space (a). *The Fighting American* #1–6. New York: DC Comics, February–July 1994.

McGurn, Garrett. *Yank: The Army Weekly–Reporting the Greatest Generation*. Golden, CO: Fulcrum, 2004.

McKenzie, Roger (w), and Dick Ayers (a). *Men of War* #6. New York: DC Comics, May 1978.

_____. *Men of War* #11. New York: DC Comics, December 1978.

McRae, John, and P. Craig Russell. "In Flanders Field." In *9-11: Artists Respond*, vol. 1. Milwaukie, OR: Dark Horse, 2002.

Meihm, Grant, and Mark Waid (w) and Grant Meihm (a). *Legend of the Shield* #4. New York: Impact / DC Comics, 1991. http://www.atomicavenue.com/atomic/TitleDetail .aspx?TitleID=17246

Meleton, Marcus, and Pete Garcia. *Pete the P.O.'d Postal Worker: War Journal*. Costa Mesa, CA: Sharkbait, 2002.

Menchine, Ron. *Propaganda Postcards of World War II*. Iola, WI: Krause, 2000.

Meyer, Richard C. (w), Martin Montiel Luna (a), and Richard C. Meyer (a). *No Enemy but Peace*. Laredo, TX: Machine Gun Bob Productions, 2008.

Micheline, David (w), and Ed Davis (a). *Men of War* #1. New York: DC Comics, August 1977.

Millar, Mark (w), Bryan Hitch (a), and Andrew Currie (a). *The Ultimates* #1–2. New York: Marvel Comics, 2003, 2005.

Millar, Mark (w), and Dave John. *Superman: Red Son* #1–3. New York: DC Comics / Elseworld, 2003.

Millar, Mark (w), and Steve McNiven. *Civil War*. New York: Marvel Comics, 2006–7.

Millar, Mark (w), Steve McNiven (a), Dexter Vines (a), and Morry Hollowell (a). *Civil War*. New York: Marvel Comics, 2007.

Miller, Frank. "The Power of Faith." In *9-11: Artists Respond*, vol. 1. Milwaukie, OR: Dark Horse, 2001.

Miller, Steve. *Gung Ho! How to Draw Fantastic Military Comics*. New York: Watson-Guptill, 2006.

Mills, Pat (w), and Joe Colquhoun (a). *Charley's War*, vol. 1–3. London: Titan Books, 2004–6.

Minear, Richard, and Theodore Geisel. *Dr. Seuss Goes to War: The World War II Editorial Cartoons of Theodor Seuss Geisel*. New York: New Press, 1999.

Montes, Bill (w), and Charles Nicholas (a). *Fightin' Marines* #78. Derby, CT: Charlton Comics, January 1968.

Moore, Anne Elizabeth. *Hey Kidz! Buy this Book: A Radical Primer on Corporate and Governmental Propaganda and Artistic Activism for Short People*. New York: Soft Skull, 2004.

Moore, Robin (w), and Joe Kubert (a). *Tales of the Green Berets* #1. New York: DC Comics, January 1967. Reprinted in *Tales of the Green Beret vol 1*. El Cajon, CA: Blackthorne Publishing, 1985.

Moore, Stuart (w), and Cliff Richards (a). *New Avengers: Fireline*. New York: Marvel Comics/AAFES, 2008.

_____. *The New Avengers: Letters Home*. New York: Marvel Comics, January 2007.

Morrell, David (w), and Mitch Breitweiser (a). *Captain America: The Chosen* #1. New York: Marvel Comics, November 2007.

_____. *Captain America: The Chosen* #6. New York: Marvel Comics, March 2008.

Morse, Ben. "Who Will Be Captain America?" In *Wizard* #187. New York: Marvel Comics, May 2007.

Murray, Doug (w), and Wayne Vansant (a). "Back in the Real. . . ." In *The 'Nam* #41. New York: Marvel Comics, February 1990.

_____. "Beginning of the End." In *The 'Nam* #24. New York: Marvel Comics, November 1988.

Museum of Comic and Cartoon Art (MoCCA). Society of Illustrators. www.moccany.org .Accessed May 14, 2011.

Nakazawa, Keiji. *Barefoot Gen*, vol. 1–4. New York: Penguin, 1990.

_____. *I Saw It: The Atomic Bombing of Hiroshima—A Survivor's True Story*. San Francisco: Educomics, 1982.

Nomura, Ted. *Pearl Harbor: The Comic Book* #1–2. San Antonio, TX: Antarctic Press, 2001.

_____. *Dictators of the Twentieth Century: Hitler* #1–4. San Antonio, TX: Antarctic Press, 2004.

_____. *Dictators of the Twentieth Century: Saddam Hussein–The Fall* #2. San Antonio, TX: Antarctic Press, 2004.

_____. *Hiroshima: The Atomic Holocaust*. San Antonio, TX: Antarctic Press, August 2005.

Norlund, Christopher. "Imagining Terrorists before Sept. 11: Marvel's GI Joe Comic Books, 1982–1994." In ImageTexT: Interdisciplinary Comics Studies 3.1, Gainesville: University of Florida, 2006.

Nyberg, Amy Kiste. *Seal of Approval: A History of the Comics Code*. Jackson: University Press of Mississippi, 1998.

O'Donnell, Kenneth. *Operatives, Spies and Saboteurs: The Untold History of the OSS*. New York: Free Press, 2004.

O'Donnell, Patrick. *Beyond Valor: World War II's Ranger and Airborne Veterans Reveal the Heart of Combat*. New York: Free Press, 2001.

O'Shea, Tim. "Interview: Joe Kubert on Sgt. Rock." Comics Bulletin. http://www.comics bulletin.com/news/106930719573960.htm. Accessed May 14, 2011.

O'Sullivan, Carol. *Television: Identifying Propaganda Techniques*. San Diego: Greenhaven, 1990.

Oirich, Alan, and Ron Randall. *Jewish Hero Corps* #1. New York: Judaica, 2004.

"Operation: Vengeance." *Atomic War* #2. Philadelphia, PA: Ace Comics, 1952.

Ordway, Jerry, and Karl Kesel. *U.S. Agent* #1–3. New York: Marvel Comics, 2001. http://www.atomicavenue.com/atomic/TitleDetail.aspx?TitleID=5012

Ottaviani, Jim. Interview on the G.T. Labs website. http://www.gtlabs.com/interview .html. Accessed June 4, 2008.

Ottaviani, Jim, Janine Johnston, Steve Lieber, Vince Locke, Bernie Mireault, and Jeff Parker, with Chris Kemple, Eddy Newell, and Robin Thompson. *Fallout: J. Robert Oppenheimer, Leo Szilard, and the Political Science of the Atomic Bomb*. Ann Arbor, MI: G.T. Labs, 2001.

Oxford Companion to American Military History, s.v. "Chennault, Claire." New York: Oxford University Press, 1999.

Parker, Jay. "You Can't Fight Tanks with Bayonets: Psychological Warfare against the Japanese Army in the Southwest Pacific." *Armed Forces and Society* 26, #2 (Winter 2000).

Pekar, Harvey. *American Splendor: Unsung Hero*. Milwaukie, OR: Dark Horse Comics, 2002.

Pekar, Harvey, and Ed Piskor. *Macedonia: What Does It Take to Stop a War?* New York: Villard, 2007.

Perlmutter, David. *Visions of War: Picturing Warfare from the Stone Age to the Cyber Age*. New York: St. Martin's, 2001.

Philips, Peter, and Project Censored. *Censored 2005: The Top 25 Censored Stories*. New York: Seven Stories, 2005.

Pilcher, Tim, and Brad Brooks. *The Essential Guide to World Comics*. London: Collins & Brown, 2005.

Powell, Thomas. "The War Writers Board and Comic Books." *Historian: A Journal of History* 59, #4 (Summer 1997).

Pratkanis, Anthony, and Elliot Aaronson. *Age of Propaganda: The Everyday Use and Abuse of Persuasion*. New York: Owl Books, 2001.

Prawdzik, Christopher. "Simulation Adapts to World Conflicts." *National Guard* 58, #1 (January 2004).

Previews. Osprey Publishing. http://previewsworld.com/support/previews_docs/Bestsellers/Top100comics_2007.pdf. Accessed February 1, 2011.

Proud, Judith K. *Children and Propaganda*. Oxford, England: Intellect, 1995.

PS: The Preventive Maintenance Monthly. U.S. Army magazine, June 1951– . https://www.logsa.army.mil/psmag/pshome.cfm. Accessed April 24, 2011.

Pyle, Ernie. *Brave Men*. Westport, CT: Greenwood, 1974.

Quesada, Joe, ed. *Amazing Spider-man #36*. New York: Marvel Comics, 2001.

_____. *Heroes: The World's Greatest Super Hero Creators Honor the World's Greatest Heroes 9.11.2001*. New York: Marvel Comics, December 2001. http://www.atomicavenue.com/atomic/IssueDetail.aspx?ID=102015

Quinn, Peter. "Race Cleansing in America." *American Heritage*, March 2003.

Raicht, Mike, ed. *A Moment of Silence*. New York: Marvel Comics, 2001.

Rall, Ted. "The Day My Train Stood Still." In *9-11: Emergency Relief*, edited by Jeff Mason. Gainesville, FL: Alternative Comics, 2002.

_____. *Generalissimo El Busho: Essays and Cartoons on the Bush Years*. New York: NBM, 2004.

_____. *Silk Road to Ruin*. New York: NBM, 2006.

_____. *To Afghanistan and Back*. New York: NBM, 2002.

Raymond, Alan. *Children in War*. Washington, DC: TV Books, 2000.

Real Heroes #1. New York: Parents Comics Institute, 1941.

Rees, David (w), and Tony Salmons (a). "Seeds." In *411* #1 New York: Marvel Comics, June 2003.

Remember Pearl Harbor: Battle of the Pacific. New York: Street & Smith, February 23, 1942.

Rennie, Gordon (w), and Randy DuBurke (a). *Weird War Tales* #1 "Tunnel Rats." In New York: DC Comics, June 1997.

Ress, Stella. "Bridging the Generation Gap: Little Orphan Annie in the Great Depression." *Journal of Popular Culture* 43, #4 (Summer 2010).

Rickards, Maurice. *Posters of World War I.* New York: Walker, 1968.

Rieber, John Ney (w), and John Cassaday (a). "Fight Terror." In *Captain America* #2. New York: Marvel Comics, 2002.

_____. "The New Deal." In *Captain America* #1. New York: Marvel Comics, 2002.

Ro, Ronin. *Tales to Astonish: Jack Kirby, Stan Lee, and the American Comic Book Revolution.* New York: Bloomsbury, 2005.

Robbins, Trina. *The Great Women Cartoonists.* New York: Watson-Guptill, 2001.

Robinson, James, Paul Smith, and Richard Ory. *The Golden Age: A Different Look at a Different Era.* New York: DC Comics, 1995.

Robinson, Linda. *Masters of Chaos: The Secret History of the Special Forces.* Washington, DC: PublicAffairs, 2004.

Roeder, George. *The Censored War: American Visual Experience during World War II.* New Haven, CT: Yale University Press, 1993.

Romita, John, Sr. "Back from the Dead." In *The Golden Age of New York: Marvel Comics*, vol. 1. New York: Marvel Comics, 1997.

Roosevelt, Franklin D. State of the Union Address, 1941. http://www.presidency.ucsb.edu /ws/?pid=16253.

Ross, Alex, and Paul Dini. *Wonder Woman: Spirit of Humanity.* New York: DC Comics, 2001.

Ross, Steven J. "Hollywood, Jews, and America." *Reviews in American History* 30, #4 (December 2002).

Ryan, Mike, Chris Mann, and Alexander Stilwell. *The Encyclopedia of the World's Special Forces.* New York: Barnes & Noble Books, 2003.

Sabin, Roger. *Comics, Comix, and Graphic Novels: A History of Comic Art.* London: Phaidon, 1997.

Sacco, Joe. "Complacency Kills." *Guardian Weekend*, February 26, 2005.

_____. "Down! Up!" *Harper's*, April 2007.

_____. *The Fixer.* Montreal: Drawn and Quarterly, 2003.

_____. *Notes from a Defeatist.* Seattle: Fantagraphics Books, 2003.

_____. *Palestine.* Seattle: Fantagraphics Books, 1994.

_____. *Safe Area Goražde: The War in Eastern Bosnia 1992–1995.* Seattle: Fantagraphics Books, 2000.

_____. "Trauma on Loan." *Guardian Weekend*, January 21, 2006.

_____. *War's End.* Montreal: Drawn and Quarterly, 2005.

Saunders, Frances Stoner. *The Cultural Cold War: The CIA and the World of Arts and Letters.* New York: New Press, 1999.

Savage, William W., Jr. *Commies, Cowboys, and Jungle Queens: Comic Books and America, 1945–1954*. Hanover, NH: Wesleyan University Press, 1998.

Schechter, Harold. *Savage Pastimes: A Cultural History of Violent Entertainment*. New York: St. Martin's, 2005.

Schelly, Bill. *Joe Kubert: Man of Rock*. Seattle: Fantagraphics Books, 2008.

Schiffrin, Andre. *Dr. Seuss and Company Go to War*. New York: New Press, 2009.

Schomburg, Alex. *All Winners #7*. New York: Marvel Comics, January 1943.

Schrier, Fred. "The Last Laugh." In *Hydrogen Bomb and Biochemical Warfare Funnies*. San Francisco: Rip Off, 1970.

Schrijvers, Peter. *Crash to Ruin: American Combat Soldiers in Europe during World War II*. New York: New York University Press, 1998.

_____. *The GI War against Japan: American Soldiers in Asia and the Pacific during World War II*. New York: New York University Press, 2002.

Schwartz, Richard. *Cold War Culture: Media and the Arts, 1945–1990*. New York: Checkmark Books, 1998.

Scott, Bob, and Mike Leffel. *Impeach Bush!* Cresbard, SD: Blatant Comics, 2006.

Scott, Cord A. "Written in Red, White, and Blue: Comic Book Propaganda from World War II and 9/11." *Journal of Popular Culture* 381, #2 (Spring 2007).

Scott, Maurice. "Shock Gibson." In *War Heroes Classics #1*. Larchmont, NY: Lorne-Harvey, 1991.

Senate Committee on the Judiciary. *Comic Books and Juvenile Delinquency: Interim Report*. Washington, DC: Government Printing Office, 1955.

Shaffer, Ronald. *America in the Great War: The Rise of the War Welfare State*. New York: Oxford University Press, 1996.

Shores, Syd, Phil Sturm, and Joe Klein, eds. *Marvel Masterworks Golden Age USA Comics*, vol. 1. New York: Marvel Comics, 2007.

Siegel, Jerry (w), and Joe Shuster (a). "How Superman Would End the War." *Look*, February 25, 1940.

_____. *Superman: the Dailies 1941–1942*. New York: DC Comics/Kitchen Sink, 1999.

Simon, Joe (w), and Jack Kirby (a). *Boy Commandos #1*. New York: DC Comics, Winter 1942–43.

_____. *Captain America*, vols. 1–2. New York: Marvel Comics, 1991, 1994.

_____. *Captain America: The Classic Years*, vols. 1–2. New York: Marvel Comics, 1998.

_____. *Fighting American*, vol. 1. New York: Marvel Comics, 1989.

_____. "League of the Handsome Devils." In *Fighting American #2*. New York: Prize Comics, June 1954.

_____. "Major Liberty." In *USA Comics #2*. New York: Marvel Comics, November 1941.

_____. "Stranger from Paradise." In *Fighting American #3*. New York: Prize Comics, September 1954.

_____. *Young Allies #1*. New York: Marvel Comics, June 1941.

Simon, Joe, and Jim Simon. *The Comic Book Makers*. New York: Vanguard Publishing, 2003.

Simpson, Christopher. *The Science of Coercion: Communications Research and Psychological Warfare 1945–1960*. New York: Oxford University Press, 1996.

Singer, Aubrey (w), and Dave Matthews (a). *Strange Combat Tales* #4. New York: Epic Comics, January 1994.

Singer, P. W. *Children at War*. New York: Pantheon, 2005.

Slotkin, Richard. *Gunfighter Nation: The Myth of the Frontier in Twentieth-Century America*. Norman: University of Oklahoma Press, 1998.

Smaridge, Norah. "Red Victim: The Story of Bishop Walsh." *Treasure Chest*, vol. 19, #2 (September 1963).

Smith, T. Alexander, and Raymond Tutlalovich. *Cultures at War: Moral Conflicts in Western Democracies*. Peterborough, Ontario: Broadview, 2004.

Smucker, Philip. *Al Qaeda's Great Escape: The Military and the Media on Terror's Trail*. Washington, D.C.: Brassey's, 2004.

Snow, Nancy. *Information War: American Propaganda, Free Speech, and Opinion Control since 9/11*. New York: Seven Stories, 2003.

_____. *Propaganda, Inc.: Selling America's Culture to the World*. New York: Seven Stories, 2002.

Spangenburg, Ray, and Diane Moser. *Propaganda: Understanding the Power of Persuasion*. Berkeley Heights, NJ: Enslow Publishers, 2002.

Specwarnet, s.v. "SEALs." http://www.specwarnet.net/americas/SEALs.htm. Accessed February 25, 2011.

Speigel, Lynn. *Make Room for TV: Television and the Family Ideal in Postwar America*. Chicago: University of Chicago Press, 1995.

Spiegelman, Art. *In the Shadow of No Towers*. New York: Pantheon, 2004.

_____. *Maus: A Survivor's Tale*. 2 vols. New York: Pantheon Books, 1986, 1991.

Spillane, Mickey, ed. *Golden Age of New York: Marvel Comics*, vol. 2. New York: Marvel Comics, 1999.

Spotts, Frederic. *Hitler and the Power of Aesthetics*. New York: Overlook, 2003.

Springhall, John. *Youth, Popular Culture and Moral Panics: Penny Gaffs to Gangsta-Rap 1830–1996*. New York: St. Martin's, 1998.

"Statistics of World Armies." In *World Almanac for 1940*. New York: New York World–Telegram, 1940.

Steranko, Jim. *The History of Comics*, vols. 1–2. Reading, PA: Supergraphics, 1970, 1972.

Stone, Kathryn. *All Necessary Means: Employing CIA Operatives in a Warfighting Role alongside Special Operations Forces*. Carlisle Barracks, PA: U.S. Army War College, 2004.

Straczynski, J. Michael. *Rising Stars*, vol. 1–3. Los Angeles: Top Cow Comics, 2003.

Straczynski, J. Michael (w), and John Romita Jr. (a). *Amazing Spiderman*, vol. 2, #36. New York: Marvel Comics, 2001.

Strömberg, Fredrik. *Black Images in Comics: A Visual History*. Seattle: Fantagraphics Books, 2003.

Sturm, Phil (w), Syd Shores (a), and George Klein (a). "Mr. Liberty and the Spirits of Freedom." In *Marvel Masterworks Golden Age U.S.A. Comics*, vol. 1. New York: Marvel Comics, 2006.

Susman, Warren. *Culture as History: The Transformation of American Society in the Twentieth Century*. New York: Pantheon Books, 1984.

Takaki, Ronald. *A Different Mirror: A Multicultural History of America*. New York: Back Bay Books, 1993.

Talon, Durwin. *Comics above Ground: How Sequential Art Affects Mainstream Media.* Raleigh, NC: TwoMorrows, 2004.

Taylor, Phillip. *Munitions of the Mind: A History of Propaganda from the Ancient World to the Present Era.* New York: Manchester University Press, 2003.

Terkel, Studs. *The Good War: An Oral History of World War Two.* New York: Pantheon Books, 1984.

"There Are No Master Races." In *True Comics* #39. New York: Parents Magazine Institute, September–October 1944.

Thomas, Jeannie Banks. *Naked Barbies, Warrior Joes, and Other Forms of Visible Gender.* Urbana, IL: University of Illinois Press, 2003.

Tieri, Frank (w), and Staz Johnson (a). *Civil War: War Crimes.* New York: Marvel Comics, 2007.

Toonopedia, s.v. "Charlton Comics." http://www.toonopedia.com/charlton.htm. Accessed March 17, 2009.

Toplin, Robert. *History by Hollywood.* DeKalb: Northern Illinois University Press, 1999.

Treasure Chest of Fun and Fact. Dayton, OH: George A. Pflaum, 1946–72.

True Aviation Stories #7. New York: Parents Magazine Institute, Spring 1944.

Tucci, William. *Razor Annual* #1. Bayport, NY: Crusade Comics, 1993.

_____. *Sgt. Rock: The Lost Battalion.* 1-6. New York: DC Comics, 2009.

_____. *Shi: Through the Ashes.* Bayport, NY: Crusade, 2002.

Tucker, Spencer. *Tanks: An Illustrated History of Their Impact.* Santa Barbara, CA: ABC-CLIO, 2004.

Tuohy, Tom. Introduction to *Punisher Invades the 'Nam : Final Mission,* by Don Lomax (w) and Alberto Saichann (a). New York: Marvel Comics, February 1994.

The USA PATRIOT Act. Act of the U.S. Congress, October 2001. www.gpo.gov/fdsys/pkg/PLAW-107publ56/pdf/PLAW-107publ56.pdf.

U.S. Army. *Five Years Later . . . Where Will You Be?* Washington DC: Government Printing Office, 1962.

U.S. Army. Special Services Division. *Pocket Guide to China.* Washington, DC: Department of the Army, 1942. https://archive.org/details/PocketGuideToChina

U.S. Department of Defense. *The M16A1 Rifle: Operation and Preventative Maintenance.* Washington, DC: Government Printing Office, 1969.

Uslan, Michael, ed. *America at War: The Best DC War Comics.* New York: DC Comics, 1978.

Usndel, Alfred, ed. *The World around Us: Spies.* New York: Gilbertson World Wide, August 1961.

Vansant, Wayne. *Battle Group Peiper.* Plymouth, MI: Tome, 1991.

_____. *Days of Darkness.* Bethel, CT: Apple Comics, March 1992–February 1993.

_____. *Days of Wrath.* Bethel, CT: Apple Comics, August 1993–June 1994.

_____. *Semper Fi.* New York: Marvel Comics, 1988–89.

Vaughn, Brian K. (w), and Niko Henrichson (a). *Pride of Baghdad.* New York: DC Comics, 2006.

Vaughn, Brian K. (w), and Leonardo Manco (a). "The Clarion Call." In *411* #2. New York: Marvel Comics, July 2003.

Veitch, Rick (w), and Gary Erskine (a). *Army at Love: The Art of War* #1. New York: DC Comics, 2009.

Veitch, Tom, and Greg Irons. "The Legion of Charlies." In *The Mammoth Book of the Best War Comics*. New York: Carroll & Graf, 2007.

Versaci, Rocco. Intro to *Two-Fisted Tales: The EC Archives*, vols. 1–2. West Plains, MO: Gemstone, 2006–7.

Verzemnieks, Inara. "Drawn to the Truth: An Interview with Joe Sacco." *The Oregonian*, October 23, 2005.

Voger, Mark. *The Dark Age: Grim, Great, and Gimmicky Post-Modern Comics*. Raleigh, NC: TwoMorrows, 2006.

Walesby, Stokes (w), and Theodore Roscoe (a). *Navy: History and Tradition*, nos. 1–4. Washington, DC: Stokes Walesby, 1959.

Waltz, Tom (w), and Casey Maloney (a). *Children of the Grave*. New York: IDW, 2006.

Waltz, Tom (w), and Nathan St. John (a). *Finding Peace*. New York: IDW, 2008.

Wax, Emily. "Back to the Drawing Board: Teaching History with Comic Books." *Washington Post*, May 17, 2002.

Week, John. "Letters to Frontline Combat Comics." *Frontline Combat* #7. West Plains, MO: Gemstone, 1996.

Weich, Graig F. Author interview. March 19, 2006.

———. *Civilian Justice* #1. New York: Beyond Comics, September 2002.

Weiner, Robert, ed. *Captain America and the Struggles of the Superhero*. Jefferson NC: McFarland, 2009.

Weinstein, Simcha. *Up, Up, and Oy Vey! How Jewish History, Culture and Values Shaped the Comic Book Superhero*. Baltimore: Leviathan, 2006.

Weist, Jerry, and Jim Steranko. *100 Greatest Comic Books: An Appreciation of the Comics and Their Stories*. Atlanta: Whitman, 2004.

Wertham, Frederic. *Seduction of the Innocent*. Port Washington, NY: Kennikat, 1954.

Whitfield, Stephen J. *The Culture of the Cold War*. Baltimore: Johns Hopkins University Press, 1996.

Winkler, Allan. *The Politics of Propaganda*. New Haven, CT: Yale University Press, 1978.

Witek, Joseph. *Comic Books as History*. Jacksonville: University Press of Mississippi, 1990.

Wright, Bradford W. *Comic Book Nation: The Transformation of Youth Culture in America*. Baltimore: Johns Hopkins University Press, 2001.

Wright, Evan. *Generation Kill: Devil Dogs, Iceman, Captain America, and the New Face of American War*. New York: Putnam, 2005.

Wright, Micah Ian. *You Back the Attack, We'll Bomb Who We Want*. New York: Seven Stories, 2003.

Wright, Nicky. *The Classic Era of American Comics*. Lincolnwood, IL: Contemporary Books, 2000.

Wylie, Philip. *Generation of Vipers*. Champaign, IL: Dalkey Archive, 1955.

Young Allies #3. New York: Marvel Comics, March 1942.

Young Allies #5. New York: Marvel Comics, September 1942.

Young, Marilyn. *The Vietnam Wars 1945–1990*. New York: Harper Perennial, 1991.

Young, William. "The Serious Funnies: Adventure Comics during the Depression, 1929–1938." In *Things in the Driver's Seat: Readings in Popular Culture*, edited by Harry Russell Huebe. Chicago: Rand McNally, 1972.

Z., Mickey. *The Seven Deadly Spins: Exposing the Lies behind War Propaganda*. Monroe, ME: Common Courage, 2004.

Zimmerman, Keith, and Wayne Vansant. *Vietnam: A Graphic History*. New York: Hill & Wang, 2009.

Zinn, Howard. *Artists in Times of War*. New York: Seven Stories, 2003.

Zinsmeister, Karl. *Boots on the Ground: A Month with the 82nd Airborne in the Battle for Iraq*. New York: Truman Talley Books/St. Martin's, 2003.

Index

The Author

Cord Scott has a doctorate in American history from Loyola University Chicago. He has written for several encyclopedias and academic journals and contributed on the book edited by Robert Weiner entitled *Captain America and the Struggle of the Superhero*. He has also contributed to *Web-Spinning Heroics* (Robert Weiner and Robert Peaslee, eds.) and the *Chicago Sports Reader* (Steven Reiss and Gerald Gems, eds.). He teaches at several institutions in the Chicago area.